INSIDE
WALL STREET

INSIDE
WALL STREET

––––––

Continuity and Change in the
Financial District

ROBERT SOBEL

W · W · *NORTON & COMPANY*
New York · London

First published as a Norton paperback 1982

W. W. Norton & Company, Inc., 500 Fifth Avenue,
New York, N.Y. 10110
W. W. Norton & Company Ltd., 37 Great Russell Street,
London WC1B 3NU

Library of Congress Cataloging in Publication Data
Sobel, Robert, 1931 (Feb. 19)–
  Inside Wall Street.
  Bibliography: p.
  Includes index.
  1. New York (City).   Stock Exchange.   2. Wall
Street.   I. Title.
HG4572.S6723   1977   332.6'42'097471   77–6696

    ISBN 0-393-00030-3
           567890

To

Robert Haack and Ted Etherington

who saw it coming

CONTENTS

PREFACE

In 1955, when I arrived in the financial district to undertake a history of the city's securities markets, there were few books available to guide novices through the area. Most works on the subject were written by academics who had no real experience in the ways of the markets, but understood the theories, or by Wall Streeters who were good at telling stories but, sad to say, not particularly adept at describing their work.

This gap in the literature became evident to me after a few weeks of reading and interviewing. By then I had concluded that almost all of my formal education had been a waste of time as far as my current interests were concerned. It was one thing to appreciate the reasons we have securities markets, for example, and quite another to understand the actual functionings of the New York and American Stock Exchanges, based as they are upon tradition as well as logic. The same was true for investment and commercial banking and other ancillary functions in the district—or at least they seemed to be peripheral in 1955. Only in such a tightly knit community, where tradition was alive, could so many deals be made based upon the honor and the word of participants, with the written agreements often being completed after the arrangement was ended.

The awareness of this came slowly, and in the process I found myself being transformed from a quasi Marxist to a moderate free enterpriser. The theories I took with me to the Street made a good deal of sense, but they conflicted with the practices I found on arriving. Still, I needed a guide, and none was available in early 1955.

As luck would have it, Martin Mayer's book, *Wall Street: Men and Money,* was released soon after, and I read it in a single sitting. In the space of slightly more than 250 pages, Mayer told me more about the way the district functioned than had all the texts I had digested during the previous decade.

The reason was obvious to me. Economists tend to evolve theories based upon logic and reason, and then seek to justify or prove them by studying the "real world," a messy place which often is not logical or reasonable. In other words, they proceed from the abstract to the concrete, and find disharmonies between the two. Faced with the choice between reality and theory, many academic economists opt for the latter; they try to squeeze events into a rigid mold, rather than revamping their ideas.

Mayer reversed the process, starting as he did by studying the people in the area and their institutions, and only afterwards formulating his generalizations. This approach, combined with natural and refined skills and intelligence, made *Wall Street: Men and Money* the best book written on the subject since the turn of the century, one that was not superseded for close to a generation.

Even then the pace of change on Wall Street was accelerating. Mayer updated his book in 1959, but by that time had moved on to new interests, and he hasn't touched it since. That *Men and Money* is outdated today is no reflection upon the book. In the same way, a work describing the federal government under Abraham Lincoln would provide little guidance during the era of Jimmy Carter. Wall Street has changed more in the past generation than it had in any other comparable period.

In the process of gathering information and ideas for other books on the financial district, as well as for articles and magazine columns, I have interviewed hundreds of individuals, from leaders of exchanges and banks to policemen who patrol the area and vendors who sell hot dogs and pretzels from carts. Some of these people changed considerably over the years and watching this happen was one of the more interesting aspects of my work. In 1956 I interviewed a freshly arrived

Harvard M.B.A. who was certain he was on his way to big things. So he was: by 1965 he was earning over $100,000 a year. In that year I met a black high-school student who had a summer job as a runner at a commission house. He was interested in learning all he could about the Street, in order to use this information to further revolutionary causes. At the time, the broker and the runner seemed the two extremes of Wall Street life.

Today the Harvard man is an insurance adjustor in Seattle; he was wiped out in 1970–73. The black student went on to graduate from Baruch College and holds a well-paying position at a Wall Street bank, while taking his M.B.A. at N.Y.U. I haven't heard from the insurance man for several years, but ran into the banker last summer. Today he is a "progressive Republican," who belongs to the service clubs in the Westchester suburb to which he moved last year.

Such twists take place in other areas of American life and work, but they are more common on Wall Street than almost anywhere else.

One of the rewards of my work in the district has been the chance to watch the evolution of such careers. To all those who talked with me about their work, thoughts, and beliefs—and to the exchanges, brokerages, and banks that opened their records for inspection—my thanks. The experiences have been most informative, and they provided the foundation for this book.

INSIDE
WALL STREET

INTRODUCTION

IT MAY WELL BE that New York is in the process of losing its position as the preeminent world financial capital. But if over the next dozen years or so, the city's financial district disgorged some of its banks and trust companies, and those that remained had to share power with outsiders—and should the two major securities exchanges decline, merge, and then become part of a national system centered in Washington or some other place—the politicians still might attempt to preserve the area for tourists.

Out-of-towners and foreigners swarm through the district throughout the year, providing the city with substantial revenues. These visitors go to the Statue of Liberty, and getting off the ferry, head north along Broadway or Broad Street to see the Subtreasury, the exchanges, Trinity Church, the Nassau Street shopping area, the South Street Seaport and Museum, and the World Trade Center. They can find the romance of history in lower Manhattan, and a flavor of time and life absent from most other parts of the city.

The streets, lanes, and alleys of lower Manhattan indicate much of the story of New Amsterdam and early New York. Visitors can wander through the district, treading on what originally had been cow paths—William, Hanover, Thames, Rector Streets and others. When the Dutch ruled, there was a large area to the west of Trinity Church that was swamp and estuary, homes for migrating birds. Lobsters and oysters were taken from the waters off Liberty, Carlisle, and Cedar Streets. At high tides, small boats meandered atop what now is the site of the American Stock Exchange, and the land to the north and east was dotted with ponds and rivulets.

Close to two centuries ago, when landfill operations began, lower Manhattan looked like a small town. The twisting cow paths were about to become streets, with small houses and shops on either side. Here lived Washington, Hamilton, Adams, and others in the national government. The cattle still came down lower Broadway and there were slaughterhouses on the west side. By then Wall Street was the city's most important thoroughfare. Farmers would take their grain down what now are Carlyle and Rector Streets, while foreign shipping docked along the East River, to discharge coffee, dry goods, and other products. The homes and offices of merchants and petty bankers were located on the Street, one of the most important commercial centers in the New World. Some of the men who lived and worked in them became securities dealers soon after, and in 1792 a handful came together to form the forerunner of the New York Stock Exchange.

Those whose lives were centered on lower Manhattan showed no inclination to alter the dimensions of their lanes and streets, and neither did the municipal governments, which they usually controlled. They erected wooden buildings there in the first half of the nineteenth century, with offices on the street level and living quarters above. Many of these were leveled by great fires. The 1835 conflagration destroyed every wooden edifice below the present site of City Hall, and ten years later a second fire resulted in widespread bankruptcies in the young insurance industry. Most of those residences that remained were razed during the next generation and replaced by office structures, as their owners moved uptown, often to the countrified atmosphere of Greenwich Village or Chelsea. The last of the wooden structures were torn down toward the end of the century, as the district underwent a major building boom and entered the skyscraper age. The periodic reconstruction of lower Manhattan continued throughout the twentieth century, with a lull during the 1930s and early 1940s, which was more than compensated for by a spectacular effort in the 1950s and 1960s. Most of the office buildings along Wall and Broad streets are pre–World War II, however, but on the periphery of this great T-shaped skeleton that is the center of the financial district there are several major examples of postwar architecture, the most obvious being the World Trade Center.

Some realtors in the district claim the Center sucked clients away from the older buildings, creating a space glut, while others say the area had been overbuilt prior to the opening, and that due to recession, alterations in the district's usefulness, and the city's problems, lower Manhattan is about to undergo a replay of the 1930s. Whatever the reason, at the time of this writing several office buildings are less than half occupied. Many can be purchased at distress prices. When Continental Can decided to leave New York, its Wall Street building was put up for sale and no buyers appeared. In order to lower its tax burden, Continental razed the structure, and now there is a vacant lot on Wall Street, for the first time in the memory of the most ancient of old-timers.

The streets remain as they were, however, and today's skyscrapers line narrow lanes through which only a single automobile at a time can pass—and that, with a measure of caution. Of course, these passageways were meant for carts, not cars, and they weren't designed, but rather were created to suit the needs of the mid-seventeenth century, and later on were paved. Their dimensions create problems for workers of the late twentieth century.

This is the key to understanding the district, its problems, and responses to them. There are significant cultural and chronological lags on the Street, as major figures strive to adapt the institutions of the past to the needs and technology of the present. That they are failing is not only obvious, but perhaps inevitable as well. One can find instances in all parts of the district, but the symbolism presented by the streets themselves is the most striking.

The people who work in the buildings that line the lanes, most of them for firms involved in the securities industry, are of all ages. The oldest of office managers probably arrived in the area during the last stages of the great bull market of the 1920s, when five and six million shares a day were traded at the N.Y.S.E. They might have started out as runners or clerks, with many of the young women working as typists and some as adding-machine operators. *Their* supervisors could remember the time when entries in ledgers were made by long rows of male clerks, green visors atop their heads, seated on stools, quills and then steel pens in hand, and the stir created when the first manual typewriters and adding machines arrived. At the turn of the century a million-share session signaled some gigantic bull or bear raid. Clerks would have to work through the night, preparing for the next day's activities. The mechanical technology introduced then was gratefully received and quickly absorbed, so that by the time of the 1920s boom, office staffs could handle whatever came their way. So they did, until the last major push in the autumn of 1929.

Still more important alterations appeared during the next half century, though by then office staffs had become accustomed to change, more blase about it, and certain that they could control technology, and not vice versa. The young men who were amazed by the telephone, and who saw in typewriters and adding machines a means of making all sorts of improvements in techniques possible, thought the electric typewriter a quicker version of the mechanical, and the calculator a more complex form of the adding machine. Then the electric office was superseded by the electronic, and still there were no changes in operations. Computerization was the key word in the mid-1960s, as brokerages and banks rushed to obtain the latest hardware, which was placed in futuristic air-conditioned settings, and which whirred along impressively for those who came to witness the marvels.

But the offices were run by individuals who came in with the adding machines, and who barely had adjusted to the electric and early electronic ages. They would attempt to make the machines fit into their designs, and not the other way around. In those days, computer experts told office managers in matter-of-fact words that their machines were capable of eliminating much of the work of the district, or to put it more precisely, an electronic device had made many workers obsolete.

This was the situation in the late 1960s. Men and women with ideas formed in the mechanical age of the 1920s supervised employees who came out of the electrical technology and were charged with utilizing machines capable of leading the district into the future—which would not include many of these individuals. The organizations for which they had worked had been fashioned and hardened in the nineteenth and early twentieth centuries, and so were as outmoded as lower Manhattan's street grid.

The financial district contains a blend of the old and the modern. Much of it is visible to tourists, who come to view the trading floors at the exchanges, tour the Subtreasury, or simply walk through the streets and lanes. All around them they can see artifacts of previous times housing the technology and techniques of the present. But the more important aspects cannot be seen, for they are evident only in the offices. Sometimes the people and technology there can come to terms. Such had been the case in the 1920s.

By the late 1960s, however, personnel and machines were at odds. A new term came into vogue at this time. Office managers told one another they had problems "interfacing" their people with the machines. Computers and related equipment were spewing forth vast amounts of information, for example, for people who were unable to use it, or indeed knew whether it could be employed in any way. New methods of accounting, created for and often by the machines, were forced upon people who did not understand, like, or trust the devices. They did not interface. The machines would churn out mountains of data, process thousands of trades in minutes, and then be turned off, because the humans who handled the next step could not keep up with them. Transactions were misplaced and lost. In itself, this was not unusual. But now they were buried somewhere in the machine's memory, and on occasion could not be retrieved, even by technicians called in for that purpose. Mistakes in coding, programming, and tabulating became commonplace. Clerks worked overtime, and then went home to quick suppers and bed, where they would dream of being buried in heaps of IBM cards and strangled by computer tape.

Wall Street had a term to describe this. It was called the papercrunch.

The Exchange had been able to handle 5 million share days in 1929, when it employed a mechanical technology which the workers understood and appreciated. Forty years later the Exchange experienced several days in which volume rose beyond the 15 and 16 million share levels, and unusual sessions during which 20 million shares and more changed hands. Yet the total number of transactions was not three or four times that of 1929, and in addition the electronic technology had been touted as being capable of handling 25 million share days.

This technology failed in the late 1960s and early 1970s, in large part due to the inability of the financial community to absorb and use it effectively. It was one of the first clues that Wall Street was engaged in an internal struggle, one that didn't place liberals and conservatives on opposing sides, or even pit the New York Stock Exchange against the rebels. Rather, it took place between rival technologies and their adherents.

Given the nature of American values which tend to favor the new and efficient over the old and cumbersome, together with the workings of our particular form of capitalism, where cost efficiencies are prized, it appears evident that the district will in time accept radical alteration. To some, this implies the end of the N.Y.S.E. as a viable institution, the replacement of the financial district's present leaders by a new set of power brokers, and even Manhattan's eventual demise as the focus for world finance.

Logic might lead one to believe that all of these changes are in the works. Rarely does logic by itself determine events, however. Inertia and momentum often are more important factors, and these must be placed in the equation when considering Wall Street's present and future.

It has been there a long time. In addition, more than most American industries, finance tends to be self-perpetuating, in that sons follow fathers into established concerns and positions. Finance in general and the securities business in particular are encrusted with tradition, and personal ties and reputations are more important in lower Manhattan than ironbound contracts complete with sinuous codicils. The people of Wall Street are accustomed to conducting business in certain ways. Over time they will make minor changes, which as they accumulate become significant alterations, but this is not a community that accepts setbacks easily or will accede to its own demise—or even to a radical transformation of functions and operations. The Old Guard will defend its institutions for as long as possible, then retreat with as much grace as can be mustered, only to regroup to fight once more. In the end it will triumph or metamorphize with its opponents. That leading members will survive should not be doubted—not by anyone who knows the history and sociology of the financial district.

This book is about the alterations in the fabric of that district, of how challenges developed and the manner in which they are being met. It is concerned with logic and technologies, but also with tradition and the power of inertia. In it there are no heroes or villains, rather individuals attempting to salvage what they can from a new dispensation and others who hope to profit therefrom. The motives of each are understandable, as are their arguments and maneuverings.

That the structure of the financial district is changing rapidly is not in question. Nor is the fact that new interest groups have arrived that rival the old. The buildings themselves are being altered, as the face of lower Manhattan is undergoing its greatest transformation since the immediate postwar period.

Only the streets remain the same.

CHAPTER ONE

1877

CHRISTMAS, 1876, and Cornelius Vanderbilt, age eighty-two, rested in bed in his Fifth Avenue mansion not far from Washington Square. Several doctors were in attendance, as they had been for the past several months. The notorious Claflin sisters, Tennessee and Victoria, were there as well. Spiritualists and stockbrokers, journalists and politicians, their interests coincided with those of Vanderbilt, who had sponsored their careers and at one time had proposed marriage to Tennessee. Now they used their magic and charms in an attempt to restore his health. The sisters had placed salt cellars beneath the feet of his bed and Tennessee was seen to mutter chants. These may have had some effect, for several times that autumn Vanderbilt was aroused from what the doctors thought was a terminal torpor.

In the downstairs parlor was Frankie Crawford, Vanderbilt's thirty-eight-year-old second wife, awaiting the end with some of her stepchildren, all of whom were older than she. Occasionally they would appear at the bedroom door to inquire about the old man's health, but most of the time they were turned away.

Vanderbilt knew the end was near. He arranged to enlarge the family mausoleum on Staten Island to receive his body and those of his children when they died. More important, he rewrote his will so as to leave the bulk of his more than $100 million estate to his son, William, who was enjoined not to sell off the major holdings. To do so would only enrich the bankers, brokers, and speculators on Wall Street, and Vanderbilt didn't trust any of them.

Vanderbilt survived into the new year, but everyone knew he couldn't last much longer. At his request, Frankie played hymns on the family organ, and the sound of them prompted rumors that the old man had died. A reporter spoke to a doctor of his suspicions. Vanderbilt listened at the door and shouted out, "That's a damn lie!" But on the evening of January 4 the doctors called the family into the bedroom to say farewell. Frankie sang "Nearer My God to Thee." Vanderbilt raised his head and whispered, "I'll never give up trust in Jesus."

Early the next morning he was dead.

All of the city's newspapers carried reports of Vanderbilt's death, and the larger ones published long articles outlining his career and assessing his impact. Vanderbilt had been born into relative poverty and had risen to become a steamboat tycoon, a leader in transoceanic transport, and a master builder. He had been a world figure, fomenting a revolution in Central America and putting together the pieces that went into the making of the New York Central and Hudson Railroad, and other Vanderbilt railroads that crossed the Mississippi. He was best known for his financial exploits, however. Vanderbilt had been a central figure on Wall Street for the past twenty years. Together with—and often in opposition to—Daniel Drew, Jim Fisk, and Jay Gould, he had created corners, manipulated major railroads, coerced politicians, bought judges, and precipitated panics. He had been one of the half dozen most powerful businessmen in America, and certainly the central one in New York. "He who was the head and front of a great monopoly has finally succumbed to a monopoly greater than he," wrote one journalist, who thought the city would reverberate with the news of his death. "How Wall Street trembled as the fact became patent that Vanderbilt was no more."

New York was too sophisticated a place in 1877 to undergo trauma at the passing of even so powerful a man as Vanderbilt, and in any case his death had been anticipated. And Wall Street did not quiver. The week prior to Vanderbilt's death, official reported volume at the New York Stock Exchange auctions had been 406,164 shares, or slightly more than 80,000 per session, while "outside" trading was not unusually large. True, a Vanderbilt road, the Lake Shore, had dominated trading, with 225,000 shares changing hands, but this was due more to unexpected losses rather than fears of a new management. Volume rose slightly when news of his death reached the Street. Still, only 98,890 shares were auctioned, with Lake Shore accounting for 36,950 of them and closing firm. The New York Central and Hudson, Vanderbilt's pride, closed unchanged, with 5,680 shares being auctioned.

With close to a million inhabitants, New York was America's largest city, and certainly its most diverse and hectic. Visitors from Europe and other parts of the nation were struck by the rapid pace of life there and the polyglot nature of the population. Four out of every ten New Yorkers had been born in Europe, while another four either were their children or native Americans who had relocated to the city. Most lived in tenements or boardinghouses, for prices were higher in New York than elsewhere. Guidebooks of the period indicate that a family of four or five could live fashionably—this meant having a half dozen servants, a livery, and participating in the social whirl—for around $50,000 a year. Those with less than $6,000 could not expect to own their houses. Decent homes in respectable neighborhoods rented for $1,800 a year, while a good hotel might charge as much as $20 a day. A few New Yorkers lived in apartment buildings, a European concept brought to the city after the Civil War, and a four or five room suite in the fashionable Stevens House on Twenty-seventh Street and Broadway—uptown in 1877—went for $3,000 a year.

High prices, urban squalor, and fears arising out of a skyrocketing crime rate led many who worked in the city to find homes in the suburbs. Some 200,000 workers a day commuted to their New York jobs from Brooklyn, Staten Island, and New Jersey. They arrived by ferries—there were twenty-five lines operating in New York waters in 1877—and the Brooklyn Bridge. The fares were high—three cents to Jersey, two to Brooklyn, and ten cents to Staten Island—but the boats were large, comfortable, and reliable, and ran on schedule. The Hudson and East rivers were frozen the day Vanderbilt died, so that many walked across the ice to get to work, while others took those lines with routes to Wall Street and the Battery, where the currents kept the ice from forming.

Wall Street was New York's business center, though the fashionable shops had moved uptown to Fourteenth Street and beyond, and

Fifth Avenue had become the prime residential area. Halfway between the Battery and City Hall, it was the focus of the more built-up part of Manhattan, and the price of land there was said to be dearer than in any other part of America. Necessarily, the buildings that lined the fifty-foot wide street were tall—most were three stories, and several four—and well constructed, even ornate. A good deal of the land was owned by Trinity Church, located at the west end of Wall Street along Broadway. The church building had been completed and consecrated only thirty-one years earlier, but it was the third Trinity to occupy the space. Trinity was High Episcopalian, and though all Protestant denominations were represented among the district's leaders, Episcopalianism had a special cachet, and membership at Trinity was a sign of class. In the churchyard was buried Robert Fulton the inventor and businessman. The tomb of Alexander Hamilton was on the south side of the Church, properly so, since he was considered the godfather of American finance, and while Secretary of the Treasury lived on Wall Street. One of his successors at the Treasury, Albert Gallatin, was buried on the north side of the churchyard and was considered more important in the district's development. After leaving the Jefferson Cabinet, Gallatin became president of the National Bank of New York and was prominent in the city's financial community. Under his guidance, the New York bankers united with the Jacksonian Democrats to smash the Second Bank of the United States, a Philadelphia-based institution located on Chestnut Street. Thus, power was transferred to Wall Street in the 1830s, and it was there when Gallatin died in 1849. Some financiers who attended Vanderbilt's funeral had also been at Gallatin's, so recent had been the dominance of New York in the business and banking worlds.

At dusk on a clear summer day, the shadow of the Trinity Church spire would point to the New York Stock Exchange, which occupied most of the block bounded by Wall, Broad, and New Streets and Exchange Place. The $2 million structure had been designed by James Renwick, one of the city's leading architects, who also had been responsible for St. Patrick's Cathedral. The Stock Exchange was made of wood, but the main entrance on Broad Street was faced with marble, and was highlighted by eight lacquered columns and a rococo cornice. The members enjoyed this look of permanence, more so perhaps because many of them remembered the pre–Civil War period when the Exchange moved from place to place every few years. The organization had prospered during the war, and the profits had been placed in the building fund. Construction began in the summer of 1864, as General Sherman marched through Georgia, and was ready for occupancy when Lee surrendered at Appomattox the following year.

The 1,100 members of the Exchange liked to observe that their organization had more in common with social clubs than with most businesses, which was to say that it was unincorporated, and so did not require a state charter. This was no accident; nor was it a matter of simple pride. Without a charter, the N.Y.S.E. could not be taxed by the state or city, and there could be no direct or indirect levies upon floor transactions. No government agency could demand access to Exchange books or records, or regulate the N.Y.S.E. any more than it might a fraternal organization. The members claimed *they* were the Exchange, and the officers merely figureheads whose positions were honorary and whose tasks were simple. Henry Meigs, an amenable gentleman of no particular distinction, was president in 1877. He had been preceded by Salem Russell and followed in office by Brayton Ives. Russell left no mark on the Street, while Ives was a prominent broker who had little time for Exchange business.

The office of president of the Exchange carried no salary and few duties. He was supposed to signal the opening of trading and close it down in late afternoon, but in practice the first vice-president handled morning trades while the second vice-president was there for the second session. Each of these men received a salary of $7,500.

The Exchange's enemies, rivals, and critics charged the organization with tax evasion. In addition, they claimed that the N.Y.S.E. used its power to freeze the status quo in its favor, by threatening those brokers who traded on other exchanges. The members denied this, but there was something to be said for both points of view, with the balance of evidence favoring the critics.

The Exchange could trace its most distant origins to 1792, when a handful of prominent Wall Street brokers and other businessmen banded together to create an organized market based upon three principles: they would trade only with one another, exclude outsiders, and agree to charge specified rates for services.* These principles were intact in 1877. A member might be forgiven almost any crime committed against clients, but reneging on a deal with another member or shaving commissions would result in immediate expulsion, not only from the financial community, but from the social life of the city.

The New York Stock Exchange Board, as it was called in the early nineteenth century, had many rivals in Manhattan, and of course there were exchanges in most other cities as well. During the Civil War, when speculation reached a new high, there had been more than two dozen separate exchanges below Fourteenth Street, including some all-night markets and two which held meetings at different places each day, like floating crap games. Members had been warned against dealing at these rival markets, and when some did go there in 1861 they were expelled. Later on, however, the transgressors were merely fined, and after a while the Exchange just looked the other way. But most of these new exchanges folded after the war when business dried up. Others were closed down by the police as gambling dens—after the N.Y.S.E. issued complaints and bribed officials. One organization, the Open Board of Stock Brokers, could not be destroyed, for it was larger than the N.Y.S.E. and more popular due to its superior trading organization and philosophy. Recognizing the situation, the N.Y.S.E. proposed a merger in 1869, and the Open Board accepted. It was from this union that the modern N.Y.S.E. originated. Thus, the Exchange in its present incarnation was eight years old when Vanderbilt died. Even if one accepts the founding date as 1792, it was born only two years before Vanderbilt.

By the mid-nineteenth century the N.Y.S.E. had perfected the three major weapons it would use against interlopers and rivals. First, there would be investigations by outside authorities, prompted by Exchange charges that the public was being ill-served. Should this fail, the N.Y.S.E. would mount a direct attack and attempt to punish members and clients who traded at the rivals. Finally, if the rival remained intact, the N.Y.S.E. would approach it with offers of consolidation, market-sharing, or even union.

* These remained the basic rules in the 1970s, and their alteration was considered unthinkable to members. Just as some believe Gibraltar will fall when the barbary apes die, so members thought the N.Y.S.E. would collapse without fixed rates.

The N.Y.S.E. was altering its methods of conducting business in 1877, and in the process demonstrating it was not a mossback organization. The most important changes were in the areas of trading procedures and scope, with the former arising from the amalgamation with the Open Board, the latter from the development of new technologies combined with an informed opportunism.

Prior to the Civil War, the Exchange had conducted its business through auctions, similar to those presently practiced at Parke-Bernet. Sellers would deposit their securities with the president prior to the auction, while buyers would await the call, and then bid against one another. This method suited the small markets of the late eighteenth century, and so was carried over into the nineteenth. When business became hectic—such as after the discovery of gold in California in 1848, when mining shares were the rage—the Exchange would add a second auction. Sometimes this did not serve speculators and investors, who would gather near the Exchange to trade "between calls." On the outside, they could also deal in those shares not listed on the Exchange, and meet brokers who were not members—in violation of the rules. There were times when more shares were traded off the auction than on, and some brokers demanded modifications of the rules to permit other means of trading. Always these were rejected, more out of respect for tradition and suspicion of change than anything else.

So the auctions continued, throughout the Civil War and afterwards. There was one at 10:30 in the morning and a second at 1:00 in the afternoon. Brokers might deal in as many as 250 different issues at the two sessions, some with a dozen or so "packets" or "blocks" of stock. Before, between, and after the auctions the brokers would trade outside, go to the bond room (where securities were offered on a continual basis), or sneak into rival exchanges to trade or simply get a feel for the market. The larger houses would station partners at the auctions, and use young clerks for other trading. This was done because the auctions provided lead prices for the outside trades—rises and falls in particular issues began there, and then were transmitted elsewhere—and because of the more hectic nature of the nonauction trading.

The Open Board had been organized by men who for one reason or another had been excluded from the N.Y.S.E. Newcomers drawn to

New York during the war, those who had been blackballed by the Exchange, and clerks at N.Y.S.E. houses who wanted to have businesses of their own, formed the majority of the membership. They united with the leaders of a minor exchange, known as the "Coal Hole"—because it conducted business in a tenement basement on William Street—and opened for trading in a rented building on lower Broad Street in 1864. Trading took place six days a week, from 8:30 in the morning until 5:00 at night—longer if trading was heavy. Anyone who paid a $50 fee was admitted, hence the name. The Open Board did not use the auction method and, in fact, had no discernible procedure at first. Rather, the brokers, clients, moneylenders, and others concerned with trading gathered in the room to deal with any securities that interested them. There was no stock list, no standards, and no organization.

This anarchical situation did not last for long. Within a few months the Open Board had drawn up a set of rules and selected an administration to enforce them, but both were ignored. By the end of the year, however, the brokers had begun sorting themselves out. It was generally understood that certain active stocks would be traded at set locations on the floor. So a broker interested in purchasing shares of Erie would head to where the "Erie Crowd" gathered and shout out his wishes—how many shares he wanted and the price he was prepared to pay. Haggling would begin, and after a while a deal was concluded.

By 1866 some brokers took to stationing themselves at the centers of the various crowds, and would remain there throughout the day, dealing in only one stock. Would-be buyers and sellers knew who they were and would come to them for quotes. Thus was born the specialist system, the heart of the Open Board and a rival method to the auctions. It did not arrive through a plan, but rather in response to a felt need. The floor was so crowded during busy sessions that the brokers could hardly move, and economy of effort was necessary to conserve time and energy. Wall Streeters knew of the system, even though it was not incorporated in the bylaws or imitated at the N.Y.S.E. or less-hectic organizations.*

* There is an N.Y.S.E. tradition that the specialist system began in 1875 when a broker named Boyd broke his leg and remained at one location to trade specified stocks. Boyd was supposed to have found it so profitable that he continued the practice after the leg

The N.Y.S.E. of 1877 had two trading floors, each of which was considered legitimate. Upon entering the building, brokers would find themselves in the "Long Room," where the continuous trading took place, complete with the specialist system. Upstairs, on the second floor, were the auctions. By then the auction prices tended to follow those at the specialist market, and as time went on the two-a-day calls received less attention. The auctions of stocks were finally ended in 1882, and the specialist system accepted by all members.* Still, what was to become the key N.Y.S.E. institution was not officially recognized in the rules and bylaws for another half century.

The specialist system enabled the Exchange to handle a far larger volume of trading than had been possible under the auction procedure. Similarly, two inventions—the stock ticker and the telephone—widened the scope of trading until it blanketed the nation. In the process, the N.Y.S.E. eclipsed the regional exchanges, put several out of business, and obliged most of the others to merge in order to remain viable. Before the end of the century the Exchange dictated policies and prices to the entire industry. Just as Gallatin and the New York bankers had utilized the impulses of Jacksonian Democracy to seize financial control of the nation, so the N.Y.S.E.'s leaders utilized the inventions of E. A. Calahan and Alexander Graham Bell among others to dominate the American securities exchange structure.

The technological revolution had started before the Civil War. Samuel Morse had invented the telegraph in 1832, and by 1856, when Western Union was founded, out-of-towners could place orders to buy and sell securities on Wall Street. Several special delivery companies, led by Adams Express, offered low rate schedules to those who wanted to send securities from place to place. Financial news columns appeared for the first time, and interest in investments grew throughout the nation. Still, the telegraph did not create much in the way of new business for the New York brokers. An out-of-towner would have to know exactly what he wanted to buy or sell prior to using the tele-

---

was healed, and others imitated him. There is no evidence that this had occurred, while there are reports of specialization prior to 1875. Like so many other old Wall Street stories, this fabrication refused to die, and is still cited today.

* There are still auctions on Wall Street today, but usually of rarely traded preferred stocks, and conducted at small brokerages.

graph, and even then he might not want to go to the expense and trouble of using it as long as another exchange was closer to his home. Western Union and other telegraph companies understood this, and soon were working on a "continuous telegraph" which would print current stock prices, in the expectation that the apparatus would be purchased by brokerages all over the country.

The first successful quotation device was invented by S. S. Laws, a vice-president of the New York Gold Exchange. It appeared in 1866, when gold trading was more active and volatile than that in securities. The simple machine printed the selling prices for the metal on a continuous basis, and by year's end fifty of them were in service throughout the city. The following year E. A. Calahan, an operator for the American Telegraph Company, perfected an improved gold quote machine which he called a ticker, and shortly after adapted it to print trades in various stocks as well. Calahan obtained financial support, organized the Gold and Stock Telegraph Company, and by early 1868 was offering his machines to Manhattan brokerages for a fee of $25 a month. Rivals soon appeared, and these were crushed by an alliance that involved Gold and Stock and Western Union. Laws' small operation was absorbed into Gold and Stock, and when Thomas Edison perfected his ticker, it was purchased for $40,000. But one firm, Commercial Telegraph, refused to submit to a takeover, and this precipitated a short but damaging price war, in which the fee dropped to $10 a month. Then the rivals came to an understanding and agreed to stop competing and raise prices in unison. This move distressed the brokers, who complained to the N.Y.S.E.

The Exchange's leaders had watched the situation with much interest. The tickers had served to expand total business, and the N.Y.S.E. knew that in time they would be leased outside of the city, and that this would increase the geographic range as well. In effect, they could serve as a spearhead for the N.Y.S.E.'s invasion of the hinterlands. On the other hand, the tickers were not under Exchange control, and this was troublesome. Not only did this mean private companies were using what the N.Y.S.E. considered proprietary information without paying a fee, but that they could sell services to nonmember firms, who then might use the information to damage the major market. For example, an out-of-town brokerage might organize what amounted to a mini-market of its own, trading off the tape. Competing exchanges within the city might do the same, and by setting their prices carefully could undercut the N.Y.S.E.*

The Exchange made several passes at controlling the activities of the telegraph and ticker companies in 1877, but failed in the attempts. Nothing much happened in the next eight years, since the N.Y.S.E. could scarcely move against a service which so added to business. Then, in 1885, it insisted upon the removal of the private company telegraphers from the Exchange floor, threatening that unless this was done, the N.Y.S.E. would establish its own telegraph company. A compromise was arranged; the companies agreed to purchase quotations from the Exchange, and accept its supervision. Five years later the Exchange took control of Commercial Telegraph, which it reorganized as the New York Quotation Company, and in 1892 Western Union was obliged to bow to the N.Y.S.E., and place tickers only in member-owned brokerages and in other places approved by the Exchange. By then members had come to understand that while their major business was securities trading, the information derived from such activities also was a valuable commodity, while those who controlled and disseminated it had a powerful weapon.

The first telephones on Wall Street were installed in 1878, the year after Vanderbilt's death. These had little impact at first, but their potential was immediately appreciated. Just as the ticker relayed price information to other parts of the city and nation, so the telephone could be used to place orders to buy and sell. But the public had little to do with the markets in the 1870s, when most of the trading was done by large-scale speculators and the Exchange members themselves. Relatively few issues were listed for trading at the time—163 stocks and 334 bonds in 1877, for example—and most of these were for railroads, banks, and local industries. The Boston Stock Exchange, not that on Wall Street, was the major market for industrial securities, for in this period few Americans thought that the industrial securities would have more than peripheral interest for the foreseeable future.

---

* The Consolidated Stock Exchange, which was formed in 1886 and which did a larger volume of business than the N.Y.S.E. for a while, actually did trade off the tape, and for forty years was successful in fighting Exchange attempts to remove the tickers from its floor.

Telephone services expanded rapidly, so that by the end of the
1880s all urban localities had at least local service. Under the leadership of Theodore Vail, American Telephone and Telegraph set out to
create interconnections between the systems—to provide a long-dis-
tance service. In time this would have a profound effect upon the
securities industry, almost as great as the effect of the ticker. This
would not be the situation until a mass market for securities developed, and that would take another half century.

Not all brokers and speculators belonged to the N.Y.S.E., or even
to any of the several other securities markets in the financial district
and further uptown. In fact, a majority of brokers belonged to no
organized securities exchange, either because they lacked the funds for
admission and membership or the social status required to enter the
club. These men traded out-of-doors, at a variety of locations over the
years. In 1877 the largest group of them congregated on Broad Street,
just south of the N.Y.S.E. These men, known as curbstone brokers,
dealt only in those securities which were not deemed suitable for trading at the central market. For the most part these were shares in
marginal and new companies, while the curbstone brokers themselves
were looked upon as marginal dealers or newcomers. Of all the non-
Exchange securities markets in the city, the Curb alone did not compete with the N.Y.S.E., and so it was not only accepted, but in some
ways encouraged. Whenever a N.Y.S.E.-affiliated brokerage received
an order for shares traded on the Curb, it would contact its correspondent house there to place the order. In return for this, the curbstone broker would present the N.Y.S.E. member with a small kick-
back. Each was content with the arrangement. The senior market knew
the Curb was a useful place to keep unwanted men and stocks until
both were ready for the N.Y.S.E., and until then would share in its
profits but not the risks. As for the curbstone brokers, they understood
that given the sponsorship of a major Wall Street house they could
become moderately wealthy—as long as they stayed in their place.

These large houses were the foundation for most securities dealings in the city. Some were known as brokerages and others as investment banks, the former implying the transaction of securities in the aftermarket, the latter the marketing of securities and the gathering of
funds for new and established businesses. In practice, the largest and

best known houses provided both services, although each tended to concentrate in one or the other area. For example, J. W. Seligman & Co., one of New York's major investment banks, had branches in San Francisco, New Orleans, London, Paris, and Frankfort, and since most offices were manned by Seligman relatives, was known as the "American Rothschilds." Seligman helped raise money for the Union cause during the Civil War, and in the 1870s had come to specialize in railroad securities. But Seligman brokers also attended the N.Y.S.E. auctions, buying and selling shares for selected clients.

Drexel, Morgan & Co., another major investment bank with overseas affiliates, was considered one of the most aggressive houses in the district. In 1879 J. P. Morgan, one of the firm's partners, was approached by William Vanderbilt, and asked to sell 350,000 shares of New York Central overseas, in such a way as not to cause the price to collapse. Morgan agreed to undertake the job. In return he obtained a large fee and pledges to maintain the dividend. Vanderbilt agreed to conduct business according to the banker's dictates. Soon after Morgan took a seat on the Central's board, and became one of the major influences there and on other railroads. Wall Street was becoming the funnel whereby funds from all parts of the nation were gathered and then distributed to transportation, manufacturing, and mercantile establishments, and the investment banks were the indispensable part of that funnel.

Seligman and Drexel, Morgan, along with a handful of other large investment banks, worked with a score of smaller satellite banks—including Henry Clews & Co., Trevor & Colgate, Osgood & Brother, and Martin Brothers—which came in on major underwritings to share risks and rewards. They dominated the field, and most remained intact despite panics and depressions, and survived into the twentieth century. They did not speculate for their own accounts, and whenever possible minimized their risks and maintained small securities positions of their own.

Other firms did little in the way of providing banking services, and instead prided themselves on cleverness in executing orders on the N.Y.S.E., usually for major speculators. Groesbeck & Co., a small firm with only a handful of clerks, was the headquarters for Daniel Drew, one of the Street's leading figures, and to serve him better

David Groesbeck had installed the district's first ticker. After the Civil War, Lockwood & Co. had the reputation of being the city's wealthiest investment bank, and also the home of several major speculators. Mills & Co. had a youthful image, and generally could be found on the bull side of the market, pushing stocks higher, attracting the business of new speculators who hoped to become the "Napoleons of Wall Street." Kelly & Co. provided special facilities for women speculators, a large group of whom had come to the district after the war and remained into the 1870s, much to the distress of the old-timers. All of these firms, and others like them, tied their futures to those of their speculator customers, lending them money and often participating in their attempted coups. They did well on occasion, but could be crippled during panics. Few lasted more than a generation. Groesbeck, Lockwood, and Kelly declared insolvency during the 1873 panic, and the others went under in 1884.

No one bothered to count the number of brokerages in the Wall Street area in 1877, perhaps because many were small, were located in out-of-the-way places, and had short lives. According to estimates, there were between 400 and 500 in lower New York, below City Hall, with a majority situated in tenements on William and New streets. Even the smallest of the N.Y.S.E.-affiliated brokerages had two partners, one whose job it was to attend the auctions and be responsible for operations at sites where continuous trading took place, the other to oversee affairs at the office, solicit business, and make certain payments and deliveries were in order. Ideally, the Wall Street representative was flamboyant, able to discern market movements, and able to keep an eye out for manipulations and attempted coups. The office partner had to juggle funds, and in the larger houses, coordinate the activities of dozens of employees. Though less visible, he was the organization's key man, which may best be appreciated by tracing a typical transaction.

Suppose a client contacted his broker and placed an order for 100 shares of Western Union, currently quoted at around 50. The office partner would fill out duplicate slips, place one in his file and give the other to one of his runners, who would carry it to the Exchange. There it would be handed to the floor broker, who would execute the order at the auction or the continuous trading area on the first floor. In either

case he would contract an obligation in his firm's name, and in return
be guaranteed delivery of the purchased shares. Along with other executed orders, he would send this slip back to the office, where the
sale would be recorded.

The office partner would earmark $5,000 for the account of the
firm from which the shares had been purchased. More than likely the
two brokerages used different banks, and so the transfer of funds
would be handled by the clearinghouse. In some circumstances the
seller might want a cash payment, and then one of the runners would
be dispatched to the office with the funds, usually after the close of
trading. Meanwhile, the selling broker's clerk would transmit the
stock certificate to the purchaser's office, or to a bank nominated by
the purchaser as a trustee. Deliveries of cash and securities were supposed to take place within a day of the trade, or in some cases, as
much as three. But the rules were flexible here, and brokers who knew
one another would make concessions for tardy deliveries, with the understanding they would receive the same consideration in return.

There were no stock-clearing facilities in 1877. One had been
organized in 1868 by the Bankers' and Brokers' Association. It was an
ambitious project, since the agency was to have cleared cash payments
as well as certificates. But the organization lasted less than a month.
Some brokers disliked the idea of using a facility whose records might
be examined by others—they abhorred this kind of publicity, especially when it related to the volume of their business and the names of
their clients. Others found it difficult to live up to the rules regarding
deliveries. The banks opposed the agency, since they lost business. So
in 1877 hoards of clerks and runners filled the financial district. They
carried messages from offices to trading areas and back again, took
cash to banks and certificates to brokers. When information had to be
transmitted the speediest of them was used; William Heath, known as
"the American Deer," was the most famous of these "express car-
riers." The clerks, called pad-shovers, were paid by the trip, and in
1877 this was ten cents within the district, and twenty-five cents elsewhere in Manhattan.*

* The arrival of the ticker obviated the need for some runners, but they were still used to
gather price information. Some brokers had regular runners to all exchanges and markets. They would collate price information to determine the best place to buy and sell

In most cases the client would purchase his shares on margin, which is to say that he would pay a portion of the price in cash, and use the securities themselves as collateral. Ten percent margin was considered not only customary but traditional. So the client in this case would deposit $500 with the broker, with the certificate used as collateral for a $4,500 loan.

Brokers welcomed and even encouraged this arrangement. The commission on purchases and sales was small—one-eighth of one percent of the stock's par value. Since par for Western Union was 100, the commission was figured on $10,000, and not $5,000, and would come to $12.50. But the interest charges on the broker's loan would be much higher, depending upon the going price for money in the city. A thirty-day loan at 7 percent would come to $57.87, and the broker would charge a fee for obtaining the loan—$50 was customary.

Occasionally the broker would lend the money himself, but most of the time he would act as a middleman. There were more than a dozen brokers' banks in the Wall Street area, which specialized in the making of such loans. One of these, the Merchants Exchange, was a key institution in the securities structure, and rumors of difficulties there sparked several minor panics in the 1860s and 1870s, in which scores of small brokerages collapsed.

Conservative brokerages content to act as middlemen had little fear of insolvency, but few were willing to limit their activities to client services. Most loaned money, speculated for their own accounts, and entered into pools with their clients. Those who dealt in stocks in 1877 were more interested in gambling than in investment anyway, and the purchase of shares was looked upon as a risky business. Prudent individuals put their surplus funds into government bonds, deposits at secure banks, or their own businesses. To own shares in a railroad far from one's home was considered somewhat daring. In the 1870s there was a huge volume of business in lottery tickets, and many Wall Street brokers were involved in that business too.

Others advertised their willingness to sell options on stocks, a form of paper that appealed to the speculative element. An option gave the

securities. This early version of the "consolidated tape" was opposed by the N.Y.S.E., but it was used nonetheless. The advent of the telephone, of course, ended the careers of many runners.

buyer the right to buy or sell a specified number of shares in a company at a stated price on or before a designated date. The brokers would create these options themselves, and so did not have to commit funds or enter into a transaction at the Exchange. The purchaser of Western Union, for example, might have bought a "call" for 100 shares at 55 which ran for six months, for which he would have paid around $200—and would not have to concern himself with broker's loans, interest charges, or commissions. Should the stock's price rise to 57, he would break even. At 59, he would have doubled his money. Should the buyer exercise his option, the broker would have to deliver the shares from his inventory, or go to the market and purchase them.

It was a chancy business. A great upward sweep or a collapse could ruin brokers who speculated for their own accounts or were deeply involved in options trading, and on such occasions some would close shop and slip out of the city, never to return, while others simply declared bankruptcy.

It was an exciting, often rewarding, and always anxiety-filled way of life. Brokers had reputations for wild carousing when successful. They would frequent the many saloons and bars in the district, purchase extravagant carriages, and provide the business for the elegant houses of prostitution located uptown. Continued losses would lead to the poorhouse, to jail, or end in suicide. It was not unusual for a broker to rise and fall three or four times in his career. None of these men had hopes of becoming investment bankers, or for that matter any desire for the status and respectability that position carried. They were gamblers in a gambling context, and content to let it go at that. Such a way of life took a toll. "It has been remarked that the men who do business in Wall Street have a prematurely old look, and that they die at a comparatively early age," noted the writer of a guidebook published in 1872. "This is not strange. They live too fast. Their bodies and brains are taxed too severely to last long. They pass their days in a state of great excitement. Every little fluctuation of the market elates or depresses them to an extent greater than they think. At night they are either planning the next day's campaign, or are hard at work at the hotels. On Sundays their minds are still on their business, and some are laboring in their offices, screened from public observation. Body and mind are worked too hard, and are given no rest.''*

There were close to 3,400 commercial banks in the United States in 1877. Most were local in scope, financing farmers and arranging for real estate mortgages, and having few interests outside of the locality in which they were situated. On occasion, however, such institutions would require services that could not be provided in their areas, and so they became the correspondents of larger banks, often those in major cities. A small midwestern bank serving wheat growers might have such a relationship with one or more Chicago banks, and through them—or directly—with a New York institution. All monetary power seemed to emanate from Manhattan. Approximately $52 billion in bank clearances was recorded in 1877, and of this, close to half was handled by the New Yorkers. Thus, most though not all of the nation's banks were bound together in a web—perhaps it would be more accurate to describe it as a pyramid, for the apex was in New York, where the large banks were within walking distance of one another, and the presidents belonged to the same clubs.

There were fifty-one commercial banks on Manhattan in 1877, and most had long histories and long records of solvency. Investment banks might fail during periods of severe panic—Jay Cooke & Co., the nation's most prestigious, had gone under in 1873. Few brokerages lasted more than a generation without experiencing at least one bankruptcy. The commercial banks held fast, however, due in large part to the same records for conservatism that had made them so powerful over the years.

The Bank of Commerce, one of the largest in the city, had a capital of more than $10 million in 1877, slightly more than the American Exchange Bank, considered second in terms of assets. Commerce had a reputation as a racy institution, since it was liberal in its loan policies and did not insist upon gilt-edge collateral or maintain a high ratio of gold to greenbacks. The City Bank was seen as a sounder entity than Commerce, due in large part to its gold position and the high social position of Moses Taylor, its president. The Chemical was the most

* James D. McCabe, Jr., *Light and Shadows of New York Life* (New York, 1872, fac. ed., 1970), p. 280.

conservative of the major banks. John Jones, its leader, once boasted that its gold reserves were twice that of any bank. Still, Chemical was looked upon as a mossback institution, since Jones would not approve of any but the most secure mercantile loans. Brokers and even the more respected investment bankers knew better than to seek his cooperation in financing their business ventures.

The commercial bankers were wary of those who frequented the exchanges and floated new issues of bonds and stocks. Commerce and City would provide brokers' loans for some of the more respectable houses, and on occasion would cooperate with major investment banks by obtaining short-term capital for their underwritings. But the commercial and investment banking communities were separate in New York. In some of the smaller cities, the commercial banks would underwrite new issues—First National City of Chicago, for example, was a leading distributor of railroad bonds. This was not the case in New York, though the situation was soon to change.

The commercial bankers feared the risk of insolvency, a condition that resulted from the shocks of the 1873 panic—one of the most severe in American history, whose effects were still felt four years later—and the currency picture. The nation had two currencies, gold and greenbacks, with the latter not convertible into the former. Greenbacks sold at a discount, their prices dependent upon faith in the nation's financial future and manipulations of major speculators. The Gold Exchange, where the metal was bought and sold for greenbacks, often was more hectic than any of the securities markets, and price gyrations there could be spectacular, as they were in 1869, when a gigantic pool involving White House figures was mounted. This was why conservative bankers like Jones maintained large gold reserves, and why they distrusted paper of all kinds, even the soundest of common stocks.

The situation began to change in 1874, when Republican moderates in Congress passed the Resumption Act, which limited greenback circulation to $300 million, but more important, stipulated that starting in 1879, greenbacks would be fully convertible into gold. The metal's price slipped steadily in 1877, so that by the end of the year it sold for 102. It was only a fraction over 100 by mid-1878, and on January 2,

1879, the Gold Exchange closed down. For all intents and purposes, the United States was back on the gold standard.

Hard money forces rejoiced, while the commercial bankers reassessed the situation. Deliberately and with some trepidation, a few of them began to edge toward the securities market and cut back on their gold reserves. In time they would unite with the investment bankers to provide funds for underwritings, and even take a hand in marketing securities overseas. The major insurance corporations arrived later on, at first as captive houses, unwilling allies of the investment bankers, and then as partners. Wall Street was about to become a major financial pump not only for the region and nation, but for the world. That much could be discerned in the late 1870s, as could be the preeminent position of the investment bankers in all of this.

Some on the Street were disconcerted with the pace of change, which appeared to be accelerating. The multiplication of exchanges during the Civil War and their declines thereafter, the N.Y.S.E.'s merger with the Open Board, the development of continuous trading and the triumph of the specialist system, could not have been anticipated in the 1850s, when most of the district's leaders had taken their first jobs. The ticker and the telephone were bound to have wider repercussions than were seen during the first few years after the death of Cornelius Vanderbilt. The nation was still in the grips of a recession in the mid- and late 1870s. There were more labor disorders of various kinds in 1877 than in any previous year, and bank failures reached a new high as bountiful European harvests resulted in a decline in grain exports. Subsequent collapses in prices resulted in increased hardships. There was talk of revolution in the Midwest and insurrections in the cities of the Northeast. The national political picture was gloomy.

Despite all of this, there was little doubt that finance capitalism would remain intact, and that its institutions, so recently reformed and still in the process of changing, would thrive. In 1877 a N.Y.S.E. seat changed hands for $4,500, in addition to which the new member had to pay a $1,500 initiation fee. Five years later the price of a seat was quoted at $33,000, as business boomed on Wall Street.

What did all of this imply? A decade and another panic after the death of Vanderbilt, Henry Clews offered an optimistic preview of what was to come. A prominent though not major investment banker, Clews had failed in 1873, rebounded, and was doing a better business than ever. He noted that the financial district's face was being altered. Along lower Broadway and across Wall Street, four and five story buildings, some only a few years old, were being razed, and nine and ten story edifices erected in their places. A decade earlier the N.Y.S.E. had dominated the district physically. Now the building seemed small and a trifle shabby, certainly far less impressive than the new bank structures that were filling the area.

Fewer people clogged the streets during the trading day, for the ticker and telephone had replaced the runner and pad-shover. After the close of trading, however, they appeared to make deliveries of certificates, and for an hour or so one could hardly walk on Broadway, Wall, or Broad Street. Clews wondered if the brokers could handle all of this business. Already there was talk of a new clearinghouse, but nothing was done for another generation. After much discussion and prolonged negotiations—and a back office crisis in 1890—the clearinghouse came into being in 1892.

"A hundred years hence the people who then occupy our places will look upon us as primitive and crude, or, in accordance with the Darwinian theory, as the monkeys from which their perfected race has been developed." So wrote Henry Clews. He thought the city's rivers would be spanned by many bridges, and the ferries replaced. Electricity would have conquered almost all technological barriers, and new inventions would appear to both speed and ease life. It would be possible to have breakfast in Chicago and lunch in New York, for travel at hundreds of miles per hour would be commonplace—accomplished by pneumatic tubes. "These tubes will spread from New York, as the blood vessels in the human body spread out and are supplied from the heart; for New York is not only the business heart of this country, but it is destined to be, so surely as God permits growth, the business heart of the world, and the money centre of the world."*

Americans like Clews were optimistic. They had come through the nation's most divisive war, political scandals, and a time of major corruption. Their own world, which centered around Wall Street, had un-

* Henry Clews, *Twenty-Eight Years in Wall Street* (New York, 1887), p. 613.

dergone a series of technological and structural changes, and had been strengthened in the process. These men had survived recessions, inflation, new recessions, and financial panics. Safe within the bastions of the N.Y.S.E.–brokerage-bank structure, they were winners in the Darwinian struggle, and they saw no reason why their sons and grandsons could not maintain their positions.

The Wall Streeters of the 1870s built better than they knew. Their world and its institutions lasted for close to a century, growing and adapting along the way, but rarely undergoing a major transformation. Then, when cracks appeared along the seams, their great-grandchildren rushed to patch up the old system. But the cement wouldn't hold. Because of this, Wall Street is undergoing its greatest alteration since the time of Cornelius Vanderbilt and Henry Clews.

CHAPTER TWO

N.Y.S.E.—THE FLOOR

THE FINANCIAL district is empty—or at least gives the appearance of being so—from around midnight to 6:00 A.M. on working days. Throughout the night, trucks and vans rumble through the district, making deliveries and pickups. The cleaning people make their rounds and so do guards, and the lights keep burning until dawn in some offices to aid them. Only a few souls, many of them artists, live in the buildings of lower Manhattan, below Wall Street, along the East River. Some of the best locations in the city in terms of accessibility and scenery are occupied by ancient, decaying structures, which house marginal people.

On the West Side Battery Park City will soon arise—assuming New York can remain solvent long enough for completion. This huge project, designed for middle-class individuals, may alter the face of the district, turning it into a residential community for the first time in almost two centuries. Some time in the 1980s, brokers and clerks may walk to their offices and return home for lunch.

Today they converge upon the financial district from all directions each morning. In 1877 there were twenty-five ferry lines to Manhattan; only one of these is in operation today. Mornings and evenings the ships that take people from Staten Island and back are filled with Wall Streeters, but only a small fraction of the work force comes into the city this way. Buses and trains carry tens of thousands of workers from parts of Staten Island and New Jersey communities that were farms in the days of Commodore Vanderbilt. Some brokers and managers live in upper Manhattan, more in Westchester and southern Connecticut, but the largest group makes the trip by car, train—and some by helicopter—from Nassau County, Wall Street's major bedroom.*

Wall Street–bound workers come in from as far as the Philadelphia suburbs. Some of the trains emanating from there and from Princeton are filled with brokers who gossip, catch up on reading and research, or play cards in the morning, while on the return trip they snooze, stare at one another over martinis, or resume decade-old bridge and poker sessions.

There is supposed to be a major Wall Street broker who lives in Bermuda and commutes from work by means of the Wall Street helicopter and a late afternoon plane out of Kennedy, with his company picking up the tab. Does he exist? Dozens swear he has made the trip for years, but none can identify him.

In the mid-1960s, the N.Y.S.E. planned to construct a new building for itself on landfill in the East River. It was to have an immense trading floor, twice the size of the present Exchange's, and other facilities to scale. The N.Y.S.E. consultants forecast that by 1975, average daily volume would be around 10 million shares, or twice that of 1964, and that the old floor would not be able to handle such activity. Nothing came of the plans, now scrapped and unlikely to be revived. The strain came earlier than anticipated—the daily average in 1968 was almost 13 million shares. The money raised for the project was spent instead on bailing out those brokerages that faltered in the 1969–70 paper-crunch and decline.

The N.Y.S.E. remains in its old quarters, which were constructed from 1901 to 1903, in a period of high optimism and security about the future. Designed by George Post and put up at a cost of over $4 million, it was looked upon not only as a major project, but as a sym-

* Most commute by car along the Long Island Expressway or take the Long Island Railroad to Penn Station, transfer to the subway, and get off at Church Street, in the shadow of the World Trade Center. Those with time and imagination, and who want to save a few cents in fare, take the L.I.R.R. to the Jamaica Station in Queens, walk a block to the BMT elevated train station, board a car which is perhaps a half century old and covered with graffiti, and then make the slow journey through the central Brooklyn slums, perhaps the nation's worst. The BMT goes over the Williamsburg Bridge and then dips underground, winding up at the corner of Wall and Broad. Within a quarter of an hour the rider has been taken from the scene of misery and squalor to the symbol of overwhelming wealth and power.

bol of the district's stability. A further sign of this was the presence on the building committee of Ernest Groesbeck, son of David, the post–Civil War broker. Power, position, and status are not transitory things in the financial district, especially on those levels just below the top. They tend to be passed along through the generations, even when some of the links prove rather weak. But there are indications that this, along with so many other practices, is breaking down rapidly today.

The 1903 building is much larger than the one it replaced, and of course quite different in design—a representation of the early Edwardian rather than the mid-Victorian age. The N.Y.S.E. no longer required separate facilities for auctions and continuous trading, and so the designers established a single one, an enormous room in which the specialists have their posts and hold court through the working day. Boardrooms and offices are upstairs, as is the dining room and some ancillary services. More of these are to be found in surrounding buildings which the Exchange erected or absorbed over the next three-quarters of a century.

The N.Y.S.E.'s front entrance at 18 Broad Street remains impressive, with its Roman Renaissance architecture, six fluted Corinthian columns, and ornate pediment, on which are sculpted, in bas-relief, six figures representing aspects of agriculture, mining, motive power, and design. In the middle stands a bountiful female figure—Integrity—flanked by two smaller ones, male, which receive and take note of the products brought to her by the others. Integrity, the just government of financial transactions, rules the N.Y.S.E., said the men of 1903, and as a result, all good things flow to her.

The symbolism is pleasing, though not one in a hundred of the 2,600 or so N.Y.S.E. employees and managers know of it, or seem to care one way or another. Even without this knowledge, the men who work in the building accept the values as a matter of course, something handed down from the nineteenth century which is still cherished. J. P. Morgan and his circle prized integrity more than financial assets, and considered their reputations better collateral than gold. This sentiment still exists in the district—though in not so strong a manifestation.

In any case, few use this front entrance today. Visitors pass by and take note of the score or so of runners and clerks in their cream-colored work jackets on which are affixed their badges, who lounge in front, smoke, gossip, and watch the women pass by. Those who want to see the workings of the Exchange floor enter through an undistinguished building to the south—20 Broad—take an elevator to the visitor's gallery on the third floor, pass through a historical exhibit, and then move along a ramp which overlooks the trading floor. The N.Y.S.E. runs a lecture series, and there are guides to answer the more obvious questions. They point out that not all of the trading floor is visible, that part of it occupies an annex to the north of the main building—2 Broad—which was constructed in the early post–World War I period to handle the increased volume.

A more interesting and accurate insight into N.Y.S.E. life may be obtained by using the entrance employed by most of the individuals who work the floor and staff the offices at 11 Wall Street, at the corner of New, just behind 2 Broad. One goes through two sets of doors into a narrow vestibule. To the left and right are banks of elevators at least half a century old. Beyond the vestibule is a small waiting room which leads to the trading floor. The entrance here is guarded; no one can enter without badges or passes. Most of the time it is crowded with specialists and clerks, out for a fast smoke, or simply sneaking a moment or two of privacy away from the floor, or there to meet friends or associates. Many of the people entering and leaving the building during the day are elderly men, respectably dressed, carrying parcels or papers. These are the descendents of the runners of 1877. The financial district provides jobs for many retired office workers, civil servants, and manual workers who take these low-paying positions to supplement their pensions.

Despite the telephone and the computer, paper remains the life-blood of the Street. Stock certificates, memoranda, contracts and the like have to be delivered in a matter of minutes, not days as would be the case if the mails were used. These elderly men fill a vital need, and this fact, as much as any other, indicates why the district survives. It cannot be dispersed throughout the nation, tied together by electronic terminals—not so long as the rulers of the district continue to require the paper flow.

The men who hustle through the vestibule and onto the trading floor seem cheerful enough, and are given to exchanging small jokes and light banter. Their great-grandfathers used to fling dollar bills out of office windows after unusually profitable sessions, while their grandfathers would toss a ball around when activity dried up in the 1930s. To relieve tensions during the great bull market of the 1950s and 1960s, their fathers would break paper bags filled with water over one another's heads, let up a whoop when someone with a flashy jacket came to the floor, or ogle pretty women in the visitors' gallery.

On the surface, at least, they do not comprise a somber or stuffy crew. But in 1977 they are the focus of rapid change within the district, and many are troubled. For while they may be able to pass their positions and portions down to their children, most suspect the system will not last much beyond the next generation, if that. Many of these fears and much of the talk of disintegration are hyperbole, for Stock Exchange figures—especially members—are given to extremes of joy and fear. Still, there usually is a basis for such sentiments, and one exists at the present time.

Seventy years ago one specialist, John Rodemeyer, called the N.Y.S.E. "perhaps the most substantial and perfect financial temple in the world." It still is there, but no longer does the edifice seem quite so substantial. Some of its staunchest defenders concede its lack of perfection. Challenges are being mounted against it by rivals in other cities and within the financial district, and even by groups of its own members. "Things fall apart; the centre cannot hold," wrote William Butler Yeats—not thinking, of course, about Wall Street at the time. With all of its flaws, the N.Y.S.E. remains at the center, and should it fall, its leaders fear, as did Yeats in another context, that "mere anarchy is loosed upon the world."

The size of a community and the methods by which it handles its work provides a rough litmus test as to the climate for change. Today there are some 120,000 individuals who own and control, work at, with, or for the N.Y.S.E., or service its member firms. Their focus— the place toward which most of their energies are directed—is the trading floor. In 1976, the average daily volume there was 18 million shares, a record. Some of the sessions, especially those in January and February, were hectic, and the floor workers and those at the brokerages had to put in overtime to make certain orders were processed and all was in readiness for the next day's business. But there were few bottlenecks, and for the most part the work proceeded smoothly.

Ten years earlier, with less than 100,000 individuals, the trading average was 7.5 million shares. In 1969–70, when brokerages were crashing in the most intensely superheated atmosphere in forty years, the N.Y.S.E. was obliged to shorten its trading sessions and for a while close down completely on Wednesdays in an attempt at containing the volume. It didn't work. Brokerages throughout the financial district put on additional help, literally hiring the clerks off the streets, raiding high schools for runners, and wheedling old-timers into delaying their retirements. Total employment rose to 144,000, an all-time peak, while the average daily trading volume was 11.6 million shares.

Some observers have credited the relatively smooth N.Y.S.E. operations today to reforms undertaken after the paper-crunch had ended. They imply that the critical situation then had obliged the Exchange to modernize operations so as to avoid a repetition of the sorry and dangerous situation. This is a plausible analysis, but only partially true. The paper-crunch was the effect, not the cause, of change. During the 1960s, the combination of a stock market boom, the impact of new technologies, the resurgence of old rivals and the appearance of new ones—and the inability of the N.Y.S.E. to deal effectively with any of these factors—created an intolerable situation. Congressional investigations followed, and the phoenixlike resurgence of the Securities and Exchange Commission, somnolent for decades, provided the precipitating element. A critical mass was achieved in the early 1970s. Then the N.Y.S.E. began to change, the metamorphosis accelerating over time. Grudgingly, the Exchange's leaders shucked off old institutions and accepted new ones. They warned of disaster should alterations take place, but when they did, these men made the best of the new dispensation. On the whole, the N.Y.S.E. has survived well. The best place to see this is on the trading floor itself, and the only method by which the convolutions can be unraveled is through an appreciation of what is supposed to be taking place there.

To the casual onlooker, and even to many investors, all members of the N.Y.S.E. seem alike. In fact, each of the members fills one of four functions, that of specialist, two-dollar broker, trader, or commission broker. All four operate within the trading area. Yet the first three are known as men of the floor, while the registered representatives, for reasons which soon will become clear, are considered "upstairs."

First—because they dominate the N.Y.S.E.—are the specialists. Each of them is responsible for "making markets" in several stocks or, to put it more precisely, is part of a team which handles them and is known as a unit. Market making is the key to the floor. It means, simply, that the specialist unit stands ready to buy or sell shares in the stock it handles, and to do so in an orderly and responsible fashion. Presently around a quarter of the N.Y.S.E.'s members, slightly fewer than 400, are specialists, and they are gathered into sixty-six units. Since the specialists deal only with other brokers, who either are buying or selling for their own accounts or are taking the public's orders to the floor for execution, their names and those of their firms are not well known beyond the district. But Wagner, Stott and Adler, Coleman are as powerful in their spheres as Merrill Lynch or Bache are in the brokerage fraternity.

On a normal day there will be some 3,000 people on the floor. To the uneducated eye, most seem in motion or, when they are not, in casual conversation or lounging at the side of the floor. The specialists alone rarely budge from their spots. Each is stationed at one of the twenty-two trading posts, there to take orders from the others: the commission brokers who handle orders from the public, the two-dollar brokers who assist them on occasion, and the traders working their own accounts. There are over 2,000 different issues listed at the N.Y.S.E. Each has its specialist post, and in time all members learn where most of them can be traded—or at least, memorize the locations of the more important and active issues.

Until fairly recently, the Exchange was the only place in New York that made large-scale markets in its securities. True, the over-the-counter traders—individuals who were not members of the Exchange—did buy and sell such issues, but almost all did so sporadically, were obliged to set their prices by referring to the last trade at the N.Y.S.E., and were not always reliable. In addition there were regional exchanges, the most important of which were the Pacific Coast (with trading floors in Los Angeles and San Francisco), the Midwest (located in Chicago), and the P-B-W (now the Philadelphia) all of which made markets in some N.Y.S.E.–listed securities. But New York was the central marketplace, the reference point, the leader of the community. Ten years ago it was not at all unusual for a Los Angeles-based broker to execute an order in Liggett-Group (then called Liggett & Myers) at the N.Y.S.E. rather than at the Pacific Coast, even though the latter was only a few blocks from his office.

This situation gave the specialist in LiggettGroup—in this case, Adler, Coleman—an effective monopoly on trading in that stock. He didn't have to seek business, for it came to him, since he ran the only game in town. A critic of the system, who at the time clerked on the N.Y.S.E. floor, recalled a specialist who "spent his entire day at play with some of his friends," engaged in what he called "the Italian finger game"—in which two players thrust fingers at one another, simultaneously shouting out guesses as to what the sum of the digits will be. This particular specialist was assigned an attractive stock. One day he told the clerk that the previous year he had earned $720,000. "I knew right then that either the finger game or the specialist's slot was extremely lucrative." Such are the wages of monopoly returns.*

By N.Y.S.E. regulations and Securities and Exchange Commission practice, the specialist is supposed to maintain an orderly market in his stock. This means he must always stand ready to buy or sell shares, and should adjust his quotes so that advances and declines are minor, and not in sudden jumps. This requires the specialist to enter the market in a trading capacity. Should there be a rush to sell the stock, he must be prepared to "eat" the shares. Conversely, when demand develops, he must sell from his holdings. In other words, the specialist on balance bets against the market. Or at least, this is the theory, rationale, and justification for the system.

The practice does not conform well to the theory. On the one hand, the specialist is supposed to perform a stabilizing function, even though losing money or foregoing profits in the process, while on the other he has the normal urge to maximize profits while minimizing risks. Should there be bad news regarding his stock, for example, sellers would rush in, and the specialist would be expected to try to maintain an orderly market by buying their stock for his inventory

* James M. Stone, *One Way for Wall Street* (Boston, 1975), p. 48.

while gradually lowering his quotes. But at the same time he has the natural tendency to sell his own shares, or at least not add stock and troubles to his portfolio. The workings of self-interest demand a rapid decline in price. The specialist realizes that should this transpire an investigation would follow. So he does the best he can. Some 99 percent of all trades in any given stock are within a quarter of a point of the previous sale. The N.Y.S.E. is proud of this "stabilization rate," and means to keep it high.

The specialist derives a good deal of his income from inventory profits, with the rest coming from a shared interest in the commissions on trades. In many ways he is a private trader, dealing for his own account. He knows the value of a good stabilization rate—that is one measure of a specialist's performance, and new issues are assigned in part at least on this basis. But it hurts to have to purchase stock while it is sliding, or sell in a market on the way up. Self-interest and duty collide every day on the floor, with the individual specialist having to weigh matters, consulting his own calculus of duty and profit. Recent studies have indicated that more often than not, specialists have decided to opt for their short-run interests. Too often, they run for cover when the avalanche begins.

Until quite recently, little was done, or could be done, about this situation. There was no secret about any of this; nor did those who profited most from the system evince feelings of guilt or remorse. The N.Y.S.E. dominated the market nexus, and the specialists controlled the N.Y.S.E. It was a closed circle. In theory, any member could try to become a specialist, but in practice few new ones were admitted to the group. Allocations of stocks were made by the Floor Committee, where friendships and tradition usually proved more important than ability. Thus, if a new listing, XYZ, appeared before the Committee, chances were that it would be assigned to an old-timer, and not a pushy newcomer. Moreover the old-timer knew this, and this knowledge played a role when he had to decide whether to eat a declining stock or let its price collapse, thus abandoning his post. He would run out, fairly certain his friends on the committee would understand. So they did.

Today even the Exchange concedes there have been major abuses in this system, and steps have been taken to reform it. One method was to introduce competing market makers, individuals permitted to make markets in stocks and deal in them alongside the specialist, in effect as his rivals. The specialists themselves were gently urged to perform better than they had in the past. To this they responded with a defense based on the record, which showed that most of the time they had carried out their functions. Critics answered by noting that the specialist was not necessary in normal markets. Like a fire extinguisher, you wanted it to work in emergencies. And on such occasions, the specialists ran for cover. Thus, they were redundant most of the time and useless when needed.

The Exchange reacted. In the mid-1970s its leaders warned the specialists that just as stocks had been assigned to them in the past, so they could be withdrawn in the future. Finally, the allocation system was scrutinized, most of all by the Batten Committee, headed by William Batten, the retired head of J. C. Penney and a N.Y.S.E. board member.

Batten is a gregarious, wholesome individual, who while at Penney had transformed it into a major retailer. He had known little of Wall Street prior to 1975, when he took a more active interest in the Exchange. Named to head the committee which investigated the specialist system, Batten found "a correlation between desirable awards and current or past service as a Floor Director or Governor on the part of one or more of the successful units." This could be explained, said the committee, "by the fact that Directors and Governors tend to be chosen from the better performing units." In other words, the large units produce the powerful figures, who in turn use their power to enlarge their units. The committee did not say which came first, the power or the performance, but clearly the specialist system produced a tightly knit fraternity, a club within the club, as it were. Batten and his colleagues recommended that specialist power be reduced, but they didn't say how this was to be accomplished. In this way, Batten became known as a reformer, but maintained his links with the specialists.

But the change was coming, the result of factors which the specialists could not control, and events to which they reacted slowly and often foolishly. Some of these men, reared in the 1930s and 1940s when months would pass without a single million share day, had been unable to adjust to the higher volume of the 1950s and 1960s. Average daily volume in 1940 had been 750,000 shares. In 1950, it was slightly below the 2 million mark. By 1961, the N.Y.S.E. was trading an average of 4 million shares a day, and five years later, over 6 million. By then the specialists were showing the strain of such an environment, and even the younger ones were having trouble keeping up with the pace.

Such a situation had existed prior to the appearance of the Open Board. The N.Y.S.E. should have recognized the signs. It was little wonder, then, that the system developed major fissures in 1971, when the average volume was over 15 million shares, or that by then the Third Market was a flourishing rival.

Another problem was the increase in the number of block trades, those orders of more than a few thousand shares—the N.Y.S.E. today defines them as 10,000 or more shares of a stock in a single transaction. Major financial institutions buy and sell blocks just as the individual deals in "round lots"—one hundred shares at a time. The institutions came to dominate trading in many key issues in the late 1950s and 1960s. The number of block trades increased, as did their impact upon the exchange system.

The N.Y.S.E. sought new techniques which would enable the specialists to adapt to block trading. Most involved a combination of off-the-floor dealings and the familiar auction system. All of these were flawed and were discarded after relatively short periods.

The specialist system demonstrated an inability to wed block trading and public responsibility. This became evident when several institutions tried to unload their shares at the same time. On such occasions the specialist would find himself having to eat tens of thousands of shares in a morning session, and perhaps more in the afternoon. Rather than doing so, he would abandon attempts at maintaining order and flee for cover. It did not happen often, and in time the specialists learned how to cross orders by locating buyers for the sellers, but by the mid-1960s, it had become evident that the system wasn't working as advertised, and either would undergo major surgery and alteration or be replaced—just as the upstairs auctions had been a century earlier.

There was much talk of automation in the late 1950s, and predictions that one day stock trades would be handled by machines, eliminating the human factor. Some of this was farfetched and exaggerated, but enough of it was demonstrably true, and it worried the specialists. Could machines make them obsolete? It was a most important question, for which they had no precise answer. But they did have a response, and that was to fight automation, especially where it involved a challenge to the specialist system.

While struggling against automation, the N.Y.S.E. had to meet the challenge from an older, more familiar set of rivals, namely the regional stock exchanges. In fact, the two battles were joined, for the regionals did automate willingly, and in other ways make their markets more attractive to those institutions that dealt in large blocks. From 1960 to 1970 the non–New York exchanges had less than 10 percent of total volume. Then the figure began rising, always at the expense of the senior market. By 1973 it peaked at 11.4 percent, leveled off, and then rose once more.

This is not to imply that the specialists at the regional stock exchanges are challenging those at the central market for domination in securities, but rather that they not only have survived but are prospering.

A more important challenge to the N.Y.S.E. specialists came from the old over-the-counter traders. These men and their ancestors had dealt in listed stocks for as long as the list had existed, and like their counterparts at the central market, they suffered severely during the depression and the 1940s, eking out meager livings by dealing in government paper and nonlisted stocks. But they did have an advantage, in that they were accustomed to dealing directly with principals who wanted to purchase or sell blocks of securities. And they weren't bound to an old system or organization, even though most were members of the National Association of Securities Dealers. These men quickly challenged the N.Y.S.E. specialists for the big block business. First they did so by using their old technology—telephones. Then they adapted to the new—computers and related equipment. In 1965 a term cropped up on the financial pages—Third Market—to describe the O-T-C traders who specialized in listed securities.* That year Third

* "In simplified terms the Third Market consists of broker-dealers, nonmembers of either large stock exchange, who actively engage as principals in buying and selling listed

Market transactions totaled 49 million shares, less than 3 percent that of the central market. By 1972, the figure had reached 327 million, well over 7 percent of the business done by specialists.

As might have been expected, the N.Y.S.E. specialists were skittish. The Third Market challenge, added to the collapse and financial disruptions of 1969–70 and the feelings of ennui prevalent throughout much of the nation, led some to conclude the end was near. The pessimists were prepared to concede defeat. Others wanted to make a last stand on the merits of their system, and purge nonbelievers; the more astute of them knew that the specialist system had flaws, and searched for ways to improve it, or failing that, to scrap the method and seek a new one.

The contest between the specialists and the Third Market began in the late 1960s, but the key phase opened in early 1971, when the traders unveiled their new weapon, NASDAQ, an acronym for National Association of Security Dealers Automated Quotation System. Through the use of electronic consoles whose essentials could be mastered in a matter of hours, O-T-C dealers could buy and sell from one another rapidly and at low cost. For years there had been talk of an electronic marketplace. NASDAQ was the first step. Its operations will be discussed in the next chapter. For the moment, and for this discussion, it suffices to say that NASDAQ's impact on Wall Street was comparable to that of the atomic bomb on warfare; after it appeared, nothing would ever be the same.

The specialists appreciated the implications of this move, even when some of the intricacies of the machinery eluded them. These devices indeed would make them obsolete. Perhaps the machines already had done so.

What weapons did the N.Y.S.E. have with which to fight this menace? For one thing, there was proximity. Within the same building and organization were specialists and commission houses, which had worked with one another for decades, even generations. Tradition was on their side. Why abandon a perfectly workable system for a new, untried one, at a time when all markets were experiencing difficulties?

securities over the counter on a continuous basis and who themselves make the markets in such listed securities." Anthony Schlesinger, "The Third Market—Challenge to the New York Stock Exchange," *Southwestern Law Journal* (Vol. 20, 1966), p. 640.

The specialists controlled the N.Y.S.E., which in turn maintained strong controls over its members, including the commission houses. These had close relationships with the trust companies, banks, mutual funds, and other powerful investors. Word was passed down that these ties of business and friendship would be strained if the large institutions utilized the Third Market's new facility. Or at least, this was the hope the specialists held in 1971.

Would the brokerages cooperate? If not, the N.Y.S.E. had its Rule 394 to brandish over their collective and individual heads. This rule, a keystone of the Exchange system, stated that member firms had to execute their orders on the floor of a recognized securities market—and this meant no dealings with the Third Market. In 1971–72, the N.Y.S.E. interpreted the rule to mean the floor at Wall and Broad, but later on stress was placed upon the fact that the members were free to use any floor—the Midwest, the P-B-W, and the Pacific Coast among others—so long as the boycott against the Third Market was maintained.

With the advent of NASDAQ an era of law suits, political pressure, large-scale maneuverings in Washington and New York, and convoluted infighting erupted. Both sides marshalled electronics to assist in their efforts, and the Exchange in particular created new organizations, so many that outsiders required a pocket glossary to understand the words behind the acronyms. BAS, AutEx, Instinet, SIAC, ATS, CENTAUR, CTA, SECURE, TAD—these were only some of the more important ones. N.Y.S.E. and Third Market leaders understood what they were supposed to accomplish as well as their implications, for their futures depended upon the technology and how it was used and accepted. They could explain the struggle to outsiders, and would do so at length if asked. But it really was a rather parochial fight, especially in its tactics. Listeners would find their eyes glazing over, their heads nodding, and would fix smiles on their faces while wondering how best to terminate somewhat meaningless conversations—at least from their point of view. Perhaps they felt foolish or stupid, for the specialists and market makers would become quite animated in the course of their monologues. Few, however, were or are able to reduce the arguments to essentials, or to convince nonparticipants that the public will be seriously affected by the outcome. As for investors, they are more interested in the fortunes of IBM, RCA, and GM than those of SIAC, NASDAQ, or TAD.

When all the infighting and electronic and institutional detritus is stripped away, what remains is a conflict between two differing kinds of securities markets, each with its own philosophy and rationale as well as its own leaders, and neither without weaknesses or flaws.

The specialist market is more costly than that of the dealers. It has a complex superstructure and services facility—the N.Y.S.E.'s 1976 expenditures were around $84 million, more than twice the 1966 figure. Too, it is cumbersome. In the Third Market, buyer and seller confront one another directly, without intermediaries. The specialist is supposed to function as an intermediary, fulfilling a public interest. This is costly. For his effort, the specialist must be compensated, and this comes in the form of inventory profits and commissions. Part of the latter is given to the N.Y.S.E. to keep it functioning and prepare for the future. Around 20 percent of the Exchange's income is derived from commissions.

This is not the Exchange's major source of income, however. Some 30 percent comes from listing and related fees, provided by those firms whose shares are traded on the floor. If the Third Market could convince America's corporate elite that there was little value or prestige attached to an N.Y.S.E. listing—and if these major corporations no longer were willing to pay for the privilege—then the N.Y.S.E. would disappear. More even than trading volume, listing is the key to the Exchange's future. And it is here that the Third Market has mounted one of its most sustained and successful attacks.

A new company accepted for N.Y.S.E. listing pays $25,000 for the entry plus one cent per share for all of those outstanding. In addition, there are yearly fees of $10,000 and one-tenth of a cent. This means that a company with 5 million shares outstanding can be listed for $75,000, and must pay $15,000 a year thereafter. The continuing fee for a large firm like General Motors—with close to 300 million shares outstanding—comes to over $300,000.

In contrast, the much less expensive NASDAQ fees are $1,000 initially and one-tenth of a cent per share, while the continuing charges are $250 and one-twentieth of a cent a year. That small 5 million share company would have to put up $6,000 for a NASDAQ listing and $2,750 annually.

What of General Motors? If that company left the N.Y.S.E. for NASDAQ—improbable and unthinkable though it may be—its annual fee would be halved. Furthermore, some companies which have opted to remain on NASDAQ claim it is superior to the specialist system. "In the over-the-counter market, we have 8 or 10 market makers, sponsoring our stock," said Douglas Curtis of the Franklin Electric Company. "On an exchange, we don't know what kind of market we would have with one specialist." Curtis went on to note that "newspaper coverage of NASDAQ stocks has greatly improved. . . . With a number of market makers, good newspaper coverage, and an accurate reliable system, we see no need to go to an exchange."

This is precisely what bothers all specialists. Not only do they fear the loss of volume in listed stocks, but they know of many over-the-counter traded securities which qualify for listing—among them Anheuser-Busch, Tampax, Cameron Iron Works, Tecumseh Products, and DeKalb Agricultural—and haven't applied, and have indicated their intentions to remain where they are.

When trading volume shrank during the Great Depression, specialists would track down companies that qualified for listing and try to talk their leaders into applying. This was not necessary in the 1950s and 1960s; then, the companies approached the Exchange, which considered itself the bearer of good news when informing the corporation that it would be admitted to the exclusive club. Today we see a replay of the 1930s. Exploratory correspondence to qualifying companies is often politely rejected, and the specialists have difficulty in getting to see chief executive officers. This concerns the specialists as much as the threatened and real loss of floor trades. No longer do they run the only wheel in town.

In order to preserve both their listings and trades the specialists—functioning through the N.Y.S.E. management—took the offensive. First of all, they attempted to retain the allegiance of the commission houses by threatening them with a strong and vigorous application of Rule 394, while fighting any attempt to alter the essentials of the Exchange structure. The Third Market responded with lawsuits, and the two sides fought it out before the Securities and Exchange Commission and congressional committees. The S.E.C. tended to favor the Third Market, while Congress was in the mood for Wall Street reforms after the 1969–70 debacle. By the early 1970s, the N.Y.S.E. leaders had come to understand that this was a losing game. By one means or another, Rule 394 would become a dead letter and they would have to accept drastic alterations in the way they did business.

Exchange President Robert Haack said as much, and for this earned the opposition of old-timers, who had little taste for his sad tidings. Haack was deposed in 1972. At the same time his opponents grudgingly agreed that his analysis of the problem had been accurate. They would have to erect a new exchange system complete with an alternate technology to that of NASDAQ.

James Needham, who succeeded Haack, led the attack. A medium-sized, heavyset and handsome man with a piercing glance, he impressed people with his ability to resolve problems by cutting directly to their roots. When he wanted to be, Needham was blunt, but he also knew how to persuade. Needham looked like a former football player turned coach, and indeed he did play the game at college. However, he became an accountant and in the early 1960s seemed headed for a distinguished but not necessarily prominent position at one of several large companies. A conservative Republican known for his criticism of regulatory bodies, he was named to the S.E.C. by President Nixon, probably as part of an attempt to counter the more liberal forces there. Almost immediately, Needham clashed with the lawyers who headed the agency—as might be expected when a conservative accountant entered such a place. But this unpopularity served him well on Wall Street, where he became known as one of the few commissioners amenable to the N.Y.S.E. point of view.

In late 1970, when the S.E.C. seemed sympathetic to the Third Market approach, Needham spoke out for a drastic overhaul of the entire securities industry, but his plan was one which met with N.Y.S.E. approval. There would be two central markets, he said. The first would consist of an exchange, formed by the merger of all present exchanges, on which would be traded only listed stocks. The other would be a market centered around the National Association of Securities Dealers, based upon NASDAQ, on which would be traded un-listed securities. "Each market will have the right to determine whether to trade a security," he said, and the issuer of the security would decide which market he preferred. Thus, competition would be introduced into the marketplace. Naturally, "both market systems will be fully automated."

This was not an attempt to create new competition, but instead a plan designed to aggrandize the N.Y.S.E. and ban the O-T-C traders from dealing in listed securities. The plan didn't get very far and served to isolate its author further still from his colleagues. But the concept, and the flamboyant and forceful way in which Needham presented it and then defended himself from attacks, impressed the Exchange's specialists. They needed a person with strong ideas, a dynamic manner, and an empathy with their point of view, who knew his way around Washington and New York. Needham was named as the first paid chairman of the N.Y.S.E.

The selection and elevation of James Needham indicated that the Exchange would accelerate its offensive against the Third Market, and in particular develop methods to refine and enhance the specialist system. This conclusion was reinforced by the release of the Martin Report, presented by William McChesney Martin, who in addition to being the former head of the Federal Reserve Board had served as N.Y.S.E. president in the 1930s. Martin had been asked by the Exchange to undertake a study of the markets and make recommendations about the need for change. Among other things, the Report favored the specialist system over Third Market techniques, frowned upon abrupt changes in the Exchange system, but called for a unification of registered exchanges. Most important, Martin saw the need for a "consolidated tape," which would transmit all transactions on all exchanges.

Several months prior to the release of the Martin Report, the S.E.C. published its Institutional Investor Study Report, which came to a different set of conclusions. It too favored a consolidated tape upon which all trades would be reported but insisted that the Third Market be allowed to continue in operation, and that its transactions in N.Y.S.E.–listed stocks be reported on that tape.

This became the crux of the argument, the battlefield upon which

Needham and his specialists would fight the Third Market. Both agreed that the electronic marketplace was about to be born; the technology already existed, and the S.E.C. was pressing to have it put into place. The vital questions were who would control the system and which forces would be included under its umbrella.

The debate and parrying intensified in 1972 and the strategies coalesced soon after. The Third Market had its NASDAQ, a system whereby market makers could communicate with one another and execute orders, but it lacked a tape readout. Its backers claimed this presented no great difficulty, and they urged Congress and the S.E.C. to give them permission to develop one. Once the two segments were connected, the electronic marketplace would be ready to go into operation, and would be based upon open access to all those who chose to join—exchanges included.

For its part, the N.Y.S.E. had the tape, but no trading consoles. It rushed to develop such a system, which would complete its version of the electronic stock market.

The task was entrusted to the Securities Industry Automation Corporation (SIAC), which was organized and owned by the N.Y.S.E. in conjunction with the American Stock Exchange. SIAC had attempted to develop systems earlier—BAS was one of these—and for the most part had done poorly. By late 1972, however, it appeared on the verge of completing at least part of the job—a system designed to consolidate all *exchange* originated sales on a single tape—which would exclude those executed on the Third Market. The O-T-C traders protested. If their trades were included, they argued, the public would be able to see just how superior they were to those of the specialists. It was unfair and unnecessary, they said, an attempt to perpetuate the N.Y.S.E. monopoly.

Wouldn't it have been more sensible to perform a wedding of NASDAQ with the N.Y.S.E. tape? It could have been done if technology was the only problem, and at a substantial saving for all. Operators at NASDAQ consoles could have obtained rival bids and asks, executed the order, and have the information fed into the tape simultaneously. As it was, the specialists completed their operations, and then placed the information on the tape. It was as though Henry Ford had placed an engine into an old surrey and had not developed the automobile. Why save the specialist system when technology appeared to demand its elimination?

Power, and not economics or even technology, was at the base of the struggle, however, and the specialists adamantly opposed such a solution. Instead, the N.Y.S.E. began installing cathode ray tube displays of its own into the specialist posts in the spring of 1974, and they were ready for operation the following year.

Why not accept the NASDAQ hardware? It could have been adapted for the use of specialists. But Needham claimed the NASDAQ terminals were too big for the cabinetry, and with perfectly straight faces the N.Y.S.E. management held to this line.

By then the S.E.C. had decided that the N.Y.S.E. would have to permit Third Market sales to be displayed on its tape, and after some wrangling Needham conceded the point. But in return he received a major concession. SIAC was granted a five year contract to run the consolidated tape—and so, in effect, exclude NASDAQ from competition for this period. Then the Third Market and the S.E.C. reacted. Unwilling to permit SIAC so much raw power, the Commission insisted upon the establishment of a Consolidated Tape Association, which would set SIAC policy and be composed of representatives of the exchanges—plus the National Association of Securities Dealers, which upheld the interests of the men of the Third Market. Furthermore participation in SIAC was opened to the regional exchanges, and there were hints that some might be offered to N.A.S.D. members as well—if they were interested in making such a gesture, which would imply a loss of confidence in NASDAQ.

Thus the specialists won both a skirmish and a major point. They too were going electronic; they were answering the NASDAQ challenge with an automated marketplace of their own. But was it a significant victory? The specialists remained; and on the surface, at least, they conducted their operations pretty much as they had in the past. Yet there were differences. NASDAQ was intact, trading listed securities often for lower net prices than those at the N.Y.S.E. or the regionals.

By early 1976 there were signs all was not well—the general public was coming to realize that the great Wall Street debate might affect the so-called little guy after all. Clients would place orders to purchase a round lot of stock at, say, 50, and be told by their broker that the order could not be completed at that price. But the following day the financial pages of their newspapers, which carried the prices on the consolidated tape, would show that the stock had dipped to 49⅞. When challenged, the broker would have to concede that the stock had traded at that figure, but not on the N.Y.S.E.—or perhaps it had crossed there on a large block. Too, the stock might have been traded at 50 or slightly lower than that at one of the regionals, or on the Third Market.

Most likely, the broker had acted in a routine fashion, following company policy, and sent the order to the N.Y.S.E. His floor representative had placed the bid with the specialist, who had entered it in his book at 50, but had not lowered his price to that level during the day. But some other specialist, on another exchange or market covered by the consolidated tape, had sold the stock at the desired price, and it had shown up in the newspaper the following day. No matter what the explanation, the client would be irate, perhaps angered to the point of taking his account elsewhere, to a more aggressive broker whom he believed capable of getting better executions by shopping around. Furthermore, it could become a Securities and Exchange Commission affair, since the broker was committed to get the best price for his client.

The matter did not rest there; on Wall Street today, technological breakthroughs are quickly mutated into economic and political issues. In the autumn of 1976, the N.A.S.D. announced that the consoles soon would be equipped so as to display quotations for all N.Y.S.E. listed stocks, from all exchanges and the Third Market as well. Known as the Consolidated Quotation Service (CQS), it would enable offices equipped with NASDAQ consoles to find out at a glance the best market in the country for any N.Y.S.E. security, and so provide operators with a far more efficient pricing mechanism than exists on any trading floor. CQS would begin operations at 9:00 A.M. Eastern time and close down at 6:30 P.M., going into service prior to the N.Y.S.E. opening bell and continuing on after the close. In CQS, the NASDAQ people would have the prototype for an around the clock market, open to those who wanted to use it at any time, day or night. How could the N.Y.S.E. fight such a system?

The N.Y.S.E. knew about CQS months prior to the official announcement, and naturally was concerned about the development, while at the same time uncertain how best to respond. The Exchange's own system wasn't working out as well as had been hoped, and other problems surfaced to complicate matters. Needham had alienated many S.E.C. commissioners and had angered several prominent congressmen and senators by his abrasive behavior. He had been hired by the N.Y.S.E. board to fight the Third Market and force it to retreat. Failing in this, he was to work for a unified exchange system, which would be led by the N.Y.S.E. and exclude O-T-C traders. Needham had lost, but through no fault of his own. Rather, he had been brought down by two forces over which he had no control. The first was the superior technology represented by NASDAQ, while the second was pressure from Washington on the part of legislators determined to press for a central marketplace based upon non–N.Y.S.E. institutions.

By January, 1976, some board members were talking of easing Needham from office, of throwing him away as a sop to reformers and as a sign of capitulation. The movement to do so began, gathered momentum in late winter and early spring, and came to a head in mid-April. Those men who once had urged Needham into battle now used him as a scapegoat for their misconceived defense of an outmoded system. Needham left the Exchange in early May, to be replaced by William Batten, author of the Batten Report, which had criticized the specialists, and a person who was granted more of a free hand in determining policy than had any of his predecessors.

Batten is an unusual kind of man for the N.Y.S.E. He is the first of its leaders to have been raised in a highly competitive atmosphere. Needham had been an accountant, and Funston a college president, while previous chief operating and executive officers were civil servants or N.Y.S.E. members. Batten had come up through J. C. Penney when it had to combat Sears, Roebuck, S. S. Kresge, Montgomery Ward, and others for the customer dollar, and do so on the basis of price and service, and not as a monopoly that couldn't be breached and which maintained fixed rates. He promised to defend the N.Y.S.E. against interlopers, but would not swear to preserve the status quo, or even try to do so. Rather, he would get the best deal possible. Rule 394 might have to be sacrificed in the process. Even the specialists might be discarded, though Batten would not say this was necessary.

Needham had been acquired to do battle. William Batten was to negotiate a surrender, or at least so it seemed. The largest securities market in America would have to come to terms with the O-T-C dealers who operated without seeing one another, through terminals and telephones. He would have to parry with a revived Securities and Exchange Commission, headed by civil servants.

Vanderbilt would have been amazed.

CHAPTER THREE

O-T-C

O NLY ONE stock issue in every ten is traded on an organized securities exchange, and fewer than half of those make it to the N.Y.S.E. The others are bought and sold on the over-the-counter market, a vast, amorphous institution comprised of three thousand member firms with six thousand branch offices.

Some O-T-C houses are as powerful and prestigious as most N.Y.S.E.–based brokerages. Weeden & Co., perhaps the best known of them, is one of the top firms in the industry in terms of sophistication, influence, and reputation. For years James Needham tried to woo Weeden to the N.Y.S.E., not only in order to have another strong firm, but to rid the Exchange of one of its most effective critics. Weeden & Co. prefers the over-the-counter market, which it considers superior to the N.Y.S.E.

Not long ago there was a status hierarchy among securities. Stocks in newly capitalized companies would be underwritten, sold to the public, and then traded over-the-counter. After a while they might qualify for listing on the American Stock Exchange, which for years served as a sort of minor league, with the best issues going on to the big time. That, of course, was the N.Y.S.E.

True, some companies rejected listing on any exchange, due to an unwillingness or inability to provide information or meet one or another technical requirements. A small handful of companies remained on the O-T-C due to perversity on the part of a founder. But this no longer is the case. As has been shown, many O-T-C stocks qualify for listing on either the N.Y.S.E. or Amex, have been invited to apply, but have opted to remain where they are.

On the other extreme, there are companies with a few thousand shares of stock outstanding, doing a local business of less than $100,000 gross, and staffed by one or two full-time workers and some part-timers. Included among these would be family businesses incorporated for tax reasons, with only a small portion of the total capitalization in the hands of the public. Months might go by without a single transaction taking place in these issues. Such stocks, too, are found on the over-the-counter market.

Similarly, thousands of small businessmen have passed licensing examinations, paid fees, and are considered registered representatives. They work for no firm—at least on a full-time basis—and may spend only a few hours a week on securities. They operate out of desks in their homes, and are not considered brokers by their friends. Of the approximately 200,000 registered dealers in the United States, only a very small percentage are employed by Weeden or other large houses. Many more run one-man offices. An even larger number tend to look upon brokerage as akin to being a notary public—handy to earn extra cash but no more than that.

This loose conglomeration of securities and dealers has diverse origins. They may be traced to those brokers who weren't asked to join the Stock and Exchange Board in 1792. Throughout the nineteenth century, there were dealers who through choice—or the lack of it—remained outside the central market and the regionals. Some came to terms with the N.Y.S.E., agreed not to trade in its securities, and later on emerged as the Curb, which in time evolved into the American Stock Exchange. Others would not accept this limitation and persisted in trading N.Y.S.E.–listed securities even while concentrating upon unlisted stocks and bonds. These men came to be known as over-the-counter brokers, because the structure in which they functioned was just that—a market where each broker worked out of his own office, dealing in securities over his counter.

There was no central market, no meshing of forces, and little in the way of cooperation, even after the perfection of the telephone, telegraph, and ticker. Should a person want to buy or sell a stock that wasn't listed on an exchange, he would have to contact several dealers, perhaps in more than one city, and then get the best deal possible. O-T-C brokers were used by speculators who wanted to accumulate or sell large blocks of shares without anyone at the exchanges knowing of it. Several O-T-C dealers held regular auctions of N.Y.S.E.–listed stocks along with unlisted issues long after the senior market abandoned the practice. As late as the 1940s there were such auctions in the Wall Street area, run by brokers who catered to the needs of estates and institutions.

The N.Y.S.E. did not trade government securities, municipal bonds, and railroad equipment trust certificates, as well as several other categories of paper. All found markets on the O-T-C. Until recently bank and insurance stocks weren't acceptable at Wall and Broad, and these two were bought and sold over the counter, as were stocks in most foreign corporations. The N.Y.S.E. listed shares in closed-end investment trusts in the 1920s and afterward, but would have nothing to do with mutual funds. That horde of salesmen that amassed more than 10 million mutual fund accounts in the quarter of a century following the end of World War II were over-the-counter brokers, most of whom worked part-time on their jobs.

Throughout American history those interested in and concerned with securities focused their attention upon the organized sector—the exchanges and the large investment banks. Doing so is akin to speaking of American civilization in 1620 in terms of the few scattered European settlements along the eastern seaboard. What of the rest of the continent? At the turn of the century, according to most accounts, the financial universe revolved around the N.Y.S.E. and ancillary institutions. New York bankers, such as J. P. Morgan and Jacob Schiff, became figures of world prominence, who not only advised rulers, but manipulated them.

At that time, however, most of the securities business in America was transacted by thousands of small dealers in towns and villages. The retired railroader who wanted a few shares in a local bank, the small businessman who thought it prudent to own some equity in the new electric utility company, and the widow who placed her life savings in government bonds—all took their business to bankers and part-time brokers, who were not members of organized exchanges. Morgan knew of their existence; when he set about creating U.S. Steel he had

70 INSIDE WALL STREET

to gain control of over a hundred small companies that were not listed on the N.Y.S.E. He recruited dozens of brokerages that sent their agents into the back country, contacted these over-the-counter dealers, and arranged with them for the acquisition of needed securities. Not until the early 1920s did these small-town bankers and brokers begin to fade from the securities scene, and they persist in it today, for some stocks and for some clients.

These individuals were adept at the cross-transaction. A seller would come through the door with a few hundred shares in a company, for which there was no market, and would ask the banker's aid in locating a buyer. The banker would do so, for a commission, or even purchase the shares for the bank's account in some situations, to be resold at a later date. That same banker might buy and sell listed shares, too, for trust accounts and the like. There was no need for an exchange in such small dealings, and none was utilized, except as a reference point for prices.

The situation changed in the 1930s, when the New Dealers set about a thoroughgoing overhaul of the entire industry. Their major target was the old symbol of finance capitalism, the N.Y.S.E., which came close to collapse in 1934–35. In contrast, the over-the-counter dealers had only minor difficulties in surviving. Since they had little in the way of overhead—no market organization, no expensive bureaucracy, not even an exchange building and a mortgage—they could cut back and still maintain themselves intact. Not until 1938, when the reform era was about over, did the New Dealers seriously consider a restructuring of that market, and then it was done as an afterthought.

How was the O-T-C to be regulated? Had the question been asked in 1934, most reformers would have answered that it should be made part of a unified exchange structure, to be controlled by the Securities and Exchange Commission. In the next four years, however, the S.E.C. had setbacks as well as triumphs, in the course of which its leaders had developed the philosophy of self-regulation. In effect, the government would oversee the exchanges, making certain they were honest, run by ethical men with professional standards and aboveboard with the public. Such was the kind of compromise it had worked out with the N.Y.S.E., and that point of view was to be applied at the O-T-C. That marketplace would be asked to form its own administrative body, which would establish principles and codes of conduct, would enforce them, and act as an industry spokesman when dealing with the government.

Late in 1938 Congress passed, and President Roosevelt signed, the Maloney Act, more properly known as an amendment to the Securities Act of 1934. Under its terms, the O-T-C dealers were called upon to create an organization, the National Association of Securities Dealers, which would function as "a mechanism of regulation among over-the-counter brokers and dealers operating in interstate and foreign commerce or through the mails." The N.A.S.D. was a federal entity, with thirteen districts, each with a governing board. It went into operation the following year, headquartered in Washington, not New York, as befitted the only such organization of its kind—a body created by legislation and operating under what amounted to a federal charter.

What kind of structure had Congress created? Although the N.A.S.D. contained within itself seeds that in time might have grown into some form of securities market, clearly it was no such thing at the time of origin. The organization did not establish standards for O-T-C stocks and lacked the power to police O-T-C dealers. And since some of the dealers were also members of the N.Y.S.E. and other exchanges, the Association could scarcely claim their prime loyalty. On the other hand, it could establish ethical and professional standards, and noncompliance could result in ejection from the organization. N.A.S.D. rules against dealings with nonmembers and special discounts afforded members, combined with later congressional enactments and S.E.C. attitudes, meant that those O-T-C dealers who tried to operate outside the N.A.S.D. would find it difficult to do so.

Was the N.A.S.D. a professional organization, such as the National Association of Manufacturers or the American Medical Association? It did bring broker-dealers together in conventions, establish policies, and purport to speak for the brokerage community before Congress and the S.E.C., and act for it in relations with organized securities exchanges.

Though unable to accept or reject securities, the N.A.S.D. did create a national list of O-T-C stocks, report on their daily volume and price changes, and distribute the material to newspapers. In order to be on the national list today, a security must have at least 1,500 shareholders in a four-district area (with 300 in each of two of them) or 2,000 throughout the country. The price has to be five dollars or more, regular reporting is necessary, and there must be sufficient brokers—known as market makers—who will buy and sell, and so insure a measure of liquidity. Local lists, comprised of securities of smaller companies of regional interest, also were created and distributed. O-T-C stocks might begin on a local list and then graduate to the national, in somewhat the same way as listed stocks go from the Amex to the N.Y.S.E.

Not even its founders were certain as to how the N.A.S.D. would function, or for that matter, what its goals should be. The organization was a hybrid as well as an afterthought, a federally chartered body which was to operate under private auspices, one that could regulate members but not the securities in which they dealt. The N.A.S.D. could draw up its stock list, set requirements for entry, but not establish an exchange. Centralized in a Washington office building, it functioned through its thirteen centers, and at first there was little coordination of efforts. Some district leaders rarely visited their offices and ignored communications from Washington; to them, the N.A.S.D. was a sop to the federal reformers, nothing more. The O-T-C dealers were not accustomed to controls and regulations, and though these were supposed to exist in the early days, the exigencies of war meant that they became dead letters from the start.

The establishment of the N.A.S.D. did not alter the relationships between the O-T-C dealers and the organized exchanges, primarily because there was not much in the way of a relationship to affect. As a matter of course, an O-T-C dealer who wanted to buy or sell shares in a listed company would contact an N.Y.S.E.–affiliated brokerage and place his order there. Should a client at a Wall Street house wish to purchase unlisted shares, his registered representative would contact a market maker on the O-T-C, and execute his trade over the telephone. As might have been anticipated, reciprocal relationships arose and continued in some instances for generations.

There was competition in special kinds of trades, most particularly large blocks. For example, shortly after the beginning of World War II, European investors and governments attempted to sell shares in American corporations in New York, so as to raise funds for their war efforts. They quickly found that N.Y.S.E. specialists, who had become overly cautious due to the depression, were unable to execute sales of 10,000 or so shares of U.S. Steel, Standard Oil of New Jersey, or General Motors, or if they could, wanted to do so at prices that were several points below the last recorded trade. The O-T-C dealer operated differently. Unlike the specialist, he was not obliged to maintain an orderly market or to take stock when there was no apparent market for it. Rather, he was out to serve his own interests, and this meant buying low and selling high, and not necessarily doing one without a clear hope of the other. On learning of the existence of a person with a large block of stock to dispose of, the dealer would try to line up customers to acquire it. Thus, he might be able to get four or five clients together, who between them could take the 10,000 shares of G.M. Once everything was in place, the dealer would contact the seller, make an offer, and then distribute the block to the purchasers, selling at a higher price than he purchased. Unlike the N.Y.S.E. broker and the specialist, he charged no commissions, making his profit from the differential between the buy and the sell.

The O-T-C dealers conducted little business in large blocks during and immediately after World War II. Then, with the rise of institutional interest in the 1950s, this portion of their trading expanded. From 1955 to 1961, over-the-counter dealings in listed securities almost doubled, advancing at three times the rate of the increase at the N.Y.S.E. Additional firms were attracted to the business. Only three N.A.S.D. members were primarily concerned with listed securities in the early 1940s. Nine more entered the area in the early 1950s, and in 1961–62, another five were added. At the same time, many more O-T-C firms which specialized in unlisted and government securities established departments to trade in large blocks of listed shares.

That the senior market should have been concerned with this development is obvious today, but the situation was different in the 1950s and early 1960s. Under the leadership of President Keith Funston, the N.Y.S.E. wooed the small investor, not the large—this was the thrust of Funston's pet idea, People's Capitalism—and did little to refine block trading. Thus, the O-T-C dealers evolved and expanded with little in the way of significant opposition.

At the time, it appeared that the N.Y.S.E. would concentrate upon the retail end of the industry, with the O-T-C dealers carving out a niche in the wholesale operations. The specialists and the large brokerages would work together; both were members of the senior exchange. Should an investor call his broker to place an order he could be almost certain it would be executed at the N.Y.S.E. or one of the regionals. For their part, the O-T-C dealers had as clients portfolio managers and trust executives, who did not do a direct business with the general public. Finally, the dealers would not attempt to open retail outlets; they would not serve as brokers to the run-of-the-mill small investor and speculator. Or at least, so it seemed in the early 1960s.

Thus, an unspoken accord existed between the two markets that dealt in the same securities. It would remain workable so long as investment conditions remained stable, or if there were no major changes. But such stasis is abnormal on Wall Street, and so alterations were bound to occur. The peace was ruptured by the N.Y.S.E., though the stakes were not clear at the time.

In 1961 the Exchange removed tickers from the offices of two Dallas O-T-C houses that had been dealing in listed securities. One of the firms, Silver & Co., sued the N.Y.S.E. for damages, charging violations of the Sherman Anti-Trust Act. Silver won its case after arguments before the Supreme Court the following year. And with this decision, the warfare escalated.

But major historic moves in this arena are not determined by Supreme Court decisions alone. Rather, such judgments act as precipitants for forces already in existence—forces which would otherwise have become evident in some other way.

Institutional trading was on the upswing, obliging the N.Y.S.E. to seek means of adjusting to its requirements. The specialist system would have to bend, be twisted, perhaps in the end be discarded entirely, so as to accommodate the institutions. By 1965, there were nine block transactions on the floor per session; by 1969, the number was sixty-one, and rising. At that time, blocks accounted for close to a fifth of all volume. The Third Market wanted these trades, and acted as though it would be able to capture them in a fair contest.

Simultaneously, the Exchange was disrupted by the paper-crunch, which was followed by the sharpest decline and quasi-panic since the end of World War II. The N.Y.S.E. commission houses, which serviced over 30 million clients, most of whom had relatively small accounts, were inundated and paralyzed, while the specialists were torn between the requirement to maintain orderly markets and the need to show profits. The O-T-C traders, who had fewer and larger clients, experienced little difficulty in keeping records, and they had no trouble at all in reconciling their profit-seeking activities with a public responsibility, since they were not bound by the latter.

The large banks and trust companies indicated that they were considering reentering the securities markets directly, by seeking loopholes in New Deal legislation. Almost four decades earlier, they had been obliged to rid themselves of securities affiliates, to separate investment from commercial banking. By the early 1970s, these financial institutions were finding ways around the laws, and doing so with little in the way of government opposition. They found it easier to work with the Third Market than with the exchanges, and even probed the possibility of creating their own marketplaces, thus bringing about new vehicles through which securities could by bought and sold, marketed, accumulated, and utilized to direct corporation policies.

Most important, there were those technological developments revolving around the computer which have been sketched above. The exhanges looked into the feasibility of automating trades in the 1950s, and rejected the notion. The reasons had nothing to do with efficiencies and profits. Rather, the N.Y.S.E. could not afford to anger the specialists and the odd-lot dealers, both of whom would have suffered losses of business and even of function had automation taken hold. But technology could not be denied for long; the machines were bound to make an impact upon the ways in which Wall Street transacted its business.

This should have been the challenge most easily turned aside, and would have been were it not for the surprisingly rigid social and business structure at the senior marketplace. The N.Y.S.E. had come to terms with the telegraph, ticker, and telephone, and had used them to expand business, activities, scope, and power. A fully automated exchange—without specialists—could have been in place by the mid-1960s, had the N.Y.S.E. made a strong effort in that direction. But this would have required the scrapping of part of the present system, replacing human decisions by those made automatically by machines.

The specialists would have none of this. They held on, and forced the N.Y.S.E. leadership to their will. Thus, the Exchange fought the computer and related paraphernalia, in what must be viewed as the greatest blunder in its history, one from which it may never recover.

The O-T-C had its own difficulties in dealing with the potentials of automation. While lacking the problems of entrenched interests that stifled change at the N.Y.S.E., it suffered from a near-anarchy insofar as the membership was concerned. Unified action could come only through the N.A.S.D., which while capable of setting minimum standards and holding conventions, could not act quickly and effectively in other areas—especially those which required funds from the common treasury.

The N.A.S.D. members were an independent and varied lot, running all the way from major investment bankers in New York City, the heart of District Twelve, to notary publics who sold mutual funds in small Missouri towns—that state, together with Kansas, Nebraska, and Oklahoma, formed District Four. Could these men agree to create an automated marketplace? Certainly they would not have done so in the early 1960s. But even had the interest existed, there was doubt that the articles of incorporation would permit such an unprecedented action.* Like the N.Y.S.E., then, the O-T-C traders studied the potential of automation, looked at a few machines, but did little else.

Instead, the first automated exchange was created by an outsider, a person who did not have to concern himself with defending the old traditions or organizing the anarchists, who could start fresh without preconceptions. Alan Kay, a computer designer who had never worked in the securities business, designed AutEx (for automatic execution) in 1968, with the idea of selling it to the N.Y.S.E. Armed with an AutEx console, the operator could transmit messages regarding his willingness to buy and sell specified amounts of stock. His offer would go out to all subscribers, like a broadcast, and should one of them be interested, he could contact the operator by telephone and

* Under its charter, N.A.S.D. was permitted ''to promote through cooperative effort the investment banking and securities business, [and] standardize its principles and practices. . . .'' But its leaders doubted this fuzzy statement could be twisted to justify the establishment of a centralized market. Or at least, this was the view in the early and mid-1960s.

consummate the deal. It was a crude system, most adaptable to the O-T-C trades in large blocks, and not the specialist system. But Kay, who knew nothing of how that system functioned and who was unaware of specialist power, took his idea to the N.Y.S.E., hoping to sell it to management; and as might have been anticipated, he was rebuffed. Undeterred, he went ahead on his own, and in mid-1969 began signing up subscribers. Meanwhile the N.Y.S.E., knowing of Kay's intentions, tried to head him off by creating the Block Automation System (BAS) which was supposed to perform the same functions through specialists. The Exchange warned members against joining AutEx, and doubtless this affected the firm's prospects. Still, within a year Kay had 140 subscribers, seventy-five of which were institutions, and thirty of which were member firms of the N.Y.S.E.

Kay's modest success encouraged another outside organization to take the technology a step further. Institutional Networks Corporation, headed by former securities analyst Jerome Pustilnik, had been working on its own version of an automated market since the mid-1960s. Unlike AutEx, the Instinet system preserved the anonymity of buyers and sellers and permitted the actual execution of orders via the consoles. The program went into operation in 1970 and quickly signed up thirty subscribers. Then Pustilnik ran into organizational and technical difficulties, which, in addition to public and private N.Y.S.E. pressures, limited his market. Instinet did not become the national automated marketplace Pustilnik hoped for, but it survived for the usual reason—it filled a need.

Without meaning to do so, AutEx and Instinet had created an embryonic Fourth Market, another rival with which the N.Y.S.E. would have to contend. This Fourth Market did not compete with the Third— at least, not directly. Instead, it offered a means through which the Third Market's traders could function more efficiently. This situation intrigued and worried the N.A.S.D., which included most N.Y.S.E. brokerages as well as the O-T-C dealers. Unless the Association came up with an automated structure of its own, many of its O-T-C members would be attracted to the new electronic network, and so create complications in that sector of the industry, and lessen the power and influence of the N.A.S.D. There was no way of predicting the reactions of the brokerages. Some already had indicated discontent with the way the N.Y.S.E. was being managed, and there was a chance they too might migrate to AutEx and Instinet, or at least transact part of their business there. This would precipitate a conflict with the specialists. Meanwhile, the Association would become redundant.

When faced with a situation like this, the N.Y.S.E. chose to ignore automation and to defend the old system. The N.A.S.D. reacted differently. For several years it had toyed with the idea of establishing some kind of automated exchange, but it lacked the money, expertise, or daring to begin work. In 1968, however, the N.A.S.D. entered into an agreement with Bunker Ramo, a relatively minor electronics company, whereby that firm would create a system for the N.A.S.D., operate it for a profit, and give the Association an option to purchase it in 1976 or afterwards.*

Work began in 1969, and was intensified after the introduction and initial success of AutEx. In mid-1970, the N.A.S.D. announced the creation of an alternate operation—NASDAQ. It was to be an electronic stock market—that was how it was billed. Even then, however, there was a great deal of uncertainty as to which securities would be traded there, and how the operations would be conducted.

Three large, powerful groups contested for control over transactions. First, there were those O-T-C dealers whose business was solely or generally in unlisted issues. To them, the electronic marketplace was an interesting but hardly vital idea. They were doing quite well without it but were willing to give the method a trial. In their minds, the system would provide a continuous linkage between their offices and their clients, the large N.Y.S.E.–affiliated brokerages, and the banks, through which better and more efficient trading could take place.

Other O-T-C dealers, those who comprised the Third Market, had a more grandiose vision. To them, the electronic market could become a weapon in the fight against the N.Y.S.E., an alternative means by which transactions in listed stocks could take place. Convinced that they could provide better executions and eager for a confrontation, the Third Market looked forward to the time when a brokerage would check out their prices prior to turning to the N.Y.S.E. floor. This

* The N.A.S.D. exersised this option in 1976, with NASDAQ, Inc. taking over ownership and operation of the system from Bunker Ramo.

could be accomplished with ease through the use of the consoles—with the press of a few buttons, the broker could discover that several dealers could offer lower net prices than the specialists. If these men had their way, the new system would challenge and then replace the organized exchange structure—it would be a revolutionary weapon, rather than one means of enhancing already existing institutions.

The N.Y.S.E. influenced the Association through its member firms. A majority of the N.A.S.D. Board and the entire executive committee were comprised of representatives of N.Y.S.E. firms, who were committed to maintaining the N.Y.S.E. monopoly of listed stocks, but whose loyalty to the specialists was less than complete. These men were interested in learning more about the machines, but were not going to scrap an ongoing exchange for an untested grab bag of electronic gear.

In late 1970, then, the technology for the new market existed, and a fierce struggle within the N.A.S.D. had begun between the Third Market and N.Y.S.E. members, with the others leaning toward the Exchange, more through inertia, tradition, and an ignorance of the stakes involved than anything else.

In the midst of all this was Gordon Macklin, the new N.A.S.D. president who had taken office only half a year earlier. Forty-two years old at the time, Macklin was a tough midwesterner, who had spent most of his life in Ohio, and was considered more a marketing and public relations man than a strong executive. At the time of his appointment, Macklin was at McDonald & Co., in Cleveland, where he was in charge of sales management and syndications, as well as being active in the affairs of District Nine of the N.A.S.D. Macklin knew and understood the situation in New York, mostly through Association affairs and his dealings with large banks and trust companies. He was no novice to the Street, then, but at the same time lacked the friendships and working relationships with the district's leaders necessary to smooth the way to compromise. Nor was Macklin certain—in late 1970—of the capabilities of his electronic market, or where it might lead. Finally, he lacked a mandate to place his stamp upon the N.A.S.D. Macklin's position was more akin to that of a secretary-general of the United Nations than a President of the United States, in that he had to rely upon persuasion and charm in dealing with members who were more powerful than he. The N.A.S.D. president would influence decisions but not force actions. As a new man too, he had little control over his Board and executives.

Originally the N.A.S.D. had decided to ban listed stocks from the electronic market, which even in early 1970 was known as NASDAQ. Some Third Market leaders, then involved in litigation against the N.Y.S.E., complained to the S.E.C., charging that pressures had been brought to bear against the Association. The S.E.C. agreed, backed the Third Marketeers, and the N.A.S.D. switched positions, now deciding to trade in listed stocks. This was the situation when Macklin arrived in Washington to take office. But by then the Board and executive committee had decided to petition the S.E.C. for another reversal, on the grounds that trading in listed stocks would create complications. The S.E.C. accepted this argument, and so it seemed NASDAQ would become a vehicle for O-T-C trades and little else.

Angered and feeling betrayed—and understanding that the S.E.C. could be swayed on the matter—several Third Market firms instituted a class-action suit against the N.A.S.D., charging among other things that the Association itself was in violation of the antitrust statutes. Macklin and the Board were angered and of a mind to give battle. How could the N.A.S.D.—a federally chartered agency—be sued under the terms of the Sherman Act? It no more could violate such a statute than might the Department of Agriculture or the State Department, each of which was supposed to have a kind of monopoly in its own sphere. Furthermore, all of the prior decisions had been cleared with the S.E.C.—was that agency to become a co-defendant in the suits?

Clearly the N.A.S.D. was in a strong position. However, such a trial could prove embarrassing, and might even move Congress to the passage of new legislation, which the Association did not want. With S.E.C. approval, it agreed to carry listed securities on NASDAQ, but only on a trial basis.

NASDAQ made its debut on February 8, 1971, on what amounted to a shakedown cruise. All proceeded according to plan, and on April 5 the system was expanded to include thirty N.Y.S.E. stocks. The event was marked by celebrations at Third Market houses, where some of the brasher executives predicted an end to the N.Y.S.E.'s hegemony within two years, with the Exchange either out of business or part of the electronic market by 1980.

There is no evidence that the N.A.S.D. leadership had such vaulting ambitions at that time, or even later on. Instead, after the system had proven itself, Macklin and his executives planned to run a three-level market of great flexibility, some aspects of which even the N.Y.S.E. has come to see as superior to the specialist system, and which in time could become the foundation for a national market.

Level I, the most basic of NASDAQ services, is primarily informational in nature. Some thirty thousand registered representatives have at their disposal consoles from which they can extract prices for over four thousand securities, each of which has a minimum of two market makers, and some as many as thirty. All market makers are obliged to feed their bids and asks into the system, which then combines the information for each security for Level I subscribers. This service is somewhat akin to the function performed by the ticker tape, when that is used by watchers to gauge "the state of the market." The important difference is that the tape records actual transactions, while Level I contains only the bids and asks.

Knowing this, and using Level I and the tape accordingly, a representative could compare price information on both markets before making a move. From Level I to the consolidated tape is not a large leap, either technologically or politically. For once Level I went into operation, there developed reasons why the N.Y.S.E. would be willing to accept some form of accommodation.

Brokers and dealers were expected to subscribe to Level II, which, in effect, provided some of the raw material which went into Level I quotes plus additional information. By pressing the right buttons on his console, the operator could learn the bid and ask prices on NASDAQ stocks offered by each market maker. Armed with this information, the broker then could telephone the market maker with the best price and complete the deal in the usual fashion. Thus, Level I is informational in nature, while Level II is for those who want to use the information to effect trades.

What Level II is for the retail side of the business, Level III is for the wholesale. This service, used by some one thousand market makers, enables them to enter as well as receive price information. The stocks and prices put into the system at Level III are shown on Level II, and go into making the price data created so as to have Level I information. All is of a piece, yet each is separate from the others, to suit the needs of each subscriber.

One might say that the N.Y.S.E. grew organically over the decades. It has a history, and it shows, in that parts of the structure no longer function as they once did. In contrast, NASDAQ is a creature of the eternal present; the past is obliterated when no longer needed, and the future can be programmed in a matter of hours.

NASDAQ simplified several important functions for the O-T-C dealers. In the 1960s, the harried broker would all but glue the telephone to his ear at the beginning of the day and pry it loose at the end. His judgment in contacting dealers was important, and speed was of the essence. In contrast, much of the specialist's work on the N.Y.S.E. floor was automatic. He would call out his prices to those who asked, make his deals, and then move on to others. The setting of prices required experience and a feel for the market, but since he knew more about his stock than anyone else, the advantage more than compensated for the risk.

With NASDAQ, several operations which once were judgmental now became automatic. A well-trained clerk could function on Level II, and a junior partner could perform most of the work for Level III.

The specialists had read about NASDAQ, listened to boasts and rumors, and started quite a few of their own. They were curious and troubled. A handful of them managed to visit Third Market houses and witness the machines and their operators in action. The sight was at the same time confusing and awesome. There, in a room not much larger than a dining facility at a good club, were several dozen traders at desks, each equipped with a console, and all facing displays. There was some shouting and badinage, but the traders were not talking to one another and making deals: this was the way it was done on the N.Y.S.E. floor. Rather, they were addressing their machines, as they had the telephone the previous year. To the specialists who watched all of this, it appeared a congenial blend of man and machine. It worked—too well by half to please the N.Y.S.E. members.

The N.Y.S.E. always has been a clubby organization. Its members tend to think of themselves as an elite, and regard outsiders with suspicion. In contrast, the NASDAQ people are outgoing, as though attempting to draw all into their network by means of consoles, telephones, and related apparatus. NASDAQ relies upon technology, whereas the N.Y.S.E. is based upon personality. Three-quarters of a century ago, J. P. Morgan said the most important attribute a Wall Streeter could possess is character. The electronic gear knew nothing of character. It is not supposed to compute such matters. NASDAQ is based upon the proper alignment of transistors, not the presence of the exceptional person in the right place.

The specialists appreciated the implications of NASDAQ, even when some of its intricacies eluded them. These machines indeed could make them obsolete. Perhaps they had already done so.

Yet many Exchange members chose to ignore the threat, while others decided it was not necessary to take measures to meet it. For that matter, the most sanguine O-T-C dealers were not certain just how far the new system could be pushed. To them, the electronic market was just the old O-T-C with transistors or the N.Y.S.E. with terminals.

Technical personnel disagreed. They spoke glowingly of NASDAQ at scholarly meetings and then wrote papers which neither the O-T-C or N.Y.S.E. members could appreciate or understand. They proceeded from technology to business structure, rather than vice versa, and did so in a matter-of-fact fashion. What they said and wrote had revolutionary implications which the technicians themselves could not appreciate, but which the brokers would have, had they the background to digest the reports.

In 1971, the N.A.S.D. had some $25 million worth of research, organization, and equipment. Most of the machines came from relatively small producers—Bunker Ramo, Ultronics, Scantlin, and Telequote. Some had been revamped systems first tried out in Las Vegas gaming houses and at racetracks. At the central NASDAQ facility in Trumbull, Connecticut, were several UNIVAC computers operated by technicians. Whether they had a feel for the market or a deep comprehension and appreciation of the virtues and flaws of the specialist system was irrelevant. They had expertise in electronics, which was more important, and they knew the potential of their machines.

In 1971, these individuals saw no reason why NASDAQ could not be expanded so as to include an infinite number of securities and market makers. In other words, given the proper computer arrangement—and the knowledge for this existed in 1971, as did the technology—one could create a worldwide securities market that operated around the clock. It was a matter of capacity, the number of terminals, the training of operators, and will—nothing more than that, at least as far as the technicians were concerned.

The specialists pondered all of this. They began by conceding that a block positioner at an Instinet console had to be skilled, even daring, and they admired the boldness of several partners working on NASDAQ's Level II. But the others were glorified clerks in their estimation. Yet they were doing the work of specialists, but getting a fraction of their total remuneration. If this was technologically pleasing, the thought was disturbing from the point of view of specialist self-interest. Even if the specialists could not be replaced by a machine, they could be made redundant by a clerk and a console.

In 1971, such individuals wondered whether O-T-C dealers were underpaid or specialists overcompensated. Here too the answer was disquieting. Market makers functioned in a highly competitive system, their wages set by supply and demand. Specialists had monopolies, and got monopoly prices for services. They had been able to get away with their price structure for as long as they had because they had functioned in what amounted to a sanctioned monopoly.

Now competition was altering the exchange structure. AutEx and Instinet were beginnings, and NASDAQ the major blow that obliged both the N.Y.S.E. and the S.E.C. to face the need for a new structure in the business. The N.Y.S.E. finally accepted competitive specialists in 1976, and hinted at more to come. William Batten's pledge to help revamp the specialist system sounded to some of the group like Franklin Roosevelt's threat to a mossback businessman that he never again would earn a million dollars a year. And this could indeed be the case in the 1980s. The specialists knew that they would have to lower their financial goals; either they would bow and adjust to new circumstance, or their businesses would shrink and then disappear altogether.

The specialists always have had a fine instinct for survival, even though their timing often left much to be desired. They accepted cuts in remuneration for services. By 1975, the Third Market's dealers had adjusted to the new technology; then the specialists came to terms with the market makers—or at least agreed to an armed truce. The evolution toward a central marketplace continues. There was no revolution along the way, and certainly no mass exodus of men and securities from the N.Y.S.E. Such is not the way Wall Street accommodates itself to changes.

NASDAQ's impact upon marketing and trading were such as to earn it recognition as the most important innovation in these areas since the development of the specialist system. It was more than that, however. By the mid-1970s, NASDAQ was linking with other forces altering the Street, plus one which threatened to dissolve the financial district, or at least result in the dissipation of power throughout the nation.

In 1969, while readying itself for the introduction of NASDAQ, the N.A.S.D. established the National Clearing Corporation, similar in design and function to that used by the N.Y.S.E. for generations. Instead of having the seller send stock to the purchasing house, the certificates would go to the Clearing Corporation in New York, which would function both as a depository and bookkeeping agency. Later on, the Corporation constructed a net clearing operation, under which balances would be "netted out" on a continuous basis. Thus, a brokerage which sold five thousand shares of a stock to several customers and purchased three thousand from others, would deliver two thousand shares to the Clearing Corporation, which would complete and allocate the shares to the proper accounts.

The system worked well, and the logical next step was to link it with NASDAQ, which was done in 1972. Now the Level II and III operators could receive net balance statements at the end of the day, and make arrangements for deliveries accordingly. By then, the N.A.S.D. leaders were talking of the possibilities of automatic clearing, somewhat akin to checking accounts. The purchase or sale of securities by Levels II and III would result in deposits or withdrawals of securities and funds from preexisting accounts.

The creation of such a system is as close to being inevitable as anything can be in the financial markets. Furthermore, the Clearing Corporation shortly will be merged with its counterparts at the

N.Y.S.E. and American Stock Exchange to create a completely consolidated entity to serve the entire industry.

A future move would appear to be the elimination of the stock certificate, and its replacement by bookkeeping entries kept in computer banks, verified and backed up by confirmation slips sent to buyers and sellers. On the face of it, this seems a modest, sensible, and harmless development. Whatever reasons once existed for the stock certificate have long vanished. Given the guarantees afforded by the Securities Investors Protection Corporation, there is little fear that a firm's bankruptcy will result in the loss of securities on the part of clients. A good many investors do not want delivery on certificates, preferring instead to keep them in their brokerage accounts, as do many institutional buyers and sellers.

In 1968, the N.Y.S.E. created the Central Certificate Service, nominally in order to ease paperwork and cut costs. The idea behind it was sensible enough; brokerages would maintain their securities at the C.C.S. instead of making and accepting deliveries. But the program was bungled. Billions of dollars worth of stock were misplaced, misdirected, or simply stolen; for a while the Street buzzed with rumors of Mafia control of the Service, and of indictments that would rival those of the 1930s. Undaunted, the N.Y.S.E. reorganized the Service, which now became the Depository Trust Company, which was supposed to develop into a central depository for all stocks and bonds. The N.Y.S.E. would offer participation in the D.T.C. to the N.A.S.D. and the American Stock Exchange, with the regionals coming in later on. But leadership would remain at Wall and Broad; the Exchange would not relinquish this under any circumstances. For should such control be lost, a vital aspect of N.Y.S.E. domination would be challenged. The Exchange leaders felt the central depository had to be located in lower Manhattan, close by the large banks and securities markets. The alternatives—placement of the depository elsewhere, scattering depository functions throughout the nation, or putting such an agency under the influence of outsiders—were anathema to these men.

Throughout all of this some technicians and a handful of exchange figures questioned the need for any depository. The certificate was outmoded, unnecessary, and even unwanted, they claimed, and should be abandoned, perhaps in stages. The N.Y.S.E. and Amex opposed this point of view, arguing that the public wanted securities, that without them confidence in markets and exchanges would be lessened. Some investors would remain away from the markets unless they knew that a few weeks after paying the price for their shares a finely engraved and signed certificate would arrive in the mail, from the company's transfer agent *via* the brokerage through which the shares had been purchased. The paper then would be placed in a safe deposit box among other valuables. The exchanges' opinion was supported by several polls.

Critics of this system responded by noting that the uncertainties caused by the collapse in the late 1960s and early 1970s—a failure that had resulted in part from the requirements to deliver security certificates—had scarred many small investors, and that once confidence had been restored, the vestigial paper could be eliminated with little trouble or trauma.

There the matter rests, for the time being at least. Yet logic and technology indicate that the certificates will be eliminated someday, that perhaps within the next decade these symbols of finance will be souvenirs and little else. Just as Americans of the 1930s became accustomed to doing without gold coins, so the investors of the 1980s will learn to do without stock certificates. When this transpires, the exchanges will have been dealt an important symbolic blow, and the N.Y.S.E.'s hold on the marketplace will have been that much eroded.

The Exchange is a Manhattan-based organization. That this is so is obvious, and would not need stating were it not for the fact that the one-time source of strength may now be another sign of weakness. The N.Y.S.E. can reach out to the provinces by means of electronics and related devices, but its heart and brain are firmly wedded to New York. And New York is a decaying city in troubled circumstances.

In contrast, the N.A.S.D., while located in Washington, is a national structure and organization. NASDAQ is in suburban Connecticut, for reasons of convenience and nothing more. There is no reason why the computer installation could not be shifted elsewhere if economics and politics dictated such a move. This is another source of flexibility for the N.A.S.D., and a problem for the N.Y.S.E.

The difficulty may best be illustrated by referring to two moves across the Hudson, one made in 1868, the other more than a century later.

In the winter of 1868, Cornelius Vanderbilt defeated Daniel Drew, Jim Fisk, and Jay Gould in one of their several contests for control of the Erie Railroad. Rather than concede defeat, Drew, Fisk, and Gould crossed the Hudson to Jersey City, where they could not be touched by Vanderbilt's lawyers. The Commodore was irate, but could do nothing about this situation. The "unholy trio" organized the Erie as a Jersey firm, exempting it from New York laws.

Jersey City was a dull place, however, though within sight of Manhattan. The conspirators found it difficult to transact business from their sleazy hotel in the dingy town. And they were homesick. In the end they worked out a deal with Vanderbilt, and with a sense of relief returned to civilization—Wall Street.

Beginning in the late nineteenth century and throughout the twentieth both New York City and State have tried to tax securities transactions to the limit, and always the brokerages, banks, and even the exchanges responded with threats to relocate. The politicians knew these institutions wouldn't move, however. It was generally conceded that financial transactions had to take place within a community. In Vanderbilt's day that was Wall Street. The telegraph, telephone, and ticker had expanded that community, but the center of attention remained in lower Manhattan.

In the summer of 1975, while in the grip of a financial stringency, New York levied a 25 percent surcharge on the stock transfer tax, payable by all sellers within the state—that is, by those who transacted business through Wall Street. As before, there were protests and threats, which were listened to but not acted upon. The tax remained in force. The relocations began.

The key move was by Weeden & Co., the largest Third Market firm, which in February of 1976 made the trip to Jersey City. Other, smaller firms followed, so that by the end of the year, there were a dozen houses in the Jersey City area, with others considering the move quite seriously. Even after New York backed down on the tax, discussions of relocation continued. Weeden reported a savings of between $100,000 and $150,000 a month on taxes, with additional costs due to relocation of only $50,000 a month. Through microwave equipment, the firm's offices on Montgomery Street in Jersey City are connected with the old offices at 25 Broad Street in Manhattan. Thus, clients can call the New York telephone number and be switched, automatically, to New Jersey. The system worked without a hitch from the first. To some, the move is viewed as one of the most ominous developments of the past decade, an indicator that not only is the N.Y.S.E. on the decline, but the entire New York financial complex as well.

That Weeden & Co. should have led the trek westward was not surprising. For the past decade or so, its president, Donald Weeden, has been the most outspoken and eloquent advocate of the Third Market and critic of the N.Y.S.E. Together with a handful of other Third Market leaders, Weeden testified before Congress and spoke to interested industry groups on the subject of the need for an electronic marketplace and the flaws inherent in the specialist system. Others of his group were more radical in their approaches—suing the N.Y.S.E. and even the N.A.S.D. to get their way—and some more astute in matters of tactics and strategy. But Donald Weeden is colorful, brash, and "mediagenic," and so became the symbol to the public of Third Market challenges to the N.Y.S.E.

Weeden's attack had three prongs. The first was the organization of Dexter Securities Corporation in April, 1975, and the subsequent restructuring of Weeden itself into an umbrella operation, Weeden Holding Corporation. Then Dexter applied to the N.Y.S.E. for membership, which led the Exchange to promulgate Rule 389, which obliged holding companies of member firms to conform to all N.Y.S.E. rules. Weeden rejected the rule, appealed to the S.E.C. for a judgment on it, and threatened the Exchange in such a way as to oblige it to accept Third Market firms on the floor. The second threat was the move to Jersey City. Weeden had originated in San Francisco in 1922, and so was not unaccustomed to relocating if business dictated change. But by moving when and how it did, and doing so successfully, it provided a model for the others—and for N.Y.S.E. firms as well—to seek the best location for their headquarters.

The third and in some ways most interesting challenge was the development of the Weeden Holding Corporation's Automated Market, given the acronym of WHAM. Utilizing existing technology plus some machines in the process of refinement, WHAM could become the basis of a national market system, including all stocks and all dealers. There appears little chance of WHAM being accepted by the exchanges, or for that matter by the commission houses and the N.A.S.D. But the prospectus does indicate that such a system is possible and, more important, plausible as well. Given the nature of technology, the political climate within and outside of the industry, something akin to WHAM could emerge as the eventual metamorphic design of the market system of the 1980s. Or at least, that is the expectation in parts of Wall Street, some offices in Washington, and several in Jersey City.

How this would come about is difficult to say. Clearly the N.Y.S.E. and the regional exchanges would fight the idea. The other O-T-C dealers would scarcely accept Weeden leadership in any attempt to institutionalize the Third Market electronically; they are too independent a group to do this. The N.A.S.D. never has had the power to force this kind of market into being, even though its experience with NADSAQ indicates it could do the job—given proper encouragement. Nor can the S.E.C. do the job on its own. Rather, the national market—when it arrives—will have to be a creation of Congress and the presidency, consulting with the industry but in the end, forcing their wills upon the recalcitrant and the reluctant. Whether this kind of market will emerge from the N.Y.S.E., NASDAQ, or some version of WHAM cannot be predicted, for the final decision will be as much political as technological. That it will come about can no longer be doubted, however, even though the implications of such a system are not yet fully appreciated.

N.Y.S.E.—UPSTAIRS

———

THERE ARE SOME New York businessmen who dawdle over three martini lunches, but few of them work in the financial district. Top executives there may entertain clients in that fashion, and semiretired partners with little else to do may sit for a while at one or another of the few decent restaurants in the district. The executive dining rooms at some of the major investment banks are excellent, but the service is fast too, and partners take little time for their lunches. Many $100,000 a year men frequent a favorite hot dog pushcart, some of which have standing lines at noon. Yet in an area so close to the rivers and bay, only a handful take the time to stroll near the ferries in the spring and summer, purchase an apple or pear from a vendor, and sit on a bench in Battery Park, getting the sun. Wall Streeters do not venture south of Beaver Street during the workday. Some of them lunch occasionally in Chinatown, a few minutes from the district.

On the other hand, several dozen clerks eat their sandwiches in the Trinity Churchyard, a few steps from Gallatin's grave. They engage in other activities as well—on a hot day in summer, with absolutely no breeze, one can catch the sweet smell of marijuana smoke, which hangs over the group as a small, miasmic cloud.

Where do the workers eat? A half century ago the office buildings on New, Beaver, and Pine streets and Exchange Place had small restaurants on the street level—there were some on Broad itself. After World War II many of these buildings were demolished to make way for more modern skyscrapers, which lacked such facilities. Few new buildings have gone up on Nassau Street, north of the Subtreasury, and there one can see the small eateries in operation. But the office workers don't go that far for lunch; that is, unless they want to shop on Nassau, which is closed to vehicular traffic during the noon period, and which offers everything from office supply stores to tropical fish emporia to porno outlets, along with Chock Full o'Nuts and pizza parlors. There are none of these further south—except a Zum-Zum on lower Broad.

The companies in the new buildings are aware of this situation. Many offer free lunches to their employees—out of the goodness of their hearts and purses, and also in order to encourage shorter lunch hours. Several have conducted an interesting experiment which has worked out to their benefit. Their lunchrooms are open throughout the day, and workers are able to go there for free food whenever they wish, and stay for as long as they feel it necessary. The employers have found that the workers eat a lot in a few minutes, and then are back to work. So a $3.50 an hour typist eats $2.00 worth of food in a half an hour, and is back to work early. The company is out a few cents, but makes it back in goodwill and friendlier employee relations. This arrangement is more important for the broker-dealer, who can earn several thousands of dollars for the firm in the time it takes him to get on and off the building's elevator.

Time and money are closely related in the economy as a whole, and nowhere is this more evident than in the financial district. It can be seen in the Luncheon Club located on the N.Y.S.E.'s seventh floor, a room open to members, key executives, and guests.

It is 12:30 on a Tuesday afternoon in March, and the Club is less than half occupied. Many of those eating at the tables appear to be members of the administration; you can tell they are because they do not seem to be under time pressure, and are dining and speaking slowly. (In addition, they are better groomed and look less harried than do most brokers.) There are a few specialists and commission brokers in the room this day. The slack business is not a reflection upon the food or surroundings, however—the Club's fare is somewhat better than average for its genre—but due to time pressures this particular session. The busier it is on the floor, the more tables will be vacant at the Club.

Some of the Exchange's old-timers claim they can gauge trading volume by the number of empty tables. His eye sweeping the room, one waiter estimates it at 12.2 million for the morning. He was off the mark—volume was 11.9 million at 12:30. On checking this, the waiter looks crestfallen, and mutters something about not having taken account of the poor weather. Come back tomorrow, he urges, and he'll do better.

The gaming and competitive instinct is ever present in the district, even among those who have no direct connection with securities and the money world.

On the far wall in the Club is a large clock, another sign of the importance of time in the district. And in the vestibule, across from the cigar stand, is a pedestal upon which rests a statue of a bull and a bear in struggle. Look at it from one angle and it appears the bear is about to crush his opponent; at another one might conclude the bull had just administered a fatal blow to the bear's chest.

Few members notice the statue or study it with any care or interest. One staff member who does glance at it whenever he passes swears his view of the contest alters according to developments on the trading floor. That day the bull seemed to be having the best of it—and the Dow was up 10.5 points at noon.

A light turnout at almost any Wall Street restaurant means business is good. On such occasions the N.Y.S.E. workers will send out for sandwiches, to be delivered to their stations, while those with a few extra minutes, who feel the need for a breather, may rush out to New Street and grab hot dogs from one of the pushcarts, and then wash them down with Diet Pepsis.

These men dine at some of the city's finest restaurants in the evening, and order $50 bottles of wine and end the meal with snifters of 30-year-old brandy. They function in a different world during the workdays, and seem to see no startling contrast between the two modes of dining.

Administrators who transact a good deal of their business over the telephone often take meals at their desks, while a key executive may dine in one of the two small private rooms on the sixth floor. Secretaries and other office workers have two cafeterias from which to select. During the early 1970s, when the situation at the N.Y.S.E.

seemed grim and many workers feared they might lose their jobs, it was common for them to brown-bag it. The return to the cafeterias in 1975 was a sign that the Exchange was recovering—that confidence had been restored.

From this general survey, one might conclude that the district's drugstores do a brisk trade in Tums, Gelusil, and Alka Seltzer. The tension is high, the pace rapid, and burnt-out cases not unusual during hectic periods. However, there is no evidence that the men of the N.Y.S.E. suffer unduly from stomach disorders, though this conclusion is not based upon scientific research. Nor do any more than a handful drink heavily during the day; those who do are quickly eliminated—they self-destruct, for a person cannot function at peak efficiency in this business with three martinis under his belt, and anything less than a complete effort is likely to be wasted.

Those who make their livings in the trading arena do complain about other physical problems, however. Their feet hurt. Some suffer from kidney maladies as well.

These are attributed to the maple surface of the trading floor, which is hard on the feet and kidneys. One commission house representative, a former college football player, claims a hectic day on the floor is the equivalent of a tough day during spring practice. Exaggerated, perhaps, but the sore feet and capacity business at the men's rooms near the floor indicate that there is some truth to this. So does the cloakroom at the Luncheon Club. Shortly prior to the opening it may be filled with members, who are not grabbing their jackets after a quick breakfast, but rather changing into their work clothes—usually an old jacket and a comfortable pair of shoes.

The latter are kept in cubbyholes in the cloakroom, and used only for floor work. Some are modified basketball sneakers and others—especially in recent years—space shoes. One member has used the same pair of shabby oxfords for over twenty years; another has golf shoes—the cleats removed, of course. Most favor crepe soles, which absorb the pounding of the maple floor.

Some of these shoes are used by specialists. The older ones, in particular, feel the need for foot comfort at their stations. But a large majority of the men who need special foot care are commission house representatives, some of whom claim to walk a total of over five miles a day on the floor. What makes a good representative? A quick mind and a subtle feel for the market are important. But as in baseball and basketball, the feet go first.

There are close to four hundred commission houses at the N.Y.S.E., all of which handle transactions for public investors. This does not mean that at any given time there are that many members scurrying from one specialist post to another filling orders. In fact, there are almost six hundred commission house brokers engaged in this activity, since the larger firms have several seats, and their volume of business is such as to keep all of them busy. Merrill Lynch, Pierce, Fenner & Smith, the biggest of them all, has twenty-two floor representatives, each of whom handles a relatively small portion of the trading. Like some basketball teams, Merrill Lynch employs the zone approach, so that one representative will have to cover only six or so specialist posts. The other large houses have far fewer men on the floor, and during hectic sessions employ the services of several of the approximately 160 two-dollar brokers.

The tasks performed by these men run from the mechanical to the complex, with the tendency in recent years toward the latter.

An N.Y.S.E. publicity brochure of a decade ago presented the classic case of a person in small town America wishing to purchase a round lot—one hundred shares—of General Motors at the market price. He gives the order to his broker, who transmits it via wire to the floor, where the company's representative there picks it up, glances at the slip, and rushes to the post occupied by the G.M. specialist. At this point he is the customer's agent; he will help decide the nature of the order's execution.

"How's G.M.?" he shouts, to which the answer might be, "65 to a quarter," meaning the specialist is prepared to buy the stock at 65 and willing to sell at 65¼. In this way, he is filling his function, that of creating an auction market in the stock. Automatically the representative replies, "I'll take a hundred at a quarter." Thus, he is carrying out his order, to get the stock at the current best offer. Each man jots down the other's number, which is printed on their identification badges, the quantity of stock, the letters "G.M.," and price information. A reporter marks an I.B.M. card and inserts it into a machine at his post. Within seconds the information appears on the tape—the purchaser in the brokerage house can see it flit across the screen. Thus, his agent has completed his assignment, for which the firm receives its commission.

In actual practice, the transaction is carried out somewhat differently. When the order reaches the floor it is handled by a clerk, who presses a button to activate the representative's number, which flashes on a large wall display. After a while the representative may notice it—he is supposed to glance at the display from time to time, but at the moment he may have been engaged in some other business, or if the floor was quiet, just horsing around. Noticing his number on the board, he would walk to his clerk, pick up the slip, and then go to the G.M. post, where he may have bought or sold shares just a few minutes earlier. The representative probably has a good idea of the rhythm of G.M. trading, and senses that he could get the stock for a slightly lower price if he waited for a little while. But the order is for purchase at market, and in any case it would not be worth his while to fiddle around for a quarter of a point or so. Thus, the order is completed and displayed on the tape for the buyer to see.

A similar situation takes place should the customer place a limit order, meaning that he will buy under specified circumstances. Perhaps he feels the price is due for a slight dip and so tells his broker to put in a buy at 64½. In this situation the floor representative transmits the order to the specialist, who enters it in his book—a pad he carries for such purchases and sales. There may be other buy orders at that price, and if so, the new one goes to the bottom of the list. Should G.M.'s quote fall to that point, the purchase orders would be triggered. The specialist knows this, of course, and so he conducts his business accordingly, bouncing orders off the book somewhat like the player of a financial pinball game.

There are some problems involved with this procedure, which have developed with the coming of the consolidated tape. Let us suppose the specialist at the Pacific Coast Exchange, or one of the dealers at the Third Market, is offering G.M. at a slightly lower price. The customer's broker is supposed to scout the markets and find the one which offers the best price, but in practice such small orders go routinely to the N.Y.S.E. So the client could see G.M. traded at the Pacific Coast at 65⅛, then the tape could show 65¼ at the N.Y.S.E., followed by

65 at the Third Market—and learn that his purchase was made at the highest price. Let this happen two or three times and the client may seek another broker—and by telling his friends, take a dozen or so accounts out of the house.

This doesn't happen very often—few clients sit around in brokers' offices watching their trades cross the tape. But the possibility does trouble the brokerages and is making the work of the floor reps more difficult now than previously.

The real action nowadays is in block trading, however, and it is here that the floor work has been altered greatly, and the role of the representative transformed. Most of the larger commission houses steer their best people into the block trading area, where they negotiate purchases and sales in their offices and then—on occasion—''bring them to the floor'' to be executed there by the company's representative. Thus, the position of the floor man has lost much of its old status. He handles small trades in a routine fashion, and more often than not is a messenger boy for the bigger ones. He does not negotiate block sales; this rarely takes place on the floor. Those who do the bargaining are in the offices, where they haggle over commissions. Veteran floor men consider this beneath their dignity, remembering as they do how it went in the long era of fixed commissions. In fact, floor representatives for large firms no longer have a strong feel for what is happening at headquarters. They are in a limbo of sorts, and this is all the stranger since that limbo is the N.Y.S.E. floor, once the focal point of finance capitalism.

A generation or so ago, the floor representatives had to possess experience in trading, a good feel for the market, and sturdy legs and feet. All that are needed now are legs and feet.

That part of Upstairs familiar to most shareholders is the brokerage office, though increasingly business is conducted over the telephone, and clients may rarely if ever see their customer's men (the term most brokers use to refer to themselves, whether male or female). So the office need not be large and ornate; most are neat, functional, and rather spartan. They may be located in out-of-the-way places, but almost all are in office buildings, in shopping malls, or tucked away in the corner of a local savings and loan in a small town. Some member firms have a single office, somewhat cramped, with only a handful of customer's men plus a secretary to handle orders from townspeople and nearby suburbanites and farmers. On the other extreme, there are offices in large cities with more than twenty brokers, each in a semi-enclosed space. There they sit, with push-button telephones, electronic displays and related paraphernalia, and comfortable seats for clients who may drop by to pass the time of day, exchange information, or watch the tape while sipping coffee. In the old days—the late 1960s are so categorized today—some firms would have star performers, who earned upward of a quarter of a million dollars a year in commissions without undo strain. They would have their own offices, and on the walls would be tasteful prints and pictures of celebrity clients, signed with messages attesting to their fondness for the broker and thanks for his assistance. Such individuals would screen their clients, refusing to accept those who came without the proper introductions. Although their names were not known outside of investment circles, they could make a splash at a Southampton party, and they were sought out for advice along with heart surgeons and corporation lawyers.

The steep declines of 1969 and the early 1970s changed all of this. Dreams of quick killings made possible by clever moves on the part of star brokers turned sour. Individuals who in the mid-1960s all but begged these men to take their accounts left the Street, perhaps never to return. The institutions, which are too sophisticated to take such razzle-dazzle very seriously, did not bring their business to such brokers in the past and are not about to do so today. The stars saw their sources of income melt. Some of them lost their own money, having made that most egregious of all Wall Street blunders—they believed their own propaganda, and thought they could do anything short of walking on water. They too left the Street. Some of the great producers of the old days are running sandwich shops and saloons, managing small retail businesses, or simply have vanished from sight. One has fallen so low as to conduct guided tours of Manhattan, cap on head and megaphone in hand.

This breed usually appears three or four times a century. They were in the district in the early 1900s, and shone brightly in the 1920s, and then in the 1960s. The next generation of Wall Street superstars still may be in the cradle or womb. That the hotshots will resurface is not doubted by any old-timer—nowadays this means anyone who managed to survive the 1960s intact. If the pattern of the past is repeated in the present, they will shine brightest just before the market collapses. By then, however, their clients either will have forgotten the lessons of previous bull markets or be ignorant of this most persistent of cycles.

The great shake-out educated the investing public as to the abilities, capabilities, and limitations of customer's men. Many now understand that for the most part, those voices on the telephone that give advice and take orders really know little more than their clients.

Wall Street is in a perennial state of flux, and brokerage always has been a boom and bust profession. During bull markets, when trading volume expands, commissions multiply and new trainees are put on the job; the firings begin and paychecks shrink after the first few months of a bearish move, when volume dries up and brokers begin lining up alternate positions. Business was slack in 1973–74, when hundreds of brokers left the field and most who remained cut back on their standard of living. There was a revival in 1975, and a bonanza in 1976; those who hung on experienced prosperity once more. It was a sorry broker who did not take home more than $20,000 that year; those who could not do better than that found themselves wondering whether they had entered the right profession. Yet even with the higher volume and prices, the commission houses failed to reactivate their trainee programs, and in this respect the 1976 boom failed to resemble those that had gone before.

The reason was no secret on the Street. Many there are convinced that the customer's man, as he now exists, may soon become obsolete. Within a few years, the familiar stock broker may no longer fill a clear and perceived position within the investment community. Before the last specialist shuts down his post and bows to the fact that he has been replaced by an electronic device, the vast majority of customer's men may find themselves either out of work or engaged in activities within the investment nexus far different from those related to the telephone and ticker.

To understand the situation one first must explore its roots. There were stock brokers prior to the late 1940s and early 1950s, but they were quite different from those who came afterwards. In their essentials, they resembled the men who associated with Henry Clews in the 1870s more than those at any N.Y.S.E. brokerage today.

Most brokers who worked at member firms in the second half of the nineteenth century filled many roles, and in fact they were more investment advisors than anything else. The stock broker had a few clients, many of them family members and close friends. He would tend their accounts, making certain portfolios were in order, remitting dividend checks, but rarely bothering clients with details. Brokers would work in harmony with lawyers for trust accounts, and would be called to death beds along with doctors to make certain the ailing person's affairs were in order. In a word, the broker was a professional, who served families and filled a niche not far removed from that of lawyer, doctor, or banker. Such men did not seek new accounts, and should a potential client walk through the door of a respectable brokerage, he would arrive with references and letters of credit.

Brokerage was a gentleman's profession in those days, with little work and much time for social life. Few Americans owned stocks and bonds, and most of those who did were interested in safety and income rather than speculation and growth. This meant portfolios comprised of government paper, railroad bonds, and a few safe rail stocks—the Pennsylvania and the New York Central, perhaps—for a bit of spice. It didn't take much work, imagination, or intellect to put together such a holding. Once this was done, the broker could sit back and relax. He collected fees for managing the account, for remitting dividends and interest, and for any advice he might be called upon to provide.

Some brokers did cater to the gambling crowd, especially in lower Manhattan. Their offices and facilities would be used by major speculators attempting to manipulate individual securities or the entire market. Others had close relations with investment banks, and were charged with creating a demand for new securities. There were hundreds of the aforementioned "curbstone brokers"—men who traded in the open, on the streets—in New York, and many of them functioned through "bucket shops"—places where clients wagered on stock movements, often without actually purchasing the shares. Several bucket shops—Jones & Baker and L. L. Winkelman & Co., among others—were large-scale operations, complete with branch of-

fices in other cities, market letters, and credit facilities. But no gentleman or lady would want to be seen at a bucket shop, or for that matter
be too close to the mob that milled around the outdoor trading area on
Broad Street. Even the N.Y.S.E. itself was considered a trifle racy.
Major investment bankers like J. P. Morgan and Jacob Schiff never
went on the floor, leaving that task to the underlings.

These different kinds of brokerage continued on into the early
twentieth century. Then came the great bull market of the 1920s, when
business expanded rapidly. Prior to World War I, probably less than
one hundred thousand Americans owned securities in firms listed on
the N.Y.S.E. By the late 1920s, there were over 3 million shareholders, with half of them buying and selling shares through brokerage
accounts, while six hundred thousand were doing so on margin—bor-
rowing money to purchase shares, and using the stock to collateralize
the loan.

Volume rose sharply—the N.Y.S.E. traded less than 175 million
shares in 1921, crossed the half billion mark in 1927, and experienced
its first billion share year in 1929. This intense activity and increased
interest in investments attracted many newcomers to brokerage. The
young men who entered the field in the middle and late 1920s had
little in common with the veterans who had arrived there after World
War I. The newcomers were aggressive, brash, and cocky—and for
the most part, ignorant of even the essentials of economics and finance. These didn't seem necessary during the great bull market. The
new brokers were able to appeal to instincts of greed and paint pictures
of lush living made possible by quick killings on the market. The old-
timers had been advisors concerned with preservation and safety; the
younger men were salesmen interested in speculation and manipulation. It was as though the philosophy and even the personnel of the
bucket shops had been spliced into the form of the N.Y.S.E.-
affiliated brokerages. And even the form changed—new accounts were
welcomed, brokerages erected client rooms, complete with the best
bootleg booze and buffet lunches.

All of this ended with the crash and depression that followed. The
brokerage community was halved by 1932, and then halved again by
1937. Volume was 425 million shares in 1932, fell to 324 million two
years later, and in 1942, 125 million. By then brokers resembled in-

surance salesmen. They would spend days, even weeks, trying to sell a client on the idea of purchasing a hundred shares of American Telephone, and days might go by without a single transaction. The old-time investment advisor-broker was gone by then—fewer families could afford portfolios, and those who could used the services of trust departments at large banks. The aggressive young brokers of the 1920s had become beaten middle-aged men who worked in other fields. In fact, there was a vacuum within the profession. The forms of brokerage still existed, but there was little in the way of content, and no rationale for the operations.

These were provided by Charles Merrill, the most powerful single influence upon the retail securities business since its beginnings close to two centuries ago. Merrill professionalized and refined this end of the industry even more than J. P. Morgan had done for the wholesale operations in the late nineteenth century. Morgan and his kind made it possible for large corporations to raise huge sums of money on Wall Street. Merrill and those who adopted his ideas—few failed to do so—transformed the brokerage house from what it had been earlier: either a privileged sanctum or a racy, somewhat shady den. Under Merrill, brokerage became more professionalized and standardized. This is not to say that the brokers of the 1950s and 1960s were better trained or more intelligent than those who preceded them. Rather, they did possess certain minimum standards and the beginnings of a code of ethics. These—together with fears of Securities and Exchange Commission investigations in cases of malfeasance—made it possible for clients to view brokers more as guides and helpers than old friends or bookies. Or at least, that was the hope and ideal.

Merrill shares one other distinction with Morgan. There is no satisfactory biography of either man. The Morgans long have refused to open their papers to investigators, as have the descendants of Charles Merrill. But both estates have contributed importantly to the public good, the Morgan through the arts, while the Merrill fortune has been used to sponsor many projects, most of them involved with the securities business. The University of Chicago's business school has produced some of the industry's most important research, and much of it has been supported by Merrill money. Just west of Trinity Churchyard, next to the American Stock Exchange, is the New York University Graduate School of Business, and many of its students have classes in its new building, Charles E. Merrill Hall. But none of the Merrill funds have been used to support a biography of the man, and the estate has refused access to papers to qualified researchers.

Still, much is known about the public man, for Merrill was a genius at self-advertising and open and gregarious with reporters. The outlines of his life may be found in dozens of magazine articles and a few histories of the district and industry. He was born in a small town near Jacksonville, Florida, in 1885, got his first job on Wall Street—in sales—just prior to World War I, formed a partnership with Edmund Lynch in 1914, went into the army, and after coming out helped make Merrill Lynch & Co. a respected middle-sized brokerage and underwriter, which specialized in selling the securities of retail firms. Sensing the good times were coming to an end on Wall Street, he sold out just prior to the 1929 crash. For the next decade Merrill flitted between Palm Beach, Southampton, and Manhattan, with only brief forays into the financial district. Always something of a sybarite, his reputation as a ladies' man increased even while memories of him as a financier faded.

Perhaps it was boredom or a sense that the time was ripe for something novel. Whatever the reason, Merrill decided to return to Wall Street in 1940. The previous year E. A. Pierce & Co., the firm that handled some of Merrill's business, had been on the point of dissolution, and one of its partners, Winthrop Smith, asked Merrill to step in and help. He did so by merging Pierce with Merrill Lynch, and adding to it Fenner & Beane, a New Orleans-based brokerage headed by other friends. Thus was formed Merrill Lynch, Pierce, Fenner & Beane, which later on took cognizance of Smith's role by dropping Beane's name and adding his.

The economy was recovering rapidly in 1949, buoyed in large part by defense spending and increased consumption in the private sector. Wages, employment, productivity—all were on the upswing, along with corporate profits and dividends. But stock prices remained low, and volume actually declined. Seeking to uncover the reasons for this, the N.Y.S.E. commissioned public opinion pollster Elmo Roper to find out what Americans thought of investments. Released in late 1940, the Roper Report showed that most Americans did not trust

Wall Street. The market crash of 1929, followed by the depression and close to a decade of antibusiness rhetoric in the press and from Washington, had fixed upon the public mind the image of the stock broker as a polished crook, and the N.Y.S.E. as a nest of thieves.

Merrill took the report seriously. His natural proclivities and the kind of underwriting he did in the 1920s had interested him in salesmanship and what today would be called image-making. Now he set about transforming his company into a new kind of operation, with a different appeal, approach, and reputation from all those that went before.

The external appearance was important, though not basic to the alteration. Merrill closed down most of the firm's offices. They looked like stodgy banks or the back rooms of supermarkets, the former designed to impress the wealthy, the latter to serve the needs of the brokers and other personnel, and neither was geared to attract new clients. In their places, Merrill Lynch constructed bright, airy facilities, on whose walls hung inexpensive but tasteful prints and oils, with small reception areas but larger spaces for the individual broker to meet with and discuss matters with clients. There was an openness about these offices; Merrill wanted novice investors to feel comfortable there, and apparently he succeeded. The difference between the old and the new was somewhat like going from an opium den or elegant salon to a malt shop. Let others take care of the very wealthy and the gamblers, Merrill seemed to be saying; our firm will cater to the middle class.

Merrill then initiated a large-scale advertising campaign, the first of its kind on the Street. In the past, brokerages had let the public know of their existence through demure ads on financial pages or garish, bold, full-page announcements elsewhere in the newspapers, while some during the 1920s took their messages to radio as well. Again, there seemed no alternative between the stuffy and the sensational. Merrill's ads were educational, telling readers how the N.Y.S.E. operated, dealing with the mechanics of investment, and in other ways indicating it was not as difficult, dangerous, or esoteric as was then believed. Much of this came from his experience with retailers. He even had a slogan, "Investigate, *then* Invest." When in 1948,

President Truman attacked "the money changers" and Wall Street in general, Merrill responded with full-page ads. "Mr. Truman knows as well as anybody that there isn't any Wall Street. That's just legend." In fact, what the President called Wall Street was any place in the nation "where thrifty people go to invest their money, to buy and sell securities." Thus, Merrill changed the image of the brokerage into that of a savings and loan or bank, a secure place for prudent people.

All this was window dressing, literally and figuratively. The truly important changes were those affecting the brokers. In typical fashion, Merrill gave them a new name—account executives—which made them appear both more client-oriented and more professional than they were at the time. Later on they were known as customer's men too, an even more public-centered designation, while the N.Y.S.E. liked to refer to them as registered representatives—as though there was some genus known as unregistered, which of course there was not.

Merrill's account executives were not supposed to be salesmen; nor were they to function as investment counselors. Or at least, this was the line as promulgated by the publicity department. Rather, the typical Merrill Lynch account executive was a bright, charming young man, who graduated somewhere in the middle of his class from a local college, where he was active in a fraternity and had many friends among the students though few admirers on the faculty. He knew how to use a telephone, how to read, and possessed a good sense of humor. Such a person would be put through a training program which stressed public relations, the ways of dealing with clients, and contained a survey of how the market operated and the more common terms used in the industry. The account executive was supposed to recommend those securities approved by the research department, and there were separate lists for aggressive, conservative, and moderate investors. He learned how to solicit business over the phone, but was cautioned against using the hard sell. The company put out a full line of research reports, all of which were available to ongoing and potential clients at no charge—another Merrill Lynch innovation. By reading these and with a little additional work, the new investors could learn as much about the market as the account executives. Merrill realized this, but shrewdly knew that such openness would impress clients, who would assume an account executive employed by such an efficient, frank, and large-scale operation not only was knowledgeable himself, but able to draw upon the best brains in the industry for support.

The Merrill Lynch brokers were to receive a straight salary plus bonuses, and would not be paid commissions; they understood this, and so did the clients. In theory, it appeared such men did not have to become salesmen. In fact, the large producers did receive excellent bonuses, and a good one at Merrill Lynch could come out as well as one at any other Wall Street house. But the advertising value of such a policy was enormous, and attracted timid clients into the offices. By 1950, Merrill Lynch had one hundred and fifty thousand accounts and was spending upward of a million dollars a year on research and market letters, both by far the largest expenditures in the industry.

What of the account executives? After their training they took examinations that made them registered representatives. These were given in the company's offices, took little more than an hour, and required about the same amount of preparation as the written part of the test required to get a driver's license. In other words, almost anyone could become a broker in the late 1940s and early 1950s. The Merrill Lynch account executive of this period put one in mind of the kind of meals sold by cut-rate restaurants in New York in the next decade—ornate surroundings, free wine or beer, an open salad bar, impressive desserts—and a minuscule and second-rate main dish, all of which was standardized. Both were what the public seemed to want. Almost every brokerage accepted Merrill's approach.

A symbiotic relationship developed between Merrill and the N.Y.S.E. In the early 1950s Wall Street spoke glowingly of the average investor—a thirty-three-year-old veteran with a wife and children, a small home and mortgage, and a $5,000 a year job. N.Y.S.E. President Keith Funston boosted "People's Capitalism," based upon the idea that stock ownership would provide a firm foundation for the American economy. The Exchange came forth with the Monthly Investment Plan, designed to enable "the average guy" to invest as little as $40 a quarter in a stock; Merrill thought "every American would do well to invest one-twelfth of his investable funds monthly in stocks." All of this would help America in its struggle against the Soviets. Or as N.Y.S.E. Vice-President Frank Coyle put it: "A regular dividend check is the best answer to communism."

Such was the situation a quarter of a century ago, as the most impressive and longest-lasting bull market in American history was about to commence. Trading volume in 1950 was 655 million shares. In 1967, 2.8 billion changed hands. The three billion mark was reached in 1968, and three years later over four billion shares were traded. The Dow-Jones Industrial Index, which in early 1950 had been around 200, flitted near the 1000 mark two decades later.

The bull market attracted many novices to Wall Street and the investment and speculative arenas. There were fewer than 6.5 million shareholders in 1953; two decades later there were over 33 million. To serve them, the registered representative community expanded swiftly. In 1950 there had been slightly more than 11,400 brokers. In the same fashion as trading volume, their numbers doubled and redoubled—24,900 in 1959, close to 50,000 in 1968, and four years later, 53,000.

Some of the new brokers came to be known as "gunslingers." This was a time when almost any new issue that arrived in the morning could be taken up and disgorged at twice its price in the late afternoon. The gunslingers liked such situations—anything that moved quickly, dramatically, was their stock in trade. They claimed to possess inside information and to have developed new techniques for selecting stocks. If enough people believed them, bought sufficient shares when they were told to do so and did likewise in selling, self-fulfilling prophecy would come into action and make the gunslingers look very good indeed. Then they would repeat the process, for an even larger audience and following.

Despite the hoopla, there were few gunslingers within the profession in the late 1960s. This was not due to a lack of trying, but rather the inability of most brokers to develop followings; they did not have the nerve or panache for the job, and in some cases lacked the necessary knowledge of the market or the requisite imagination. Whatever the reason, the vast majority of brokers continued in the pattern set down by Merrill and his imitators. To be sure, their wages advanced dramatically in the 1960s, as did their status. At the same time, however, there was a marked decline in the levels of intelligence and ability within the brokerage profession. This was to have been expected, given so rapid an expansion.

The young people who had entered the field in the early 1950s had scraped for their livings. This was not necessary in the mid-1960s when new waves of clients swept in at every upsurge of prices, and there seemed plenty to go around. In the early days of the Eisenhower presidency a broker might make two or three dozen telephone calls a day soliciting business, and end up with nothing to show for it. In the high noon of the Lyndon Johnson administration, such brokers would sit at their bank of telephones and wait for them to ring. There were periods when two or three clients would call at the same time—not to seek advice, but to place orders—and then the broker would have to hang up abruptly. There had been a time when brokers prided themselves on rapid action, and would call to confirm purchases and sales. When volume was high in the late 1960s, there would be no confirmation calls, and clients rarely complained. To do so might incur anger on the part of the broker, and in those days, a good one was hard to find—or so it was believed.

The situation began to change in 1969–70, as dozens of brokerages collapsed and the industry was in chaos. Stock prices fell sharply— when most investment advisors and brokers thought they would rise. Over 300 points melted from the Dow Industrials in six months, and though much of the ground was recovered in 1971–72, and the Index went to a new high, the sparkle of the bull market was gone. Charles Merrill's "little guy," the backbone of the post–World War II market, had been hurt badly; he might never return. Every generation of Americans has seen at least one bull and one bear market. The cycle had been completed for this group. Perhaps it would not begin once more until the next generation was ready for a spin.

But trading volume did not decline appreciably. There were modest falloffs in 1973 and 1974, followed by excellent results in 1975 and 1976. These were due to increases in large block transactions, however, and not to the orders of small investors. There are three million fewer of them today than there were in 1970.

Charles Merrill's thirty-three-year-old World War II veteran now is close to retirement age. He entered the market gingerly in the early

1950s, became bold in the last years of the decade, and bought and sold with abandon in the "soaring sixties." Then he lost a good deal of his savings in 1969 and after; he is not about to risk whatever is left in a new foray. In all probability, he and his cohorts never again will become major investors. As for his children, they show little inclination toward common stocks. This troubles brokers, for that huge baby boom bulge of the late 1940s now is of the age where its members should be considering their first stock purchases and seeking out help in making them. It is not happening.

All of this is reflected in the number of registered representatives employed by N.Y.S.E. commission houses—less than 43,000. This population has declined sharply since 1970—by about 20 percent. Despite excellent price action and volume in 1976, there seems no indication that the commission houses will rush to fill the depleted ranks.

Disillusionment with stocks is only one reason for this situation, and in some ways is of minor importance. After all, moods do change on Wall Street, and sometimes with amazing rapidity. Under the proper circumstances, a new bull market—complete with hordes of clients—could materialize, and Charles Merrill's heirs could write about the young Vietnam veteran, with children, house and mortgage, making $15,000 a year, who puts part of his savings into securities. Even if this does take place, however, there are reasons to believe that Merrill's kind of account executive is obsolete. Their departure may be delayed for several years, perhaps for as long as a decade. But the account executive—or if you will, the customer's man or registered representative—is on the way out, doomed by alterations in regulations and laws and a developing technology over which he has no control, and only now is coming to understand.

The regulations and laws involve commissions. One of the reasons for the establishment of the N.Y.S.E. in 1792 was the desire on the part of some brokers to form a cartel in which there would be no price competition. The founders pledged not to buy or sell stocks "at a less rate than one-quarter of one percent Commission on the Specie value," and although the schedule became more complicated over the years, the principle held—at least until the late 1960s, when the Third

Market opened its assault against another part of the 1792 agreement, in which the brokers vowed to ''give preference to each other in our Negotiations.''

The members of the Third Market claimed they could execute orders at lower net costs than could the N.Y.S.E. specialists, and asked the Securities and Exchange Commission to take steps to end this cartel. The attack had nothing to do with the commission brokers. On the contrary, the Third Market hoped to form a nexus with the brokerages, in which its broker-dealers would execute public orders and in this way supplement and eventually replace the N.Y.S.E. The contest opened the entire industry to investigation, however, and in 1968 the Department of Justice began questioning the right of the Exchange to establish fixed commissions. The interrogation resulted in a prolonged debate, which continued through the market decline of 1969–70 and afterwards. In the process, the public learned how the major Wall Street houses competed with one another for clients.

The small accounts were obtained through advertising, word-of-mouth, family and friendship relationships, and reputation. Merrill Lynch, Bache, Reynolds, Paine Webber, and all the others did not deviate a cent from one another in the matter of commissions. Nor could any of them claim to have better executions; there was no accurate way to check on this. So they competed in nonmonetary ways, such as the personality of the broker and claims regarding the value of research reports. And there was no rule preventing a registered representative from sending a valued client a case of Haig & Haig at Christmas time.

It was different in the upper reaches, among the institutions which bought and sold thousands of shares at a time. There were no discounts on volume; a five hundred share purchase of I.B.M. carried five times the commission of a one hundred share exchange, and since it required only slightly more work, was highly prized, both by the house and the broker. Institutional clients received special treatment, in the form of special research reports, invitations to parties at which pliant females were provided, vacations at expensive resorts, and the like. Although discounts were not permitted, the commission houses could enter into reciprocal relations with large clients, and so they did, with the knowledge and approval of the N.Y.S.E.

The government attacked these and related practices, and beginning in 1968 won victories for the cause of negotiated commissions. First the S.E.C. banned certain reciprocal arrangements, and then it insisted upon negotiated commissions for large orders. Finally, on May 1, 1975, all public commissions became fully negotiated. In stages, over a period of almost seven years, competition had been brought to the commission house business. And with this, the registered representatives trained in the Charles Merrill mold found themselves working under a new set of rules, to which many found it difficult to adjust. The more astute representatives began wondering whether they filled a vital role in the industry.

What kind of people worked as registered representatives at this time? Coincident with the arrival of "Mayday," the N.Y.S.E. released a report of the industry based upon interviews and questionnaires sent to a cross section of the community.* From this study emerged a picture of a man, slightly more than forty years old, a college graduate who majored in business subjects or general liberal arts, and who upon receiving his degree obtained a position in sales. Either he did not do well in his first job or he wanted more money, so when he was about thirty years old he decided to enter the brokerage field. After a quick orientation program the broker-to-be took the N.Y.S.E. examination—in the mid-1960s, the height of the bull market, one in four scored a grade of C or lower on that simple test. Then he was turned loose on the public, invited to scramble for new accounts, perhaps to bring in some from his family and friends.

A large number of the representatives interviewed indicated dissatisfaction with the training program, and indeed with their own preparation for the job. "I thought I would take orders—customers would give me tips," said one broker, while another "thought the people I was going to contact were going to be guinea pigs for me to practice on." Most representatives had a low opinion of their research staffs, yet conceded that this branch of the business was their chief source of ideas. They saw themselves as salesmen, who were insecure about their service. "Salesmen are what we are—responsible for selling a product, ourselves," thought one respondent. "Basically, all the job

* The New York Stock Exchange Research Department, *The Registered Representative: A Look Above the Bottom Line* (New York, 1975).

entails is getting out to the people and selling," was another response. "The business setup is geared only to selling stocks—the broker is not qualified to give broad financial advice," thought a low-volume producer, while a highly successful broker said: "My sales function can be described as persuading someone to accept a point of view that has been professionally determined . . . diplomacy is essential."

Although not putting it quite this way, most respondents seemed to think that there were three kinds of brokers—investment advisors, salesmen, and order takers. Few placed themselves in the first category, either because they felt constrained from so acting by lack of training, or through fear of transgressing company rules.* Most were content to remain salesmen. But what were they selling? Not research and expertise; by their own admission this was not the case. Was it personality? Perhaps, though it might not be enough. When commissions were fixed, the ability to tell a joke and empathize with a client's problems could be important. What was that worth in terms of dollars? By judicious shopping, the client would learn that he could obtain discounts on some sales, that haggling was possible, and that the representative really was a tool of his manager in these areas, and not at all free to make his own deal. Each brokerage seemed to have its own plan, often convoluted and difficult to comprehend. The leading firms still advertised their research capabilities, but increasingly there were hints of discounts, with clients urged to operate under the terms of one or another plan.

This competition also resulted in the creation of a new kind of brokerage, the discount house. The customer's men there were neither investment advisors nor salesmen—in fact, they refused to do anything but take and execute orders. Firms like Source Securities and Brown & Co. had no research arm, operated from spartan offices, and made their money on quick turnover and volume. Those clients willing to accept what amounted to plain-pipe-rack services of this kind were able to realize a savings of fifty percent or so on commissions. These discount houses would execute orders on the N.Y.S.E. through a member firm, or at one or another of the regional exchanges or the

---

* Some brokerages limited the stocks to be recommended to a list prepared by the research department. Should the representative suggest others—and should the client sue claiming bad advice—the company would not defend the broker.

Third Market. And with their advent, the order taker—undisguised and unabashed—began to threaten the salesman.

The typical registered representative at a conventional brokerage receives from 20 to 40 percent of the commissions he generates—more in the case of small houses, less at the larger firms. Beginners may have a draw against commissions, around $800 a month. A medium producer—in 1976, this would be one who brings in $80,000 or so in commissions—would then receive $16,000 to $32,000 a year, depending upon where he worked. In addition, many brokerages pay their representatives a bonus in December, usually figured on profits and based upon the number of years of service at the firm. In order to earn this money, the representative is expected to sell, and so he does. When these men spoke of order takers of the 1960s, they referred to a broker who sat back and waited for the phone to ring. He did nothing to earn his commissions—that is, he did no selling as such.

However, the broker at the discount house is expected to be an order taker. Such a person need know little about the market. He does not have to be a salesman. Certainly he would require none of the training of an investment advisor.

Recognizing this, the discount houses employed what conventional brokers sneeringly called "glorified clerks." They were remunerated accordingly—in terms of a percentage of commissions received or on a straight salary, with the latter becoming more popular over time. They were not there to lure clients, but to serve those who called, attracted by newspaper ads or by word of mouth. The conventional houses catered to insecure investors, newcomers for example, and those who for one reason or another liked the way a particular broker talked or functioned. At a time when few new accounts are being generated, and those who are in the market are veterans of 1969–74 (when brokerages performed miserably) the future for discounters seems bright.

Even before the first discount operation appeared, however, Wall Street buzzed with talk of "unbundling," considered the key method by which the conventional houses would meet the discount challenge. The firm would charge a basic fee for simple executions, and then add charges for other services, such a record keeping, the storage of securities and transmission of dividends, research, and the like. But there were problems in such an approach. What would be the difference between a bare-bones execution at Reynolds and one at Source? Given the current investor mood, those would provide the bulk of transactions once unbundling became widespread. When and if that occurs, why would brokerages want to retain the services of its old-time reps, the salesmen of the 1950s and 1960s? The future for such individuals appears bleak indeed.

There is one final step to be made, perhaps in the 1980s, which is even more intriguing. Most of the technology already exists for fully automated brokerages, and the rest will come into being in the next two or three years. Then all that will be required is a brokerage willing to pay out the money and put it into operation.

Imagine a commission house staffed by a guard or two and a single receptionist—no account executives, no researchers, no clerks and typists, no branch manager, not even a telephone. Instead, there are small booths, each with a computer console and a cathode tube display, while on the far wall is a mini-theater, showing the consolidated tape and the Dow-Jones news wire to several clients. One of them rises, prepared to purchase one hundred shares of General Motors. He enters one of the booths, sits down, turns to the console, and punches in the symbol, GM. Almost instantly he learns that the stock can be obtained at several exchanges and from a half dozen market makers on the Third Market. The best price is from a specialist at the Pacific Coast Stock Exchange, $70½. The client is satisfied with the quote. So he punches in his account number, the GM symbol, a button for one hundred shares, and the symbol for the Pacific Coast Exchange. Within a minute or two he receives a direct confirmation from the console, and of course his account is debited $7,050 plus commission.

Already the N.Y.S.E. has a technology in place known as Designated Order Turnaround, which enables a representative to send small orders directly to the trading floor, where they are immediately filled by specialists. Some major and minor brokerages have adopted D.O.T., but Merrill Lynch, the leader, is waiting to see what transpires. On its own, Merrill Lynch is developing a system known as the National Market System, which embraces all markets and exchanges. Part of the N.M.S. is a new method of transmitting and filling orders—the key terms are automatic execution and electronic auction.

Within the N.M.S. is the capability to do away with the registered representative entirely.

A generation ago, Charles Merrill created the account executive, a new kind of broker who prevailed during the era of People's Capitalism and persists in the present. But such individuals have become anachronistic, as the result of negotiated commissions and technology. A new kind of brokerage is being fashioned, by many forces, among them Charles Merrill's other creation, Merrill Lynch, Pierce, Fenner & Smith.

RESEARCH

———

C ULTURAL anthropologists inform us that in many societies man initially had faith in magic and only later turned to belief in religion. Primitive humans thought the deities could be manipulated by means of incantations, the use of potents, and the like.

As societies evolved in the West, mankind turned to the study of the way the gods functioned. Some tried to read heavenly design in the convolutions of a sheep's liver or the paths of stars and planets. Others developed a more philosophical approach, hence the birth of theology. A God-centered civilization deeply concerned with the afterlife came to its height during the Middle Ages, when the implications of theology were paramount and signs of God's will were analyzed by priests and wizards. Upon such things kingdoms rose and fell and bloody wars were fought.

Wall Street is based upon the marketing and pricing of securities of various kinds. This is the central business of the community, and so there should be little wonder that several theologies of investment arose there. The goal was not an appreciation of what might transpire to the soul after death, or the mysterious workings of the cosmos, but rather where the market was heading the next hour, session, week, or month, and the real or perceived patterns of trading therein. What divine will served for struggles in medieval Europe, the proper analytical formulas do for Wall Street today.

The district's period of manipulation—the analogue of magic— began in the early nineteenth century and all but ended in the late

1920s. At first there were few investors and fewer traders, and so it was possible to control the price of a stock. Some giants could influence the course of the market itself. There was no need for theology then, but rather brute buying power and daring. Individuals such as Jacob Little, Russell Sage, Jay Gould, Cornelius Vanderbilt, James Keene, and others could cause the price of a stock to rise or fall by as much as 50 percent in a session. During a titanic struggle in 1901, E. H. Harriman and James Hill caused Northern Pacific to advance hundreds of points while all other railroads collapsed, in one of the sharpest panics in Wall Street history. Should an investor see large price movements and activity, he could assume that one or another speculator had entered the market, and more often than not, this was the case.

The arena was too large for individuals to dominate in the 1920s, but still small enough for manipulation by syndicates. Jesse Livermore, Arthur Cutten and Joe Kennedy would gather together friends and associates, create a pool of millions of dollars in cash, and then push a favorite stock up or down, getting out when the goal was accomplished, taking a short vacation, and then returning for the next foray.

The manipulations continued after the 1929 crash, only now they turned to the bearish side of the market. "Sell 'em Ben" Smith, a colorful character who was the master of the short sale, was one of the last of this breed. The passage of the Securities and Exchange Act, the all-but-dead markets of the 1930s, and tightened N.Y.S.E. regulations, combined to bring an end to the century of stock market manipulation. By the time interest in securities had developed once more, the theologians were in command.

St. Thomas Aquinas, perhaps the greatest Church philosopher, offered several proofs of the existence of God. One of these was based upon the concept of order in the universe. There is such an order, said Aquinas, and so he inferred the presence of a giver of order—God. Later on this became known as the clock-clockmaker demonstration. If one finds a clock on a barren beach, one must conclude that there exists a clockmaker. Everything hinges upon finding a pattern in the universe. Once this is accepted, all the rest follows.

Charles Dow, founder and first editor of the *Wall Street Journal,* believed he had found such a pattern in the fluctuations of N.Y.S.E. stocks. Others had considered the matter before him, but not in a systematic and carefully worked-out fashion. Nor did any of his predecessors possess the audience Dow reached. Furthermore, in S. A. Nelson, William Peter Hamilton, and several others, Dow had disciples who spread the gospel throughout the community and beyond. Today Dow Jones & Co., which he founded in 1882, is to Wall Street news what the Catholic Church is to Christianity—the first and the largest.* It turns out the most-respected and best-followed newspapers in the field, the *Journal* and *Barron's*. Meanwhile, the Dow Theory has managed to hold sway against rivals that have appeared over the years. It remains the keystone theory, and from it one can trace all varieties of what is known as technical analysis.

Dow arrived on the Street in 1880, to accept a job as reporter and editorialist for the *New York Mail and Express* and the Kiernan News Agency, which specialized in business news. He was not quite thirty years old, but already a veteran journalist, having written for several newspapers in Providence, Rhode Island, after which he reported on the hectic activities in the silver mining areas around Leadville, Colorado. Though tall and well-built, Dow was not a dominating figure. Rather he was quiet, self-effacing, and a trifle pedantic; he was a kind man apparently, for all who remembered him in this early period say as much. And of course, he was fascinated by the stock market. After two years on his own, he joined with Edward Jones of Kiernan's to form Dow Jones & Co., which rented offices at 15 Wall, a shabby building next door to the N.Y.S.E. Together they put out a newsletter, which contained closing prices, reports from overseas, and talk of the financial district. From this emerged the *Wall Street Journal,* which published its first issue in 1889, really little more than an augmented newsletter.

While writing for and editing the *Journal,* Dow served as a partner in the N.Y.S.E. house of Goodbody, Glynn & Dow, which he joined

---

* Standard & Poor's, Dow Jones major rival, is a close second, and some Wall Streeters believe it a more important agency. As will be seen, its origins were in the area of news, and not theory. The S & P stock average is considered a more accurate reflection of market movement than the Dow Industrials, but the power of the *Wall Street Journal* is such that the older average is still the best known and most widely used.

in 1885 and where he remained until its dissolution six years later. More than any other financial journalist of this period, Dow could claim to know the Exchange inside and out. He saw the speculations, manipulations, and on occasion, outright thievery. At that time, Dow wrote that anyone who believed he could make money through day-to-day speculation was a fool or a knave. A broker who claimed the ability to perform wonders for his clients was a fraud, he wrote, "because if he could, he would surely trade for himself and would scorn working for ⅛ commission when he could just as well have the whole amount made." Some brokers said they would include their clients in pools, and so make them privy to secret, inside information. Dow scoffed at the idea. "Speculation is not at its best a simple and easy road to wealth, but speculation through people who advertise guaranteed profits and who call for participation in blind pools is as certain a method of losing as could possibly be discovered."

How then should the small investor function? Given the nature of the market manipulations, was there any guide available? Dow thought there was, and in his columns and editorials attempted to instruct the investment community on what he perceived as patterns of behavior in human life, the economy, and the markets. Under his leadership the *Journal* became a combination newspaper and textbook, with its editor the master teacher. As a result the newspaper prospered, and Dow's concepts became influential.

Dow stated his essential idea regarding patterns in 1899. There are three basic movements in the stock market, he said. "The first is the narrow movement from day to day, the second is the short swing, running from two weeks to a month or more; the third is the main movement covering at least four years in duration." The first two waves are man-made. The daily action reflects the hunches of traders while the second is the result of manipulation. The third swing develops out of economic forces, and is beyond control by any group of speculators. "Reports from all directions are that business is active, labor is well employed, and businessmen are making money" may cause an upswing of great power, while opposite news causes prices to fall steadily. "There is a pronounced difference between bull markets that are made by manipulation and those that are made by the public," he wrote. "The former represent the effort of a small number of persons;

the latter reflect the sense of the country on values." Speculators may affect public attitudes for a few weeks or even a month or so, but no longer than that. "The sentiment that endures and sweeps away the strongest interests which oppose it is invariably founded upon general conditions which are sufficiently universal and sufficiently potent to affect the opinions of practically everybody." To Dow, the stock market was a barometer, and not a thermometer, in that it reflected changes in sentiment before they became evident to all, rather than the feelings of the moment. And since "business moves in cycles," one can trace upswings and downswings by studying the market and prices.

These are affected by three forces—sentiment, manipulation, and facts, and of these, sentiment is by far the most powerful, and the basis of the third movement. "When it is widespread [it] will defeat the strongest speculative combinations which may be working against it." Quoting William Vanderbilt, who did his share of speculation and manipulation, Dow noted that "Everybody is stronger than anybody."

In order to measure these movements better, Dow created a stock price index, which appeared in the first issue of the *Journal* in 1889. This average of twelve leading stocks—ten railroads and two industrials—was hardly "scientific" or even very meaningful. But it was a start. Dow knew this, and so he experimented with it, making alterations over the next decade. The familiar industrial and railroad indices were "perfected" in 1896, but changes continued to be made into the twentieth century. Dow also augmented his theory. A major bull or bear move cannot be said to have begun until the two averages confirmed one another by moving into new high or low ground. Other refinements came later on, but by 1901 all the essentials were in place.

Dow did not believe he had found a magic key to success on Wall Street. "The first thing that is necessary to note is that in dealing with the stock market there is no way of telling when the top of an advance or the bottom of a decline has been reached until some time after such top or bottom had been made," he wrote in May, 1902.

Dow died seven months later, at the age of fifty-two. Like other pioneers, he had stimulated interest in his field and had suggested more questions than he could answer. He managed to demonstrate that there were patterns in stock movements in the aggregate, but had not asked why individual stocks moved as they did, except to note that for short and intermediate periods they reacted to manipulation. Dow noted that the market's movements could be correlated with that of the economy, but did not explain why some stocks moved counter to the general trend. Nor did he suggest that the individual could purchase or sell the general average; he knew investors were more interested in their own stocks than the rest of the market. And for such people, he wrote that it might be well to disregard all three waves. "Individual opinions may differ as to what stocks are cheap, or are improving in value, but the buyer should have his own mind clear on this point, so that in case the market declines instead of advancing he will have courage to average his holdings under a conviction that the value of the stock owned will assert itself in due time."

This seemed to imply that the investor should look into the workings of the company whose stock interests him. Then, if the stock seems underpriced by the market, he should buy. On the other hand, Dow suggested that the patterns traced by the market as a whole might exist for individual stocks as well. And if they did, would it not be wise to extrapolate the patterns, and buy those stocks that were headed upward and sell the decliners? Dow tried to combine the two ideas, but never succeeded. After his death the philosophy of investment became bifurcated, and the differing schools opened a debate which has never ended.

The first group—the one that attempts to uncover undervalued stocks—operates on the assumption that the market can be and often is wrong, while the economy is the best guide available. Suppose investigation reveals that Apex Machines, which earned $3.00 a share two years ago and $3.50 last year, has fine prospects, a conservative balance sheet, and excellent leadership in a growing field. Based upon all of these factors, you foresee $4.50 a share for the coming year. Yet the stock sells for only 30; in your view its record and prospects haven't been fully appreciated by the market.

Individuals in this group might purchase shares, and then await a recognition by others of Apex's values, at which point the stock will rise. Because they are interested in the economy, political climate, and related factors—the essentials that go into making a company a success or failure—such people are known as fundamentalists.

The second school comprising the technicians holds that the market price of any stock always reflects the total accumulation of good and bad news, and so is never wrong. The technician would look at Apex, selling at 30, and claim that fundamentals notwithstanding there must be a good reason, or perhaps a set of reasons, for the price. Perhaps the fundamentalist has seen only one side of the story, or it could be that his information is incomplete. The technician might note that according to his charts, Apex is in a downward pattern. True, some good news could alter this, and when the reversal takes place it will show up on the chart. At a certain point—when the stock breaks through a resistance level—he might be willing to buy some shares himself.

In other words, the technician looks at the market and individual stocks, and from the patterns they trace on his charts deduces what might be taking place in the economy or the company. In fact, some technicians aren't very interested in either; they buy and sell on chart patterns, not hard news. In contrast, the fundamentalist cares little if the market as a whole, is headed downward. If the particular stock which he is following seemed underpriced, he would buy.

Generally speaking, fundamentalists are most in vogue during bear markets, recessions, and depressions. When prices decline, when all is in disarray, investors seek advice from analysts who appreciate the worth of tangible assets, the firm's position in its industry, and depreciation schedules. In such gloomy periods those remaining in the market need assurances that only can come from the record of the past, indications of a stable present, and visible signs that the business behind the stock certificates is not erected upon dreams and fantasies.

The greatest era for fundamental analysis was in the 1930s, when such matters as the book value of common shares, dividends and return on investment, and management were of prime importance. Fundamentalists of that decade and after wanted to know if the company's finances were in good shape, if the dividend was secure and what were the chances of its being increased in the near future, and the like. Analysts held out the hope of an advance in the stock's price, but they were primarily interested in safety and yield.

Such individuals had their gurus and texts, and the most popular were Benjamin Graham and David Dodd, whose *Security Analysis:*

Principles and Techniques, was released in 1934, a perfect moment for a new work on fundamentalism on Wall Street. In their preface, Graham and Dodd wrote of their decision to place "much emphasis . . . upon distinguishing the investment from the speculative approach, upon setting up sound and workable tests of safety, and upon an understanding of the rights and true interests of investors in senior securities and owners of common stocks." These were the kinds of words the battered investors wanted to hear, and what they expected from analysts. That is what they got for most of the next generation.

The technicians flourish during periods of prosperity, when stock prices are rising and trading profits relatively easy to come by. During such bullish phases, investors and speculators have their sights aimed at the future, and not the past or even the present. As a confident atmosphere envelops the nation, fundamentalism comes to be viewed as old-fashioned and even reprehensible, somehow antiprogress. It is then that analysts begin extrapolating positive curves, and ask investors to focus upon the situation as it will be—assuming all goes well—in a decade or so. Stock prices rise, discounting the next few years, and then decades—and finally, as one analyst of the late 1960s put it, the hereafter as well. Fundamental analysis offers no guide to such realms, and in their search for justification, investors seek more esoteric methods. Dow and others talked about the patterns traced by the market and individual securities. They also assumed that the patterns recurred and could be comprehended. If so, then the charts can provide answers.

Just as fundamentalists had their own vocabulary which stressed economics, so the technicians developed terms to describe movements on the charts—head-and-shoulders top, flag, runaway gap, trend channel, spiral, and island reversal, among others. And they, too, had their gurus and benchmark books. R. D. Edwards and John Magee, Jr., wrote and privately published *Technical Analysis of Stock Trends* in 1948, at a time when a glimmer of confidence was returning to the marketplace. Garfield Drew's *New Methods for Profit in the Stock Market* appeared in 1954, when several major advisory services based upon technical analysis were signing up new clients with relative ease. By the late 1960s, the technicians were in full command on Wall Street; fundamentalists not only had a hard time getting a hearing, but were not being hired by any agencies except the banks and trust companies, or those brokerages who wanted their brand of interpretation to buttress that of the technicians.*

Technical analysis started to go into an eclipse in the early 1970s, when the bear market sentiment broadened and deepened. But the technicians were never routed, and today they share remnants of power and authority with the fundamentalists.

Why remnants? Because in the early 1960s a third philosophy of investment, known as the Random Walk Theory, made its appearance. It did not fit in well with the confidence of the bull market, but the decline of the late 1960s, combined with the growing sentiment of pessimism, distrust, and rootlessness, gave it new life. Some investors of this period turned to fundamentalism once more; the more modern and hopeless were intrigued with Random Walk. It even had a theological analogue in the "God is Dead" movement, which made a splash on college campuses and talk shows in the late 1960s.

The Random Walk Theory holds that price changes in individual stocks are independent of the sequence of previous price changes. At any given time, the price reflects the sum of all information known to the investment community—in this, the random walkers agree with the technicians. But they go one step further. There is no method to predict what news will come to the market next, and so one cannot make investment decisions upon patterns the technician claims to perceive. Indeed, the random walkers deny that such patterns exist—except in the imagination of the technicians, the same kind of people who can see any of a dozen shapes in the configurations of a cloud, they imply. In other words, there is nothing in the history of stock price movements that can provide a guide for present and future decisions. And so this school upset not only the technicians, but the bedrock of analysis itself, the Dow Theory.

Random walkers trace their origins back as far as the turn of the century, when a French mathematician, Louis Bachelier, formulated the idea in his doctoral dissertation. As is the case with most such tomes, it gathered more dust than interest. But others did pick up the idea in the 1920s and 1930s, though most of them were in universities,

* Many brokerages prefer fundamentalists, because on the whole, they write better than technicians, or at least in such a way as to be comprehended by clients.

and not on Wall Street or in journalism. It was an intriguing though somewhat arcane theory, and one that was not demonstrable until after World War II.

Three factors combined to create a plethora of random walk investigations on university campuses—the invention of the computer, the birth of a major bull market, and the availability of foundation support for projects that combined the first two. Researchers infatuated with the computer's potential fed stock market data into the machines, and what came out appeared to verify Bachelier's hypothesis. Young technicians and doctoral candidates at M.I.T., the University of Chicago, and Berkeley applied for and received grants for studies that were studded with sigma signs, complex variables, and far more mathematics than economics. Eugene Fama, Paul Cootner, Sidney Alexander, Michael Jensen, and others were able to parlay their dissertations into good positions at prestigious universities, but few knew very much about the actual day-to-day operations on Wall Street, investor psychology, manipulation, or branches of financial economics. "The purchase and sale of a single grain futures contract is worth four years at M.I.T.," sneered one Wall Street old-timer, clearly referring to these academic newcomers. Yet he and others like him didn't really understand the methodology of the computer studies, since they lacked the mathematical backgrounds, while the professors lacked an appreciation of the human element in investment. Each talked past the other; rarely was there true contact.*

The technicians lashed out at the random walkers—but only after some simplified versions of the doctrine appeared in popular financial magazines. At first, they were incredulous. Were the professors saying that throwing darts at the financial page was as good a method of selecting stocks as any other? The answer was an unqualified "yes," and delivered with a blandness and matter-of-fact attitude that infuriated the Wall Streeters—and dumbfounded them too, as the random walkers threw in more equations they couldn't comprehend. "The point is, the technicians often play an important role in the

* A few of the academics did filter into Wall Street, however. One of these, Victor Niederhoffer, became quite successful at arranging corporate deals and selecting securities. Ironically, random walker Neiderhoffer came to specialize in the isolation of patterns in trading.

greening of the brokers," wrote random walker Burton Malkiel of Princeton a few years prior to departing for Washington and service on the Council of Economic Advisors. "Chartists recommend trades—almost every technical system involves some degree of in-and-out trading. Trading generates commissions, and commissions are the lifeblood of the brokerage business. The technicians do not help produce yachts for the customers, but they do help generate the trading that provides yachts for the brokers." Thus, the technicians are little better than allies to those who churn accounts. Malkiel concludes by observing that "until the public catches on to this bit of trickery, technicians will continue to flourish."*

Malkiel and others like him have kinder words for the fundamentalists, and many random walkers are willing to concede that in the long run, stock prices do reflect economic changes. How they know this is difficult to say, since fundamentalism does not lend itself well to most computer-based studies. Nor do the random walkers indicate how they go about selecting securities for their own portfolios.†

The battleground of investment philosophies today can be compared with that of Europe during the bloody first half of the seventeenth century, when religious wars decimated the population. The Catholics and several Protestant groups, led by Lutherans and Calvinists, contended for mastery. Each claimed to comprehend the nature of God and had powerful forces at its disposal. As for the rest, they were called agents of the devil or fools. The wars ended in a draw. Nothing was decided in the theological realm; we know not a particle more about the heavenly design today than we did when the wars erupted. But each dogma was able to stake out a territory, where it became solidly entrenched. And so it is in analysis of securities. The random walkers dominate the universities, while the Wall Street houses hire technicians and fundamentalists.

This is not surprising. An investment house following the random walk approach would have to fire its research staff and inform clients

* Burton C. Malkiel, *A Random Walk Down Wall Street* (New York, 1973), p. 131.
† Most of the random walkers interviewed for this section appear to use a fundamental approach in handling their own investments, perhaps due to their antipathy to the technical philosophy. On the other hand, almost all are interested in "inside information," and are willing to speculate on occasion. As one of them put it, "Don't think I'm foolish enough to risk my money on my theories."

that their guesses are as good as anyone else's in selecting securities. No brokerage will entertain such an outlandish notion—except the discounters, who may yet put out propaganda to that effect.

There is no record of which firm hired the first securities analyst, or who that person might have been. Nor is there any clear evidence as to the origins of the profession. Most likely one or several brokers of the 1850s eavesdropped on his runners' conversations, and in that way learned of gossip at the Stock Exchange Board. By the 1870s this practice might have become institutionalized, the runners being instructed to report back with any rumors heard in their travels. Prior to the Civil War the *New York Herald* had a fine Wall Street page, often written by publisher-editor James G. Bennett himself, a man who distrusted Wall Streeters, but was fascinated by the district. Soon there were financial reporters on almost all the city's major morning newspapers. Some wrote about rumors on the Street, but none in an organized fashion, or to recommend purchases or sales.

Market advisory letters similar to those put out by racetrack touts appeared at this time; known as "flimsies," they were sold at newsstands and by subscription. None have survived; we know of their existence through contemporary reports. The paper Charles Dow put out with Edward Jones was considered a flimsy, and from it emerged the *Wall Street Journal,* which in its early days was looked upon as a combination fact sheet–market advisory–neighborhood newsletter.

Still, no brokerage carried a person labeled as "analyst" on its payroll—or if it did, we do not know of him today.

There were magazines devoted to particular industries, and brokers relied upon them for information. Some contained articles designed to provide advice for speculators and investors. Henry Varnum Poor, whose *American Railroad Journal* could be found in many Wall Street brokerages, ably analyzed the nature of the industry, attempted to predict future trends, and isolated those roads that were doing better or worse than average. Poor's *Manual of the Railroads of the United States,* a compilation of statistics for the industry, had five thousand subscribers by the early 1880s, and most of these in the financial district.

By that time some large houses employed statisticians, whose tasks it was to gather information for the use of brokers. There is no indication that these individuals put out buy and sell recommendations, but the first step was made. One of these, John Moody, left his brokerage and followed Poor's example by becoming an editor-publisher. His first *Manual of Industrial Statistics,* released in 1900, performed for that category of stocks what *Poor's* had accomplished for the railroads. Moody and Poor would analyze balance sheets, provide reference materials, and create a handy statistical source book for brokers. Those who consulted their volumes did so to buttress their preconceptions or to find information to support hunches. The same broker might try to gather data on his own, from colleagues in the field, or read several of the flimsies, some of which were becoming quite sophisticated. C. W. Barron, a Boston analyst, had one of the best. Beginning as a handbill in 1887, Barron's service outlasted all of the others, and by the end of the century had developed a reputation for accuracy and dependability.

Still, there was no move on the part of the brokerages to hire analysts of their own. The business was centered around the sales and investment banking functions, and given the small markets for the former and the nature of the latter, analysts weren't deemed necessary or desirable.

The first stock analysts who can be identified as such were the products of two developments that took place simultaneously. The first was the Yukon gold rush of 1898. Visions of great wealth dazzled the investment community, which sought information and advice on new mines and spread rumors regarding forthcoming explorations. In itself this was not unusual; there had been mineral rushes and booms throughout the Far West from the 1840s onward. But the district and the speculator population had been relatively small during the California, Nevada, and Colorado bonanzas, and so there had been less of a market for advice. By the turn of the century, however, there were more investors and a rapidly increasing speculator population made possible by prosperity. Several firms decided to capitalize upon the demand by turning out their own flimsies—a combination advertising and advice newspaper, aimed at attracting new clients and encouraging the old to trade.

Most of these firms were bucket shops, places where speculators could lay bets on whether a stock would rise or fall. Such gamblers relied upon rumors, and so the bucketeers provided them. The advisories were prepared by brokers who signed their names and indicated that additional information could be obtained by contacting them at their offices. In this way, the broker would be repaid for his efforts by additional commissions.

The newsletters did not progress much beyond this stage until 1912 when Jones & Baker, a midwestern bucket shop which belonged to the Curb Market, came to New York and set up a lavish office in the Wall Street area. Jones & Baker was the largest brokerage of its day, with branch offices throughout the Northeast and Midwest, a training program for its personnel, and most important and unusual, a statistical department and an information bureau, which could dig out advice on almost any small mine or railroad in the nation.

Shortly after arriving in the city the company began publishing the *Jones & Baker Curb News,* which originated as a weekly that was distributed free to clients, and might be considered the first brokerage-originated market letter on the Street. The *Curb News* was a huge success, drawing an increased volume of trades from old clients and encouraging new ones to open accounts in order to get copies of the advisory. Other bucket shops began putting out their own small newspapers. Then the N.Y.S.E. brokerages did the same. On the eve of World War I, almost every large and medium-sized house had a range of information brochures and newsletters, offered as a lure to potential clients.

Little is known of the people who wrote these advisories, since none was signed, and no strong personality emerged from the back offices. It seems fairly certain, however, that few brokers became analysts, at least at first. A successful broker had to know how to talk, how to charm, and how to make friends. These qualities were useless to an analyst, whose skills had to stress the ability to write, interpret information, and present it in a clear and persuasive fashion. As might have been expected, most were recruited from the newspapers and the flimsies; rarely did a broker make the switch to analysis. From the first, these two essentials were separate and distinct—as in a manufacturing concern, where one set of workers produced the goods, and another sold and distributed them.

In those pre–S.E.C. days the analysts were free to falsify and ex-
aggerate, but at the same time they knew how to be circumspect. All
understood that mistakes and misstatements—especially advice that
went sour—would harm the brokerage and result in firings. So these
individuals were wary, particularly in the way they made recommendations.

This changed in the 1920s, when many analysts became corrupted
by the bullish atmosphere. Some of them took bribes, either in the
form of stock or cash, to boost securities, and the rising market could
be counted upon to make their predictions good.

As was the case with the flashy account executives of this period,
these analysts were flushed out of the financial district after 1929.
There were few of any kind at the brokerages during the 1930s and
early 1940s, simply because the houses couldn't afford their salaries.
Some newspapermen moonlighted by writing market letters for several
firms. Special reports came out under the name of a vice-president in
charge of research—more often than not, a man in charge of a one-
person office. This was the heyday of fundamental analysis; Graham
and Dodd ruled, and any average economics senior could both understand the approach and apply it, using statistics gathered from the
companies, *Standard & Poor's, Moody's,* and the financial press,
while the writing could be done by a cub reporter.

The situation changed after the war, and once more, the leader was
Charles Merrill. Along with providing a new face for the brokers,
Merrill tried to innovate in analysis. Here he concentrated more upon
form than content. Merrill Lynch would put out a greater volume of
securities analysis than any other house, stressing listed securities and
the "old warhorses." Merrill Lynch's recommendations could hardly
be called daring. Clients might not make fortunes, but at least they
could be fairly certain their portfolio values wouldn't melt in a bear
market.

The advisories would be clearly written, not a great change. But
what was new was their costs—Merrill Lynch reports were free for the
asking, to anyone who wanted one. This innovation surprised the other
brokerages—why give away something of value, without even the
hope of a foot in the door for sales? But as had been the case with the
Jones & Baker Curb News two generations earlier, the approach

worked and was imitated, though with modification. Potential clients were urged to write for special reports, and a few days after receiving them, would hear from an account executive, who would follow up with an attempt to sell the security.

The registered representative has to rely upon his analysts for ideas and recommendations, then, while the function of most analysts is to provide fodder for the brokers to feed the clients. But this symbiotic relationship goes no further than that. The division between these two central positions and professions remains as wide today as ever, and the gap probably will increase appreciably over the next few years.

Registered representatives are made, not born. Prestigious brokerages take amiable young people of no particular intellectual distinction, put them through a training program and a series of examinations, and then turn them loose upon the public. Analysts undergo a quite different preparation. Many attend superior colleges and universities where they achieve better-than-average grades while majoring in economics or business—only one out of every twenty analysts is not a college graduate. Slightly more than half of those analysts working for Wall Street brokerages hold a master's degree, while one out of twenty is a Ph.D. These individuals are not trained by their brokerages; rather, analysts are expected to arrive there prepared to begin work immediately.

The registered representatives function in the front of the office, often in lush surroundings. Analysts can be found at the main offices, usually in cubbyholes, surrounded by reference books and file cabinets, and in shirtsleeves. Representatives at branch offices may never see the analyst whose stocks they push, while a majority of analysts rarely speak with clients. In lively markets, while volume is high and prices rising, the representative and the analyst have good words for one another. In dark and angry periods, the analyst may look upon the representative as a leech, while those in the front office blame the analysts for not calling the turn.

The analysts have the better of the argument—or at least have superior sneering rights by virtue of their standards and attempts at professionalization. The Institute of Chartered Financial Analysts, almost twenty years old, has created and administers a series of examinations in accounting, economics, analytical techniques, and portfolio management. When a candidate passes all of these, and after having a certain amount of field experience behind him, he can qualify for the title of chartered financial analyst. Of the approximately fifteen thousand members of the Financial Analysts Federation, a national professional group, only four thousand or so are entitled to put the CFA initials after their names, and this provides a cachet missing in registered representation.*

Even the largest firms maintain relatively small staffs of analysts. Merrill Lynch has fewer than one hundred, and in an average year will take on a dozen or so, to fill gaps left by retirements and resignations and to provide new expertise. In contrast, this firm hires over one thousand account executives a year, for the same reasons. The compensation tells the story too. A new account executive can expect to receive $800–$1,000 a month plus bonuses based upon sales—in effect, a draw against commissions. The senior analysts in a middle-sized or large firm earn around $50,000 a year in addition to bonuses. Junior analysts, without the CFA but with a master's in business administration, will come in at around $15,000 a year.

Junior analysts at large firms can expect to perform a variety of tasks, and write reports on many companies in several industries. The newcomer might be asked to update an advisory on an industry giant—General Mills, Ford, U.S. Steel, Burroughs—but not make the final determination on recommendations. Or he could be asked to investigate a slow-mover on the over-the-counter market or the American Stock Exchange, or perform what amounts to general housekeeping duties when things are slack, such as posting new statistical information and going through the files to make certain all is in order. He could be sent to some analysts' meetings, learning the process and also making "contacts" with public relations men and other analysts. In the process the newcomer would be familiarizing himself with his surroundings.

This done, the analyst will be assigned coverage of a particular in-

* There are continual attempts to lower standards as well. The New York Society of Security Analysts, the largest component of the FAF, is lobbying for passage of state legislation to create the category of Professional Security Analyst, which would be awarded to anyone who had three years or more service at the time of passage, and afterwards be granted after licensing examinations. Should the measure pass and be signed into law, there doubtless will be infighting between the PFAs and CFAs as to the pecking order.

dustry, or group of them, such as the steels, the oils, utilities, banks, and the like. Often the job is derived from the analyst's own interests—he might have been hired with the ultimate assignment in mind. Or he could move into a vacancy created by a departure, retirement, or death. In the best of circumstances, interest and opening mesh, and if they do, and assuming the analyst does well, he could be locked into his position for life.

The "work-up" on a company is time-consuming and often requires a good deal of special knowledge, but in general the process follows an established pattern. The analyst either is familiar with the background of the firm, or makes himself knowledgeable through a session or two with the files in the library. Assuming he already understands the industry, he need not do any work in that area, but a brushup is always safe and sensible. Some analysts then would contact public relations men at competitive firms and talk with them for a while, rarely if ever divulging the reasons for the call. Of course, all information gathered from company sources—at any company—is treated with suspicion and caution; half-truths and glosses are quite common in this area. Then the analyst is ready to speak with representatives at the firm he wants to report upon. This may be done through telephone contact. A trip to one or several facilities may be necessary, and of course, analysts welcome jaunts—company-paid, of course—if the firm happens to be located in a resort area or some other interesting locale.

Along the way the analyst might call upon the industry lobbying group for facts and ideas, and in some cases, where government regulatory aspects are present, he could speak with political figures as well. All the while he would be scouring the files, reading reports written by other analysts. Most Wall Street firms exchange information, and idea-borrowing is not uncommon. Finally, the analyst would be watching the technical charts to find clues as to price action. No report nowadays is considered complete without at least passing mention of the technical position.

The analyst, then, is Wall Street's equivalent of the investigative reporter at a newspaper. His job is not as glamorous, but it does involve research, legwork, interviewing, and not a small amount of detection.

In the end, the analyst is expected to prepare his report—or really two of them, one for internal distribution to registered reps, the other for clients. A large commission house will grind out periodic reports on more than three hundred companies, will maintain lists of recommended stocks which are given special attention, and will obtain information on all other companies for clients who ask for it.

The report the client receives is written in fairly simple prose, reflects the fundamentalist philosophy (with a shading of technical analysis) and concludes with a hedged recommendation. The phrases here are trite and timeworn, and all speculators and investors learn most of them after a short exposure. "This situation should turn out well for patient investors," translates into "the stock doesn't move with the market, but should rise a trifle given a decent break over the next six months." "Businessman's risk" indicates a "pale blue chip" stock the analyst expects to act well in the near future. "Should outperform the market" is a hedged recommendation—what if the market declines sharply? "Recovery candidate" indicates a stock with a good technical chart or a forecast for better earnings. And so it goes.

The registered representative reads these reports carefully, for the stocks discussed therein will become his basic inventory, the merchandise he will attempt to sell to his clients. There is an old Wall Street cliché to the effect that no broker can be better than his research department, and to a degree this is so. Perhaps a more accurate way to put it is that conservative and prudent brokers are reflections of their researchers; those who take chances with their own stocks wind up either fired or in the executive suite.

Registered representatives meet with their analysts regularly. The former ask questions, the latter have the opportunity to expand upon ideas presented in reports and muse upon the nature of the market and what the future might bring. Each takes the measure of the other, but the advantage at these sessions is clearly on the side of the representatives, for the analysts have the problem of defending past positions that went sour and going on the record with new ones. In addition, the representative can call upon the analyst for additional information during the working day, in effect using his services to help clinch a sale.

Should the analyst have a much better than average record over time, he can expect raises and perquisites. After a while he may become something of a celebrity, called by *New York Times* and *Wall Street Journal* reporters for thoughts on the market after the close, invited to seminars in resort areas, and asked to submit articles to trade and related publications.

At the pinnacle is the assignment to write the firm's weekly market letter, which goes out to most clients. These often are free-form affairs. The chief analyst, now a vice-president, can write about the nature of the universe, the latest developments in rock music, the hobbies of a president or pope, and in the end come up with generalized investment advice, and perhaps a few concrete suggestions. These market letters are strategic tools; the reports put out by the lesser analysts are designed for tactical purposes. The chief analyst sits on the war board; the rest are in the bunkers, behind the front line—where the registered representatives engage the public.

Why don't the brokers function as analysts? The answer is that they do, at least to the extent of answering clients' questions regarding stocks not on the recommended list, reading of them in *Standard & Poor's* and *Moody's,* and perhaps, at the bare minimum, glancing at recommendations in some of the better known advisory services. A handful of representatives—very few of them—leave their desks and telephones and go into the back office, to become analysts.

This transformation is rare. Those brokers with imagination, flair, and the right personality can make much more money out front than in back, and status in this industry is measured in terms of total remuneration, not titles. Brokers who lack sophistication and talent at research cannot make the switch, but often can do fairly well with their clients. It should be obvious that a first-rate analyst making $50,000 a year could double his take by selling his knowledge and abilities at retail rather than wholesale—by becoming a registered representative. Why is he content to transfer his recommendations to brokers, who will then use them to earn wages in the six figures?

The answers can be found in personalities and preferences, or at least they could until fairly recently. The ideal registered representative has to be outgoing, and by nature a risk-taker; he can be fired in bad markets, and most of them rely upon commissions for the bulk of their earnings. In contrast, the introvert is not at a disadvantage employed as an analyst in the back offices. A good deal of his work will be with typewriter and paper. Most analysts use their telephones to obtain information, not give it. And until recently, all of their selling has been to their peers, and not to clients. Furthermore, analysts have job security; unless their records are horrendous, they can stay where they are for life. To them, this seems a fair deal. The public sees and deals with representatives; most analysts are anonymous. The bright representative may be lionized at a Southampton cocktail party by individuals who do not realize that his information comes from an analyst—who is busy broiling steaks for his family a few miles down the road, uninvited and perhaps unknown.

This situation is changing rapidly, and in such a way as to favor the analyst over the registered representative—a necessary corollary of the drift from retail to wholesale securities markets, and the emergence of the institutional investor and the relative decline of the small investor. Complicating and accelerating the changes have been actions by government agencies—the S.E.C. in particular—and legislative enactments by Congress.

During the booming 1960s the large Wall Street houses had difficulty competing with one another. Commission rates were fixed by the N.Y.S.E. and at that time sanctioned by lack of laws to the contrary. So the brokerages worked out a series of ingenious methods of cutting costs for favored clients—and others they hoped would join their ranks. Ways were found to remit part of the commissions, usually indirectly, and so lower rates for major institutions. A most important device was "soft dollars," which meant bonuses granted to clients, not in the form of money, but credits to be exchanged for goods and services. As previously indicated, these might be trips to Las Vegas, automobiles, antiques, high-priced prostitutes, and the like. Or it could be in the form of special research attention. The best and most famous analysts would be on call, as it were, prepared to devote time and company resources to the needs of special clients.

Suppose a large insurance firm with a multi-billion-dollar portfolio wanted a report on particular aspects of the semiconductor industry, preparatory to investing in several securities. It could have drawn upon the expertise of various brokerages, not to provide basic, essential information, but to prepare reports responding to specific questions the insurance company's analysts and portfolio managers wanted answered. These reports would be paid for by soft dollars, earned by previous commission sales and purchases made by the insurance company through the brokerages.

In theory at least, the big institutions received more careful attention in the way of research than the small investors. To make this possible, brokerages had to have two groups of analysts, or as was more often the case, have the same analyst prepare two separate reports, one for the general public, the other custom-made for the institutions seeking information and advice.

In those days prior to negotiated rates, when institutional business was eagerly sought after and highly profitable, sophisticated analysts able to meet special needs were in great demand, and their salaries and bonuses rose accordingly. This situation was not altered appreciably by May Day, 1975, when fully negotiated rates came about. But even prior to that benchmark date, brokerages had plans for future operations that would benefit their analysts.

This is where unbundling, which has already been discussed, became a key concept. Until quite recently the large firms (and most small ones as well) offered clients a wide variety of services, with research being one of the more important of the lot. Did the Bache client want a report on U.S. Steel? His customer's man would not only send on his in-house report, but xerox copies of those put out by rival firms as well.

The discounters are providing basic services for fractions of conventional commissions. Now, in order to compete, the Merrill Lynches, Reynolds, Bache Halsey Stuarts, and other giants of the industry will have to get into the same arena. This means charging fees for ancillary services—and for research reports.

Reports that are to be sold must be quite different from those provided free. The latter have always tended to be two or four page items, sometimes mimeographed, written in an uninspired prose and meant to be read quickly and in such a way as to prompt a telephone call to the broker. In other words, the traditional report was designed to serve as the trigger on the gun.

The research report of the future will be the entire gun—perhaps arsenal would be more accurate. It will resemble investment magazines such as *Barron's* and *Forbes* more than the conventional reports available today. After all, why purchase a one dollar report from E. F. Hutton when for the same price you can obtain a copy of *Forbes* from the newsstand? This is not to say Hutton and other firms will publish magazines, complete with advertising, special features, pictures, and graphics. Rather, the investment report–newsletters of the future will be multi-paged, contain signed columns by senior analysts, have statistical summaries, and perhaps political analysis and economic forecasts as they relate to the general market. And of course, there will be blurbs praising the firm's services and informing readers of other aspects of the company which might be of interest—such as short courses on how to use options, complete with lists of brokers to contact in order to obtain further information.

This new forum will highlight the analyst, putting him in closer contact with clients than ever before. Under negotiated commissions, a record of proven success will count for more than the services provided by the registered representatives. In the future analysts will receive higher remuneration, while representatives will be placed on straight salaries. The firm's total payroll should be the same as today, but the balance will favor analysts.

Finally, many analysts will find themselves in the business of managing portfolios. The market is too dangerous for most substantial individual investors to enter alone, what with the boom of the 1960s, the bust of the early 1970s and the subsequent recovery, the growth of institutional investors and traders, the growing complexity of the market, and recent tax laws. Within a period of less than two years old-time stock investors had to learn about the intricacies of commodities trading, gold, and options. Unable to do so effectively, they have sought advice on management of their portfolios. Unwilling to settle for mutual funds and conventional trust accounts, they would like special treatment from brokerages. Investors realize that their old registered representatives lack the training, and oftentimes the inclination, to undertake such tasks. There are firms that do provide asset management services—Argus Investors; David Babson; Danforth; Loomis, Sayles; Lionel Edie; and Stein, Roe & Farnham are among the larger and better known—but some investors are intimidated by them. Charles Merrill and his followers have accustomed clients to the brokerage house, and they will not leave unless and until the brokerages prove unable to adjust to the times.

This will not occur. Some brokerages have entered into arrangements with consulting firms to manage large portfolios, but most are busily developing their own management services, which means the training of analysts to become mini–mutual fund directors. In the process, of course, they will become the key men at their brokerages—in a way a throwback to the nineteenth century, when the broker was expected to be a portfolio manager—while the registered representative evolves backward and emerges as a glorified clerk.

Whether or not this will be translated into more profits for clients remains to be seen. For if the random walkers are correct, it makes little difference who manages the portfolio—a registered representative with charm or a Ph.D. from the Wharton School. But whatever happens, and whichever philosophy of investment is in vogue in the 1980s, the analyst clearly will be the central figure on the Street. He may work at a brokerage, a bank, or in journalism. Or as many believe will occur, he could become the star of his own firm, hiring salesmen to peddle his wares and advertising agencies to spread the word of his record and abilities. Analysts could combine with others to offer clients a combination of income management and asset development.

Young people considering Wall Street careers certainly should develop their senses of humor and sales abilities. More important, however, will be a knack with the written word and a knowledge of investment techniques.

CHAPTER SIX

OPTIONS FOR THE AMEX

———

A T FIRST BLUSH the American Stock Exchange seems a vestigial remain of J. P. Morgan's Wall Street, when leading brokers wore cutaways and silk hats to their offices and limited clienteles to the right kind of people. In those late Victorian days, a N.Y.S.E. seat implied membership in the city's finest clubs, an Ivy League education, Cunarders to Europe in the spring or long weekends at Newport, junior partnerships for sons and coming-out parties for daughters, dinners at Rector's with brandy and cigars afterwards.

This was the image; the reality was quite different. Only a few specialists could be categorized as "gentlemen," though all aspired to be thought of as such. They had to work with some of the most important businessmen in America, and so had to look and act the part.

In such a period and atmosphere, there was a need for a market where less than reputable individuals could transact business in marginal securities. One existed, an out-of-doors market known as the Curb, the direct ancestor of today's American Stock Exchange, which old-timers at the N.Y.S.E. still look upon as a junior partner with shady antecedents.

The social and economic distinctions are gone today, wiped out by the leveling forces of the past three-quarters of a century. The separate markets remain, however, though no one at either can come up with a rational set of reasons for this. Inertia and a compound of ancient prejudices prevented a merger of the N.Y.S.E. and the Amex in the 1960s and early 1970s, and of course individuals at each are concerned about their job security should unification take place. Still, there have always been ties between the exchanges, and in fact there never has been a period in which the two did not cooperate. In the past, this has been in the fashion of master and servant, even noble and serf. In the more egalitarian atmosphere of the late 1970s, N.Y.S.E. and Amex officials and specialists talk as equals—perhaps even as partners, both of whom have gold keys to the washrooms. Still, the faint outlines of the old attitudes and structure remain; Amex veterans feel the urge to tug at their forelocks when a prominent N.Y.S.E. figure comes into view.

The American Stock Exchange has its own building at 86 Trinity Place. Constructed shortly after World War I, it was conventional for the time and is not particularly impressive today. The Amex is separated from the rest of the financial district by Trinity Churchyard, which is elevated above Trinity Place by several feet. Standing in front of the Amex, one can look ahead and see the dark stone wall of the churchyard, and steps leading from the street upward. Beyond, across the burial ground, is Broadway and Wall Street. But these cannot be seen from the Amex steps. Trinity Place is a quiet street, even during busy sessions—visitors often remark on this, and on how the Place looks more like a part of Dayton or Cleveland than New York. The New York University Graduate School of Business Administration occupies two flashy buildings next door to the Amex, and the students on the street and in the nearby restaurants almost always outnumber the clerks, specialists, and floor personnel. The University, not the Exchange, gives that part of Trinity Place its special flavor and atmosphere.

That this is so does not bother many Amex members, few of whom even notice such things. For most of their working lives, these men have preferred anonymity.

Every Wall Streeter knows the story of the N.Y.S.E.'s origin—the prominent members gathering beneath the buttonwood tree, signing their pact, and then moving indoors. None can say when the Amex's forebearers made their appearance, and this adds to the feeling of illegitimacy which that exchange used to evoke. One can trace them, indirectly, to those brokers who did not sign the agreement, because they weren't asked to do so, and who remained outdoors to trade. By

the 1850s, the indoor brokers of the New York Stock Exchange Board
had admissions requirements for members and listing criteria for securities, thus guaranteeing both to the public. The outdoor brokers had
neither—anyone could deal in any security on the street, where they
met in rain and snow as well as on sunny days. These men were
known as curbstone brokers because for some of them, literally, their
offices were on the curb.

Several curbstone brokers competed with the Stock Exchange
Board, and later on the N.Y.S.E., for clients and securities. They
would trade in listed shares, thus provoking the aristocrats to anger
and inviting retaliation. Some were to be found in the bucket shops,
others went indoors after a while and became the antecedents of the
Over-the-Counter Market, and later on, the Third Market. A large
contingent formed their own exchanges during the Civil War, and afterwards united to create the Consolidated Stock Exchange, which at
the turn of the century was the N.Y.S.E.'s major competitor, but
which went out of business in the 1920s.

As has been shown, one group of curbstone brokers decided to cooperate with the N.Y.S.E., agreeing to accept a limited business in re-
in return for protection and security. These men agreed, first infor-
mally and then through an association, never to buy or sell N.Y.S.E.-
listed securities, but to concentrate instead upon those not yet on the
list. They would cease all dealings in one of their stocks the moment it
was accepted for trading at the senior market. In all matters pertaining
to the district, the men of what came to be known as the Curb Market
agreed to follow the N.Y.S.E.'s leadership. And in return for this, the
aristocrats would permit them to exist—even to prosper—and the
member firm brokers would execute their trades in Curb securities at
the Curb Market.

By the late nineteenth century, the Curb had emerged as a financial
district ghetto, in that it was a community separate from the main
stream, with its own special structure and pecking order. At the top
were major specialists in stocks of prominent firms which did not wish
to be listed on the N.Y.S.E., such as Standard Oil of New Jersey and
other trusts, and at the bottom were two-dollar brokers who were one
week's earnings away from poverty. The Curb had its own ethnic
flavor too. East European Jews and Irish Americans, not acceptable at

the N.Y.S.E., found places at the Curb, where they formed partnerships with one another and were able to make decent livings from the gleanings of the central marketplace.

By then, the Curb was located on Broad Street near Exchange Place, within hailing distance of the N.Y.S.E., which the members knew they could never hope to join. The curbstone brokers would execute orders in the street, receiving them from their clerks who sat on the ledges of nearby buildings, telephones in hand to receive instructions from clients. It was a rough life, and the men of the Curb were crude enough both to survive and to enjoy it.

The curbstone brokers of that period were either uneducated in the traditional meaning of the term or were sons of prominent families who didn't live up to expectations. Their vacations were spent at Long Branch or the Catskills rather than Palm Beach or Newport; out-of-the-country vacations meant a boat to Cuba for cockfights and women, with side trips to business offices in search of securities to trade, for the Curb had more foreign stocks than any other American market. The N.Y.S.E. aristocrats would play polo, attend the Kentucky Derby, and talk of improving the breed; the curbstone brokers of the early twentieth century preferred baseball games at the Polo Grounds, buckets of beer and plates piled with steamers at Coney Island on Sundays, and nights spent playing poker or watching a prizefight.

Clearly there was no community of interests between the N.Y.S.E. and the Curb. Each agreed to leave the other alone, and the N.Y.S.E. was assured that the Curb knew its place and would not consider a challenge to the district's leader.

This did not mean the curbstone brokers lacked ambition, both for status and power. Some of the community's leaders formed an association which attempted to regulate trading and eject from the outdoors market unwholesome men and securities. In order to accomplish this more efficiently, and also to enhance their status, the association's leaders worked for and eventually obtained their own building, complete with indoor offices and a trading floor. For some the roof was the symbol of a new respectability. The door was more important, however, for now the Curb Market could use it to regulate the quality of men and securities admitted to the floor.

The community debated the matter of standards throughout the boom 1920s and bust 1930s, and into the post–World War II period, when the Curb Market prospered greatly, changed its name to the American Stock Exchange, and wondered about its place in the financial firmament. Always there were two forces, one favoring more stringent requirements and higher standards, the other demanding the lowering of both. This was not the familiar, simplistic debate between reformers and old-timers, and it did not involve status and profits alone. Both sides were more concerned with survival. From the first the Curb, and then the Amex, had to consider the possibility of being wiped out by a crash or a scandal or destroyed by rapacious rivals, and even now such fears underlie some of its actions. On the one hand, this created and perpetuates a jittery atmosphere on Trinity Place; while on the other, it has obliged Amex leaders to innovate and create far more than have their counterparts at the N.Y.S.E., who until recently had no such fears or troubles.

Those who spoke for low standards made a good case. Such a stance would prevent competition with the N.Y.S.E., while at the same time enabling the Amex to obtain additional listings and so transact more business. But this position would cause trouble with the Securities and Exchange Commission, open the doors to shady dealers, run the risk of scandals, and in the end, might mean the destruction of the market. Low standards did result in excellent business in the 1950s—and a major scandal in the early 1960s, when for a while it seemed that the government might take a direct hand in running the Amex in order to keep it honest.

This was not necessary. A new leadership took over, the corruptionists were flushed from offices and the floor, and standards for both men and securities rose. This created a new set of problems. While the Amex listing requirements remained far below those of the N.Y.S.E., its specialists functioned as well as those at the senior market. No longer was it unusual for a person to leave the Amex for an N.Y.S.E. career—or to prefer to remain at the Amex and reject overtures from the N.Y.S.E. The sons of the curbstone brokers graduated from N.Y.U. and Boston University, and their sons went to Princeton and Harvard. By the late 1960s, Amex brokers had become almost indistinguishable from their counterparts at Wall and Broad. To some, they were superior, for while obtaining a veneer of education and a measure of sophistication, they retained the toughness of their fathers and grandfathers.

Meanwhile the reform movement showed results. During the 1950s and early 1960s, Amex stocks that qualified for the N.Y.S.E. made the move as soon as possible. Syntex, one of the most active Amex stocks, received the word from several N.Y.S.E. specialists: the company's application would be approved if submitted. Amex officials learned of this and entered into the contest, trying to retain the stock despite fears of retaliation from Wall and Broad. Syntex elected to remain, as did other Amex stocks. This was a double triumph for the reform element—not only did the N.Y.S.E. fail to obtain desirable stocks, thus losing income, but the financial world began to wonder which market's specialists were superior. This, at a time when the N.Y.S.E. was contending that its specialist system offered more benefits than the dealer operations at the Third Market.

The Amex leaders and specialists were circumspect in their euphoria, so accustomed were they to deferring to their N.Y.S.E. counterparts. Privately they rejoiced, and as the list of Amex stocks that qualified for the senior market grew, so did their confidence.

This celebration was short-lived, however, coming to an end with the market decline of the early 1970s and the souring of the investment and speculative climates. There was no possibility of an immediate Amex bankruptcy or financial failure, despite a string of quarterly deficits. But declining volume and a paucity of new listings did create concern, and with it a search for solutions.

One was the often-discussed merger with the N.Y.S.E. At various times in its history, the Amex considered such a union, and had always rejected it. During boom periods, the senior market showed little interest in merger, while in bad periods it wanted Amex securities but not its men and structure. The bringing together of these two markets would not be a merger, but a disguised liquidation of the Amex.

The Amex had become accustomed to such situations after a half century of independence indoors, was adept at matters of survival, and prepared to reject overtures in such a way as not to anger the

N.Y.S.E. In any case the Wall Street community did not press the matter, while feelers from the S.E.C. were brushed aside with relative ease.

Instead, the Amex initiated an aggressive search for new business. This approach was fully in keeping with its tradition. During the early 1920s, several prominent brokers had become major bookies; financial district gamblers knew they could place a wager on almost any sporting event with several specialists and two-dollar brokers at Trinity Place. The curbstone brokers always had cultivated foreign corporations that could not qualify for N.Y.S.E. listing—witness those trips to Cuba—and in the late 1920s developed the idea of the American Depository Receipt, which enabled domestic speculators and investors to deal in receipts for foreign stocks deposited overseas. By the end of the decade, the Curb had more foreign issues than all American markets combined as well as dominating the aftermarket for foreign bonds. When in the early 1930s margin loans were hard to come be, the Curb established a money desk, where funds could be borrowed at rates arrived at competitively.

Given regulations, policing, and the higher status of the Amex, gambling was out of the question in the early 1970s, but versions of the other two vehicles were explored in an aggressive fashion. President Paul Kolton wanted to admit U.S. government securities to trading, claiming that his specialists could afford greater liquidity in this area than did the O-T-C traders. Together with several key staffers, he visited European exchanges in an attempt to obtain foreign listings. Eventually the Amex did trade in Treasury notes and bills, but this was a small, barely profitable business. Nothing came of the idea of trading large numbers of foreign issues. So Kolton and his associates were obliged to look into new areas.

They found one, not in London, Paris, or Frankfort, but in Chicago, where a new kind of market had developed in a modern version of an old speculative and hedging vehicle: options.

On April 26, 1973, the Chicago Board Options Exchange opened for business. This was the first important American securities exchange to be formed since the organization of the Amex itself, and was also the beginning of a new chapter in the sporadic contest between New York and the hinterlands for market leadership. Significantly the challenge was met not by the N.Y.S.E., but by the hungrier Amex.

Before exploring the ramifications of the contest and the Amex response, one must appreciate the functions of options in securities trading, why they created new interest in the late 1960s and early 1970s, and why the Chicagoans beat the New Yorkers to the draw.

Simply stated, an option is the right to purchase or sell a specified number of shares in a designated security at a stated price within a fixed time. The purchaser has the option to exercise his right, hence the term. There were two kinds of options. Puts were for those who wanted the right to sell the shares—for individuals who thought the price would decline—while calls gave the owner the opportunity to purchase them at a stated price and he, of course, believed that the price would rise.

Initially options were vehicles whereby speculators could wager on stock movements without having to go to bucket shops, and to do so with relatively little money and a great deal of leverage. Thus, XYZ Inc., trading at $50, could seem a bargain to a speculator. If he bought the stock at that price, and it rose to $54, he would have an 8 percent profit, and some would be content with that.

Let us assume that the speculator decided instead to purchase an option on XYZ. He might have to pay $300 for the right to purchase 100 shares of XYZ at $50 a share within the next six months. If XYZ rose to $54, and the option holder exercised his right at that point, he would have a $100 profit, or a 33.3 percent increase in value over the $300 he paid for the option. And what if the stock went to $58? The person who owned the shares outright would have a 16 percent profit, while the buyer of the option would be able to show an earning of $500 on his $300 investment, for an advance of 166 percent.

Of course, the option buyer pays a price for this leverage and his small investment. If XYZ did not reach $53, or go beyond that point, the option would be worthless—hence the reason for its being classified as a wager, and not an investment, by most Wall Streeters at the turn of the century.

The put is the mirror image of the call. The purchaser believes XYZ will decline, and so he obtains the right to sell the stock at $50, again paying around $300. In this case if the stock fell to below $47, he would have shown a profit. An option exercised at $44 would mean a doubling of the wager.

In their crude forms, options existed in the late seventeenth century in London and Amsterdam. They were used, rarely and fitfully, in American markets prior to the Civil War. Then, in the postwar period, options were institutionalized by Russell Sage, one of the leading speculators of the day. A shrewd gambler himself, Sage realized that most of the small fry lost money and wound up in the gutter. Anxious to benefit from their ignorance of market forces and their penchant for wagers, Sage became a put-and-call dealer—in effect, one who was willing to book their bets.

Others followed Sage's example, and by the early twentieth century they added a new wrinkle. Now it became possible for a client to sell a put or call as well as purchase one. In practice, this meant that the owner of XYZ who suspected it might rise—but not beyond three points—and wanted to make some additional money, would sell a call to a person who wanted to buy it, using the dealer as an intermediary, for which he received a commission. The selling of options—especially calls—was looked upon as a fairly conservative act. Should the stock remain where it was, move upward slightly, or decline, the owner would have his dividends plus the money he received from the sale of the option, which would not have been exercised. To refer to the earlier example, should he have sold an option on the $50 stock for $300, and the stock did not rise above $53, he would have had additional income of $300 minus commission. If the stock went to a price somewhere between $50 and $53—say, $52—the owner would have the dividends and the $300 from the sale, but would have to sell the stock to the option owner (and now exerciser) for $50, thus relinquishing it for $200 below the market price. In this case, his $300 from the option sale would provide him with only an additional $100 ($300 minus $200) in income.

Of course, had the price gone much higher—say to $60 or $70 a share—the owner of the stock would have had to forego a nice capital gain, which would have accrued to the purchaser of the option. But to conservative investors, the risk seemed worth the reward—that extra $300.

In any case, puts and calls never were a big business in periods of depression, and the volume of trading was not particularly high in boom eras. Not many investors knew about options, cared to take the time and trouble to learn how they could be used, and to master techniques that might be employed to maximize profits and minimize risks—in short, undergo what amounted to an education in speculation, complete with statistics and a bit of mathematics. Others who did understand their use shied away from options for a variety of reasons. Among the more important of these was the lack of publicity and liquidity. Would-be options buyers and sellers learned of prices from advertisements placed in the business newspapers and financial pages of other sheets by several dealers—there were fifty or so in 1900, and only fifteen in New York a half century later. The Put and Call Brokers and Dealers Association was a chummy organization, consisting of firms marked by a high degree of expertise, small client lists, and a high profitability factor. Registered representatives at the conventional brokerages knew of puts and calls, but barely; they did not deal in them as a matter of course. Should a client inquire as to how they operated, he might be sent a brochure filled with textbook answers to only the more obvious questions. Most brokers knew as much as their brochures, and no more than that. The representative might handle the sale or purchase of a put or call and charge a small commission for his work, which consisted of sending the order to a member firm of the Put and Call Brokers and Dealers.

The options could not be traded easily. They were not listed on any exchange—the N.Y.S.E., Amex, and regionals did not consider them to be worthy vehicles. Nor could options be disposed of easily on the O-T-C market. This meant that the purchaser was locked in. He had to hold on, either until the option could be exercised or it expired.

All of this was well-known within the industry, and the Put and Call Brokers and Dealers Association recognized the need for an organized market and the benefits to be derived from liquidity. Whether or not that organization ever seriously considered establishing one is not known, but it never took steps in that direction, for the members saw no reason to act. They had a monopoly, the N.Y.S.E. and Amex demonstrated no desire to challenge them, profits were high, and the customers appeared satisfied. Besides, the creation of a new market would be a costly affair, and the Put and Call Dealers Association had limited means, while the members would have refused the necessary assessments to set up a new exchange.

Admittedly such a move would have involved risks. There was no way of knowing whether clients could be drawn to options trading should an organized market for it exist, or whether veteran buyers and sellers of puts and calls would want to speculate or deal in them. An ambitious educational and advertising program would be necessary in order to give the market a chance of success, and this might prove even more expensive than the administration of the exchange.

But even if all of this was done, options trading was bound to be cumbersome. The expiration dates of traded options would have to be standardized in order to create classes of options to be traded. Specialists and/or registered traders would have to stand ready to buy or sell when no one else appeared on the other side of the trade; would they be willing to take this kind of risk? There would have to be a clearing corporation too, one which guaranteed that stocks or cash would be delivered at the expiration or exercise of the option. And all of this would have to survive government regulation, probably by the S.E.C.

Why bother? The securities industry was prospering in the late 1960s, and the options dealers were no exceptions. Lacking financial incentives to act and encased in more than a half century of tradition, the members continued in their established ways of transacting business. Like the N.Y.S.E., the Put and Call Brokers and Dealers lived in the sunset of the old system without realizing the precariousness of their position. Already the N.Y.S.E. and Amex were being threatened by the Third Market and NASDAQ was only a few years from completion. New York's put and call options business would be crushed by the challengers from Chicago.

This generation of investors does not recall the last time outsiders threatened Manhattan's dominion over securities trading. For that matter, there had been no truly serious challenge since the 1830s, when Wall Street had replaced Philadelphia's Chestnut Street as the nation's financial hub. There had been skirmishes with the mining exchanges of the Far West, and at the turn of the century Boston held brief sway over industrial securities. In the end, however, Wall Street humbled its rivals, often in a way they found humiliating and offensive. Yet there was nothing to be done about this situation, especially during and after

World War I, when New York replaced London as the world's financial capital and entered its golden age.

Chicago mounted the greatest and longest-lived challenge, one that took several forms throughout the late nineteenth and twentieth centuries. At one time, the leaders of that city boasted that just as New York had replaced Boston and Philadelphia as the nation's leading metropolis, so Chicago's day was about to dawn. Its location in the center of the continent made it better suited for such a role, its industry was strong, and the city's banks powerful. And ambitious. Chicago was popularly known as "the second city," and the ranking irritated businessmen on State and LaSalle Streets.

The leaders of the Chicago Board of Trade did not feel inferior to their Manhattan counterparts. They always claimed the Chicago Board was to commodities what the N.Y.S.E. was to securities—the leader. This was not strictly so, for while the Chicago Board did dominate trading in many commodities, from wheat to plywood, several other markets—among them the New York Commodity Exchange and the New York Mercantile Exchange—did a larger business in others.

But the Chicago brokers were more aggressive, and to a degree, more imaginative as well. In the 1920s, several of them backed Harold Stuart of Halsey, Stuart, when he attempted to wrench leadership in the underwriting of utilities securities from J. P. Morgan, and they were not deterred by his failure. The Board's leaders dominated the small Chicago Stock Exchange and later on helped transform it into the Midwest Stock Exchange. But the Board of Trade's executives weren't really interested in securities. They knew and understood grain contracts—fast moving, mercurial, and exciting. In the late 1960s, the grain markets were dull, while stocks were booming. The Chicagoans searched for a vehicle which combined the action of grain futures with the glamour of securities, and they settled on options.

In 1968, the Board took on a new president, Henry Wilson, who had been one of Lyndon Johnson's administrative assistants. Wilson was charged with several tasks, one of which was to maintain a close liaison with Washington. Then the Democrats lost the White House and Wilson turned elsewhere for ways to justify his salary.

Although a novice on LaSalle Street, Wilson proved a quick study, and he had an instinct for the business. In 1969, while Wall Street sped along in the superheated last stage of the great postwar bull market, Wilson engaged the services of Robert R. Nathan Associates, which explored the feasibility of an organized options market. The Nathan Report was encouraging, but it did note a major problem area: without a method of guaranteeing deliveries and performance, there could be no options exchange.

Nathan Associates suggested the establishment of a clearing corporation, whose primary function would be to make certain each options purchase was covered by a sale or commitment to deliver. The clearing corporation was to be the guarantor of execution. In effect, it would become the buyer from the seller and the seller to the buyer—the middleman.

The system made sense, and was adopted. It was more than that, however. Perhaps without meaning to do so, Nathan Associates had developed a variant of the Third Market's dealer structure with an overlay of the specialist function.

The Board and its consultant also were uncertain as to how organized options trading would affect activities in the primary market. More important insofar as the Amex was concerned, the Chicago leaders had been told that options trading might have a major impact upon dealings in low-priced speculative issues—and most Amex issues fell into that category. For example, would the speculator prefer to deal in five-dollar shares of Amex-listed firms, or purchase an option on a stock of the caliber of Exxon? A five point change in Exxon could occur in a single session, and result in a decent though hardly spectacular move in that high-priced issue. On the other hand, such an advance could double the quote for the option in the stock. In the early 1970s, this kind of performance was rare for Amex issues, which had lost their speculative attractions.

N.Y.S.E. leaders concluded that such trading might result in higher volume for their market. Conservative investors might purchase stocks in order to sell options on them, while those who bought options would come from the small fry—the kinds of individuals who played the numbers, frequented off-track betting parlors, or dealt in chancy Amex or O-T-C issues.

Nor could the senior market take the leadership of the new exchange too seriously, or the place where it was to be located. For the first president of the Chicago Board Options Exchange, Wilson selected Joseph Sullivan, a thirty-five-year-old former newspaperman whom he had known in Washington, and who had come to Chicago as a troubleshooter at the Board of Trade. Sullivan was considered sharp and pliable, but he knew next to nothing about finance and had no experience at a major market. In fact, this would prove a blessing, for he was not encumbered by old ideas, and could start fresh. Sullivan led the search for a market location that would suit his small budget—most of the money allocated by the Board of Trade had to go into the clearing corporation. In the end, he settled on renovating a members' lounge and rest room in the Board of Trade Building. Seats were purchased by 284 individuals representing 121 firms, each of which paid $10,000 for the privilege of dealing and trading in options on sixteen stocks listed on the N.Y.S.E. Since the C.B.O.E. was the first in the field, Sullivan had selected active, popular, and fast-moving items, and he promised efficiency—and action.* But most of the initial membership was skeptical and dubious. After all, if options were that desirable, why hadn't some other exchange—the N.Y.S.E. in particular—entered the field long before? Many of them went along out of curiosity, a desire to please Wilson, and the chance that the situation might turn out better than anticipated. Sullivan promised to add more securities once the shake-out period had ended—and when the S.E.C. had been convinced that all was proceeding as pledged.

Whether due to its novelty or a realization that options could provide fast action, speculators were attracted to the market on the buy side, while investors were informed by their brokers of means whereby they could enhance their net returns by selling options on securities already in their portfolios.

This marriage of the plunger and the prudent troubled some C.B.O.E. figures, for the system could not work well without both of them. Gamblers were certain to appreciate the value of the market, but conservative investors might stay away through fear of novelty. Unless investors provided options for the plungers to buy, their prices could

* The volatility of a security made the option written against it desirable; quality was secondary, and dividends didn't matter, since options holders did not receive them. Thus, the first securities to have options traded were the big movers, and the C.B.O.E. and other options exchanges went down the list toward the more sluggish items.

rise to the point where they would not be attractive, and the entire system could collapse.

As it turned out the new exchange had opened at a most fortuitous time. The Dow Industrials, which were at ·1020 at the beginning of 1973, had lost seventy points by mid-April, and continued downward, irregularly, for the rest of the year. Options buyers did badly, but they didn't abandon the exchange, hoping to recoup their losses. Few of the options sold by investors were called, and so this group did well insofar as actual cash returns were concerned. Their "paper losses" were assuaged by funds received from options sales. Investors offered new options on their securities, and some purchased additional shares so as to be able to sell more of them. As for the plungers, a number of them switched to selling "naked options"—options on shares they did not own—hoping the decline would continue and so make their transactions profitable. New hedging techniques were learned, several the outgrowths of old experiences with puts and calls. In this way, a good balance between buyer and seller developed. The system worked better than anticipated.

The C.B.O.E. reported a loss of over a million dollars during its first full year of operation, much of it due to start-up expenses. Business was excellent—on some days the number of shares represented by sales of C.B.O.E. options was larger than those transacted at the Amex. Crowded and cramped in small quarters, Sullivan searched for a new facility, and in the end decided to erect one within the Board of Trade Building itself. This was completed by December, 1974, at a time when trading was expanding rapidly. The exchange reported a profit of $850,000 for 1974–75 and greater ones thereafter, thus doing well at a time when the N.Y.S.E. and Amex were showing deficits. Additional seats were offered and taken up at premium prices. By late 1975, the C.B.O.E. had over one thousand members, while seats changed hands at $80,000—more than those at the N.Y.S.E. Over a hundred different stocks were represented by C.B.O.E. options in early 1977, with others in various stages of admission. Furthermore, the Chicago Board was readying a plan to offer put options as well as calls, while some toyed with the idea of trading strips, straps and straddles, along with additional speculative esoterica.

None of this implied that Chicago was about to replace New York as the financial center of the United States. Nor was there any thought that the C.B.O.E. could replace the N.Y.S.E. After all, options were traded against the prices of their underlying securities, and almost all of these were listed on the N.Y.S.E. Rather, the new exchange's success indicated that the Wall Streeters had lost much of their old competitive edge. There seemed no reason why the N.Y.S.E. and Amex, combined with the Put and Call Brokers and Dealers Association, could not have established an options exchange in lower Manhattan, and run it between them. All of the components were present—except leadership.

The New Yorkers conceded as much and offered excuses and explanations for their lapse. Their attention had been diverted by the failures at major brokerages, by the NASDAQ threat, and by regulatory tangles of various kinds. In the beginning, of course, most thought the risks in options not worth the potential rewards. Along with the rest of the investment and speculative communities, however, they soon changed their minds. Then some New Yorkers set about attempting to catch up with the C.B.O.E., and eventually—if possible—subduing the upstart midwesterners.

As indicated, the C.B.O.E. traded in only a small handful of options in 1973 and the S.E.C.—still helping New York recover from the traumas of the past three years—was most cautious in permitting others to be listed. The Chicagoans selected the more volatile stocks from among those the regulatory agency would permit to have options written against, and Sullivan proved adept at getting them approved. Still, there were plenty to go around, as well as many questions that required consideration. For example, did the parent company have any rights in deciding whether options should be written against its stocks? Did the Securities Act have to be amended to cover the new trading? Were options insured? While answers were considered, rivals might enter the field and compete with the C.B.O.E. for listings. In time they might attempt to trade in the same options, and in this way offer brokers competitive markets as well as dealers.

The investment community of 1974 viewed options trading in somewhat the same way as Europe's monarchs considered the New World in the sixteenth century—wild, uncharted, potentially of great value, with plenty of room for expansion. The C.B.O.E. became the new school for the industry. Leaders of foreign stock exchanges who used to travel to America to explore New York's trading methods and automation techniques began bypassing Kennedy Airport for O'Hare. British, German, French, Canadian, and Japanese exchange personnel milled about the C.B.O.E., observing, questioning, noting, and then returning home with briefcases filled with mimeographed reports and brochures. Brokers and specialists from American exchanges also visited the C.B.O.E., somewhat to the embarrassment of the N.Y.S.E. and to the delight of the newly important Chicagoans. The C.B.O.E. realized that it could not obtain a monopoly over options and appreciated the fact that there were no secrets in this area. That exchange enjoyed its moment of triumph, confident that when the competition began, it could be met successfully.

The key to victory was not financial muscle or reputation. There could be no recourse to tradition, and a good deal of experience in other categories of securities markets did not apply to options. The C.B.O.E. leaders knew they had an opportunity to create a different kind of market, and they considered the situation exciting. For its part, the S.E.C. was in a quandary. It was required to enter a wholly new area of activity, a challenge that in some ways was greater than that of 1934, when the agency made its first appearance in the district. Then it had all the problems of a new agency having to regulate an old, established market. Now the roles were reversed: the hoary S.E.C. had to confront this newborn exchange, and due to its inability to develop a set of strategies rapidly, there was a measure of uncertainty, confusion, delay, and error.

The N.Y.S.E.'s leader did not make the Chicago pilgrimage, though the men of Wall and Broad kept themselves informed of developments at the C.B.O.E. Chairman James Needham indicated that "at some future time" his exchange would consider options trading, but then turned to other matters. In fact, the senior market had no intention of entering the context. This was not due to hauteur or a failure of imagination, but rather the perplexing regulatory and organizational difficulties options presented at the N.Y.S.E. Clearly specialists could not deal in options written on their stocks—the possibilities of manipulation in such a situation would be tremendous, and the S.E.C. would never approve of the arrangement. Nor could other specialists—or a new group of specialists on the floor—deal in the options, for the proximity to the stock trading would present similar regulatory difficulties. And what of those companies that did not desire options to be traded against their stocks? There were some of these, and the C.B.O.E. could afford to ignore them. It would be different at the N.Y.S.E., where the companies could retaliate by delisting their stocks and using the Third Market. The establishment of a New York Options Exchange might have resolved the matter. The N.Y.S.E. could have owned shares in such an organization and even dominated it, but the personnel and structure would have been independent, and the trading facilities located at some distance from Wall and Broad.

There is some indication that such a solution was considered. Needham did consult with Marsh, Block & Co., the biggest put and call dealer in New York, and there was talk that together they would open a market dealing in options on over-the-counter issues. Nothing came of this. Instead, Needham concentrated on fighting the Third Market for domination of equities. There was little doubt that a national exchange system was in the making; the only major question was how it would be organized. Needham wanted the N.Y.S.E. to lead the way, while the Third Market, several key congressmen, and an influential faction of the S.E.C. spoke in terms of a different kind of electronic marketplace, perhaps one that emerged from NASDAQ.

Needham's stance provided an opening for Amex chairman Paul Kolton, and at just the right time. For the Amex was in bad financial shape. Low volume had resulted in deficits, and the end of the bull market meant fewer companies were listing their shares for trading. Additional business was needed, for without it the Amex would have to initiate severe cutbacks. Kolton was interested in options, and had watched the preparatory stages in Chicago with interest. But he did not act. As was traditional and customary, the Amex initially deferred to the N.Y.S.E., and was prepared to follow its leadership in the matter of options trading. But when it became evident there would be no leadership—and no N.Y.S.E. retaliation for a separate Amex move—Kolton went off on his own. A special Amex task force studied the Chicago market, and in 1974 drew up proposals for trading in New York. In January, 1975, trading in options commenced on the Amex.

Kolton had led the Amex into options in order to provide his specialists with a new trading vehicle, one through which they could realize additional profits. Nothing more than that had been considered, though many at the Amex had long chafed under some of the more intransigent positions taken by the N.Y.S.E.' and yearned for independence. By this move, Kolton had set the Amex upon a new course, the full implications of which were not realized initially. The foray into options could alter the institutional and power relationships in lower Manhattan as much as, or even more than, the N.Y.S.E.–NASDAQ contest.

Again, the comparison of options trading today with events in the western world after the discovery of the Americans may be illuminating. At the time, most continental nations didn't realize how important the New World could be, and how it might alter the power structure. France, the Germanies, Spain, and other European powers struggled for dominion in central Europe, and all the while Britain established its primary footholds in a more important area, North America. Analogously, the N.Y.S.E. and the Third Market combated one another for leadership of the central market in stocks—the old basic trading vehicle—while the C.B.O.E., the Amex, and other exchanges expanded into options, which in the end may prove more valuable a prize.

The issue revolves around the question of why we have securities markets and exchanges, and why individuals and institutions purchase and sell securities—two matters which once were joined but have not been connected for decades. Ask an exchange executive, market maker, or specialist to justify his existence, and he will talk of the need for liquidity in securities. Go a step further and you will hear of the need to provide a market for new securities, for without one, who would purchase fresh stocks and bonds? And Wall Street's primary purpose is to allocate funds for capitalist enterprises. In other words, markets in old securities make it possible for investment bankers to raise money for new ones. On a more mundane level, Wall Streeters note that few investors would purchase shares in XYZ Corp. without the certain knowledge that they could be sold at an exchange or market during trading hours on any business day. Needless to say, speculation could not exist without formal or informal markets.

Two decades ago Wall Street urged the nation to own shares of

American businesses, as though this would be a way to participate in its benefits and fight Communism. Organizations appeared to lobby for "shareholder democracy," and even now Ralph Nader speaks of the need for pressures upon managements and shareholder responsibilities. Some investors—usually newcomers—actually believe this, but most arrive at a different view of affairs shortly after coming to the Street. The owner of 100 out of the more than 600 million shares of American Telephone & Telegraph would be foolish if he thought he was patronizing his own establishment when he made a dime call; similarly, the purchase of a Chevrolet by a General Motors shareholder who did so in order to help his company is somewhat naive, considering there are close to 300 million shares outstanding.

This is why options may be more in tune with true investor and speculator interests than are their underlying stocks. Prior to the arrival of the C.B.O.E., speculators would wager on the rise or decline of a stock, and investors bought them to increase the yield on their funds. In different ways, the same can be done by means of the purchase or sale of options.

This is not to say that the securities markets will shrivel and die—after all, there cannot be options trading unless there are stocks to set the price. Rather, in time the dealings in options may eclipse those in stocks, a most graphic example of the tail wagging the dog. Already there have been days when total options trading stated in terms of the number of shares represented by the options have been greater than volume at the N.Y.S.E. Doubtless this trend will continue, especially in bull markets, and so enhance the value of the trades, to the advantage of the C.B.O.E. and other options exchanges throughout the country.

Equally important was the manner by which the Amex entered the field. Initially at least it would not compete with the C.B.O.E. for listings; just as the Amex hadn't dealt in N.Y.S.E. issues, so it would respect the rights of others to such a temporary monopoly position in its options. But there was a difference. The N.Y.S.E.–Amex relationship had been cemented by tradition and mutual self-interest, and from it the Amex had emerged as a junior partner. The nexus with the C.B.O.E. was supervised and regulated by the S.E.C., and in it the Amex was a full partner. Indeed, it had more status by virtue of its age, experience, and location in Manhattan. It would become, in fact, the leading options exchange in the city, and this pleased the Amex specialists and administration.

The Options Clearing Corporation became the key institutional link between the two exchanges. Organized by the C.B.O.E. as a vehicle through which contracts were insured and many aspects of trading were regulated, the Clearing Corporation was at the heart of the operations. In a transaction supervised by the S.E.C., the C.B.O.E. sold a half interest in the Clearing Corporation to the Amex, and it quickly became the vehicle through which the two exchanges coordinated their activities. The Pacific Coast Stock Exchange initiated options trading in 1976, but prior to the first trade became a full partner in the Clearing Corporation through the purchase of stock from the Amex and C.B.O.E. Then the Philadelphia-Baltimore-Washington Stock Exchange initiated options trading, and prepared to enter as well. By 1976, too, several options—among them Walt Disney and RCA— were traded at two exchanges. Competitive markets appeared, a decade prior to initial expectations.

The C.B.O.E. did not adopt the specialist system. This embarrassed the N.Y.S.E., which at the time was arguing that specialists were superior to market makers. The dealer function at the C.B.O.E. was performed by market makers, who operated in much the same fashion as they did on the Third Market, the difference being that the C.B.O.E. had a central location, while the Third Market was an electronic exchange. C.B.O.E. brokers executed customer orders, but could not trade for their own accounts. What emerged was the kind of system the N.Y.S.E. might have should it scrap specialists and go over to market makers—something the New Yorkers swear they never will do, but a move which could seriously cripple the Third Market.

Thinking the specialist system could be adapted to options trading, the Amex initially assigned the new vehicles to the floor veterans. representatives of brokerage houses would bring their orders to the specialist, and the byplay between them was much the same as it had been for stocks. But this system did not result in the kind of liquidity required for efficient trading. Some other method had to be devised.

The Amex next permitted certain members to function as registered traders, who in addition to their other activities were permitted to deal in options for their own accounts under strict guidelines, and in this way make contributions to volume, interest, and liquidity. Finally, the Exchange approved a plan to create a new kind of operator, the options principal member, who like the registered traders would work through his own account. Unlike them, however, he would not be a full member of the Amex, or be allowed to deal in stocks, warrants, or bonds. This new category was presented "as a means of providing increased trading capability and depth in the Amex options market."*

It was more than that. Cautiously, the Amex was edging toward the kind of market maker system employed at the C.B.O.E. To be sure, the Trinity Place specialists still were at the center of options trading, but a parallel mechanism was being fashioned, and in time the old specialists may be replaced or at least substantially augmented by options principal members, should only a slight alteration be made in their functions and rights.

In these ways, then, the Amex drifted away from the N.Y.S.E. and began charting its own course. Clearly some form of declaration of independence was being fashioned on Trinity Place in the bicentennial year, for the ties with the N.Y.S.E. were becoming attenuated. One sign of this was persistent talk that the Exchange was planning a move to New Jersey to avoid New York taxes. There was little substance to this rumor, but the fact that the Amex would consider such a move without prior consultation with the N.Y.S.E. was looked upon as a further indication of the impending divorce of the two markets.

Far more important was the announcement in early July, 1976, that the Amex no longer would automatically end trading in those of its issues that transferred to the N.Y.S.E. In other words, companies considering such a switch would be encouraged to retain their Amex listings, and so have the shares traded at two separate exchanges within the same city. The Amex board presented the change in policy as simply another step in the direction of the central market. Given the consolidated tape, there was no reason why such a development should

* In the spring of 1976 the Amex conducted an investigation of specialists' dealings in options, and discovered instances of "painting the tape"—which meant that phantom trades were being reported so as to present the public with a false picture of the volume of trading. Soon after the S.E.C. investigated the matter, and several observers noted that such a problem could not have developed at the C.B.O.E., where there were no specialists involved, and where tape-painting would offer no return to broker-dealers.

not have taken place. N.Y.S.E.'s William Batten signaled his agreement. "The N.Y.S.E. supports the constructive action begun today by the American Stock Exchange that may in the future permit simultaneous trading of certain stocks on both exchanges." Had Needham remained at his post, such an action, and reaction, would not have taken place, or at least not in that way. Needham had insisted upon the primacy of his Exchange, which implied a subservient role for the Amex. Batten gracefully stepped aside, conceding that the old ways would have to change, and that the N.Y.S.E. would have to consider its former junior partner in a different light. In time, Amex and N.Y.S.E. specialists will make markets in the same stocks—not only a handful, but many of them. That the Amex will seek out N.Y.S.E. stocks for listing is not in doubt—the only question remaining is when it will take place. And should a corporation be willing to pay two listing fees, it may be able to watch the rival specialists slug it out, and then determine the winner. All of this in the same city—it would have been unthinkable as recently as ten years ago.

The Amex remains at Trinity Place, across the churchyard from the N.Y.S.E., though no longer in its shadow. That there will be a place for it in any new central market that may be created is not in doubt. While it is true that in form the Amex is a vestigial remain, in terms of content it has become something quite different. Unless the N.Y.S.E. finds some way to trade options on its floor—a likely situation given the Amex actions on dual listings—it could see even more of its business drift away. Would the Amex accept a merger? A decade ago such a development, with members of both being equals, would have been welcomed at Trinity Place. Such is no longer the case.

Instead, the Amex, the C.B.O.E., and the Pacific Coast will form its own shadow central market, one in options rather than underlying stocks. Barring the birth of a major bull market—on the order of that which developed in the mid-1950s—there will be no rush of new issues, no advance in Amex listings, and so a stabilization of them at the N.Y.S.E. and throughout the exchange nexus. All the while the number of options listed for trading will increase, and a new generation of speculators will learn to use puts and calls rather than margin.

A century ago the curbstone brokers dreamed of respectability and prosperity. The former would be obtained by a close association with the N.Y.S.E., both on an individual basis and collectively, as an organized market. As for prosperity, that could come only through dealing in questionable, speculative securities—perhaps working with the bucket shops. At different times in its history, the Amex pursued one or another of these two goals, rarely being able to achieve both simultaneously. Throughout all of this, Trinity Place was focused upon the N.Y.S.E. and trading in stocks and bonds. And in this arena, there was no hope for a proper mix of prosperity and respectability.

One of the side effects of options trading may be to provide both for the Amex and its members, and in a more permanent fashion than had seemed possible a few years ago. For this to occur the exchange will have to function more independently of the N.Y.S.E. than it has in the past, convince the S.E.C. of the desirability of easing restrictions on options trading, and further cement its relationships with the C.B.O.E. and the regional exchanges. If Kolton and his successors can do this, they will have reinvented their marketplace. Right now Kolton is Sullivan's equal, even though the Amex trades only half the options business of the C.B.O.E. Indeed, he can be the senior statesman of options and emerge as a national spokesman for that nexus. To Needham and Batten, he would always be the man from across town.

Adaptability and a willingness to experiment always have been prerequisites for survival at Trinity Place. There seems no reason to believe these qualities will be lacking in the last years of the decade, especially when the descendants of the curbstone brokers have so much to gain and so little to lose.

CHAPTER SEVEN

S.E.C.

AT NO TIME IN history—not even the glory days of the 1920s or the superheated 1960s—was Wall Street more confident and optimistic than in the Eisenhower era. Despite three minor recessions—the price paid to halt inflation and then keep it down—the economy appeared strong and established upon a permanent upward course. There was peace and prosperity under the aegis of a man most Americans admired and trusted.

Ike was good for business, and brokers and clients had reason to love the man. They gloried in his talk of free enterprise as the foundation of national greatness and noted that American military might—needed to fight communism—benefited selected industries and firms, while the highway program was invigorating the rest of the economy.

Wall Street flourished in the Eisenhower years. The markets were strong, and the Amex led the way. There was nothing unusual in this. In times of renewed confidence, investors and speculators tend to seek new companies in developing industries, the very kind of business the Curb, and later on the Amex, catered to and sought. In 1950, the Amex had slightly more than 400 listed stocks and an average daily volume of little over four hundred thousand shares. Ten years later there were 726 stocks on the list, and the turnover was well over a million shares a session on the average.

At the time the Amex was still dominated by people who had fought their way up from the streets. The young men who had gone indoors after World War I, made fortunes in the 1920s, lost everything in the 1930s, and suffered through the becalmed markets of the 1940s, were now close to retirement, and they grasped this last chance at the brass ring. The Amex specialists always were a tight group, and now they divided the new business among themselves, after which they would engage in illegal floor operations that netted them fortunes. Manipulations of prices and sales took place, securities which did not qualify for listing were taken on to please powerful specialists, unregistered securities were bought and sold by men who knew they were breaking rules and laws, but also understood they could get away with almost anything, since those who policed the area were blind and dumb.

In this period the Amex was both headed and symbolized by Edward T. McCormick, who arrived at Trinity Place with a great flourish in the spring of 1951. McCormick was a gregarious, bubbling native of Arizona, who was both a natural salesman and a Ph.D. in economics. It was McCormick who changed the institution's name from the Curb to the Amex, sought out and obtained new listings, spoke of extended trading hours—and after initiating them, obliged the N.Y.S.E. to follow his lead—and became a major district spokesman, the first leader of his exchange to be considered as such. McCormick knew of some of the violations of laws, rules, and ethics, and in fact had engaged in some dubious trading himself. Among his friends were several shady characters. Some of them wound up in jail, while others fled to Brazil to escape indictments. Most had used McCormick and prominent specialists as their tools in manipulating securities and realizing profits. It was an Amex investigation—and exoneration—of one such activity that alerted Wall Street to the nature of this situation. The S.E.C.'s Division of Trading and Exchanges began its own investigation in the spring of 1960. For a while, McCormick cooperated with the Commission, but as the inquiry moved on, it became clear that he was implicated. In late 1961, McCormick left the Amex, under a cloud and in fear of indictment himself.

Later on, McCormick pleaded ignorance of what had transpired at the Amex, claimed to have been betrayed by false friends, and attempted to justify his policy of what today might be called benign neglect, especially of Amex specialists. At no time did he claim to be ignorant of the law, or of the ways of the Securities and Exchange

Commission. McCormick hardly could have done that. He had written a book on the subject, *Understanding the Securities Act and the S.E.C.* Moreover, during the two years prior to arriving at the Amex, Ted McCormick had served as one of the five S.E.C. commissioners.

The investigation of the Amex lasted more than a year, during which time the S.E.C. uncovered a wide vein of corruption, and worked with Amex reformers in restructuring that market. Most of the work on the government side was handled by Ralph Saul, the associate director of the Division of Trading and Markets, who cooperated with Amex President pro tem Edwin Posner in writing a constitution and then selecting the new president, Edwin Etherington. After Etherington resigned in 1966, Saul—who had left the S.E.C. for a vice-presidency of Investor's Diversified Services the year before—was named the second president under the constitution he had helped frame.

The manner in which the Amex corruption had been uncovered, the role played by the S.E.C., and the careers of McCormick and Saul (and that of James Needham, who went from the S.E.C. to the N.Y.S.E. chairmanship) illustrated the place of the Commission on Wall Street, its powers and its problems.

Of all the New Deal agencies created in Franklin Roosevelt's first term, none began life with more publicity, interest, and glamour than did the S.E.C. In these respects it could be compared to the congressional committees investigating Watergate corruption and considering impeachment. Roosevelt had come to office at the bottom of the worst depression in American history and the nation's greatest crisis since the Civil War. The public already had its scapegoat—Wall Street—and was convinced the bad times had been signaled by the Great Crash of October, 1929. The public demanded action, by way of punishment and reforms. F.D.R. was prepared to offer both.

Only the most intransigent Wall Streeters opposed reform at that time. The others—a clear majority at the exchanges and brokerages—were willing to accept changes even while denying culpability. They differed, however, as to what should be done, who should do it, and how far the alterations should go. One very small group thought government control or at least direct regulation would be required. A second approach was self-regulation, whereby the exchanges would institute reforms on their own, expel wrongdoers, and change the rules so as to prevent manipulations and outright thievery. Most thought a combination of outside and inside controls and regulation would be required, though few could agree as to the proper mix.

What Wall Street got was the Securities Exchange Act of 1934, which was designed to regulate the practices of brokers and dealers and insure that the public received sufficient information regarding securities and trading methods so as to make intelligent investment decisions.

Finally, there was created a Securities and Exchange Commission, consisting of five members, which was to enforce the provisions of the Act and subsequent legislation. That was all the S.E.C. was entrusted with. The writers of the Securities Exchange Act of 1934 operated on the assumption that clearly defined abuses existed in the 1920s, and that once corrected, they would not recur—or that if they did, the S.E.C. would set things aright. Congress had no intention of altering the basic structure of the marketplace, and indeed could not foresee the need to do so. There were some who talked of the desirability of eliminating securities-based capitalism, but they comprised a small minority and had nothing of importance to do with the writing of the new law. What Congress accomplished, then, was the creation of a corrective mechanism for an unchanging securities district, with the S.E.C. present to make certain the system functioned efficiently and honestly.

Did this mean that the S.E.C. was not to formulate policy? So it would appear; that job was retained by Congress. Thus, the agency would prove incapable of leading the district into new paths once the need for changes in direction became clear. Four decades later, Wall Streeters would criticize the S.E.C. for overly zealous application of laws, while reformers considered the agency a weak reed, incapable of effective action. Yet the S.E.C. wasn't designed for leadership, while the ardor of the agency's personnel in the mid-1970s was due to lax application of laws in earlier periods.

For his first chairman, F.D.R. selected Joseph Kennedy, a former speculator himself, who only a year before had engaged in practices outlawed by the Securities Exchange Act. Roosevelt relished the idea of setting a wolf to catch other wolves, but there was more to the selection than that. For all his flamboyance, Kennedy was a moderate, who would be able to work with the district's leaders and effect some kind of compromise between control and the old anarchy. Wall Street's Old Guard resented the notion that the public had to be protected from finance capitalism run amok. At the same time, the more fervent New Dealers and those seeking to smash the symbol of business misadventures were disappointed in the Commission and its leader.

As for the S.E.C., it was housed in a small, dingy Washington office, and its members and staff did a good deal of talking and telephoning in the early days, but most of the time was spent in conferring and complaining about shortages of personnel and the absence of power. In fact, the S.E.C. was understaffed and lacked adequate financing for the tasks of patroling the district. But Kennedy had no intention of performing a thorough job. Rather, he would appear on Wall Street occasionally, deliver a speech regarding the need for a new spirit in lower Manhattan, and then return to Washington. The young lawyers on his staff ached to start the work of indicting N.Y.S.E. and investment house leaders on criminal charges. Kennedy never gave the signal to begin. He understood that the lawyers had flimsy cases, and that even while wounded, Wall Street had the strength to withstand outside pressures for reform from the puny S.E.C. Changes, if and when they came, would have to develop out of an alliance of Washington and the district's own reform element. The time wasn't ripe for this in 1934 or 1935.

More was expected of Kennedy's successor, James Landis, who was after all no recycled Wall Street plunger but a liberal architect of the Securities Exchange Act and a former Harvard law professor. But Landis, too, did little to reform the Street, and his inaction resulted in the resignations of most of the S.E.C.'s young firebrands.

Landis was followed into the chairmanship by William O. Douglas, another liberal law professor, whose rhetoric pleased and encouraged some reformers, but whose actions were mild. In public addresses Douglas excoriated the N.Y.S.E. and hinted at a takeover unless that organization wrote a new constitution which democratized the structure and opened it to public view. Privately he maneuvered and soothed the district's moderates. Like Kennedy and Landis,

Douglas lacked the money, staff, and power to carry through on the threats.

But the N.Y.S.E. did change, though not as a direct result of S.E.C. pressures. Former President Richard Whitney, both the leader of, and symbol to, the Old Guard, was indicted on criminal charges— not relating to activities in the 1920s, but a sleazy misappropriation of securities. Whitney was found guilty, sent to jail, and the Old Guard caved in. The moderates gained power, wrote the new constitution Douglas had demanded, and selected a reformer, William McChesney Martin, as its first president. Douglas was pleased. So were the moderates. Both had the substance of change without a major upheaval.

The securities markets recovered somewhat in 1933–36. Then the nation experienced one of its sharpest and most severe economic collapses. Stock market volume and prices declined once more. Never before, not even in the early 1930s, had the district been so dispirited. In the early part of the decade there had been hope of recovery; this was gone by 1936–37, for even the New Deal appeared unable to revive the capitalist spirit.

Wall Street seemed a desert, with half-empty buildings and shuttered stores and restaurants. There were few scoundrels in the district, simply because there was no business for them to manipulate, no clients to gull. The exchanges no longer required reforms—why alter a corpse? The S.E.C., originally called "the policeman at the corner of Wall and Broad," appeared unnecessary. In 1938 the district seemed more in need of an undertaker than a crime fighter.

Douglas delivered several speeches that year, in which he called for the self-regulation of the financial community. Henceforth, the S.E.C. would stay on the sidelines, prepared to act in obvious cases of lawbreaking, but otherwise remaining aloof from whatever action there was. The Commission would try to make certain that the rules of the game were fair, and were carried out by decent and honest individuals. In effect, the policeman at the corner would be replaced by a call box, with an occasional foray into the area by a patrol car.

This new direction—so it was called at the time—was both sensible and practical. In the first place, the N.Y.S.E. reforms, the clear honesty of the Martin administration and its counterparts elsewhere in the district, and the becalmed nature of the securities business, made intense observation and demands for change unnecessary. Too, the S.E.C. lacked the funds and staff to have done the jobs, even had they been deemed desirable. Finally, Douglas was planning to move on and wanted to mend fences with the financial community before doing so. He described himself in early 1939 as "really a pretty conservative sort of fellow. . . ." Roosevelt named Douglas to the Supreme Court a few months later, and the nomination sailed through the Senate without a protest from the Republican side.

After a short interlude during which the S.E.C. was headed by an interim leader—and some staffers packed and left—Jerome Frank assumed the chairmanship. An orthodox New Dealer who wanted to press for additional reforms, Frank was frustrated by the lack of cooperation from Wall Street. By then the district's elite had come to terms with self-regulation, and knew that the era of purge and renewal had ended, with relatively little accomplished. So long as they obeyed the laws already on the books, they should have no fear of new ones. Frank fulminated and threatened, but nothing happened. He resigned in early 1941 to take a seat on the federal bench, and was succeeded by Edward Eicher, a former congressman from Iowa and a Commission member since 1938. Eicher lasted only nine months. He was followed by Ganson Purcell, who had risen through the ranks and was deemed one of the ablest men on the Commission. Thus, the S.E.C. traveled the familiar path taken by most regulatory agencies—from reform to politics to bureaucracy. Purcell was scrupulous in applying the laws and regulations, and was respected on the Street. In the late 1930s, he helped clean up a mess at the Curb Exchange and kept a wary eye on speculation on the N.Y.S.E. But he did not try to alter the nation's financial institutions, or suggest major reforms. Even had he the desire to carry a big stick, Purcell lacked the political clout to swing it.

The S.E.C. faded from view during the next generation. As late as 1940, it had been considered a major force in the capital, and employed a staff of 1,700. Then came the war and the end of the New Deal. Purcell was called in one day and told that his agency had to relocate to Philadelphia for the duration, that his offices would be needed for more vital defense work. So the move was made, and the

S.E.C. almost forgotten. The old Washington offices might have been taken over again in 1946, but the White House didn't feel that the relocation would be worth the effort, and so the agency remained in Philadelphia. By 1949, the S.E.C. had fewer than 1,000 employees and had become accustomed to regular budget cuts and the departure of its best people for well-paying posts elsewhere.

In fact, the Commission had acquired the reputation of a training ground for ambitious lawyers, which even now it hasn't been able to shake. They would go there from law schools, work in the district for a few years, making contacts and learning the ways of finance, and would then jump to a position at a lower Manhattan firm. Some Wall Street law firms went so far as to suggest to bright young men that a few years at the S.E.C. wouldn't do them any harm, treating the agency as a form of graduate school. In this way, too, the S.E.C. and Manhattan law firms intertwined, as regulators and regulated appeared to merge, at least on the personal level.

Purcell's successor, James Caffrey, was an amiable man of limited abilities and vision, with no discernible ambition or imagination. He left no mark upon the Commission or the financial district, and indeed had not wanted to do so on assuming the post. The same could be said of Edmund Hanrahan, who followed Caffrey into office. Hanrahan was as silent and invisible as could be; old-timers who were on the Street in the late 1940s find it difficult to recall his name or remember what he looked like, said, or did.

By then the district's conservatives no longer viewed the S.E.C. as a major threat to free enterprise capitalism. Rather, they joked about what had come to be perceived as a toothless tiger. The move back to Washington took place in 1947, but few outside of the individuals directly involved noticed it. "The S.E.C. may be moved from Washington back to Philadelphia," wrote the *New York World Telegram and Sun* in 1950, creating a rumor in order to make the point. "Its slumber will be as profound in one place as in another."

Dwight Eisenhower had little interest in Wall Street and its institutions, while his advisors looked upon the S.E.C. as one of the New Deal's vestigial remains—important as a symbol of the old days, perhaps, but easy to ignore. In the four years from 1952 to 1955, the Commission had four chairmen—Harry McDonald, Donald Cook,

Ralph Demmler, and J. Sinclair Armstrong. These were able men, but largely ineffectual, due to low budgets and White House disinterest. Cook was an outstanding businessman who rejected an offer of the N.Y.S.E. presidency and went on instead to become the leader of American Electric Power. Demmler was a novice at Washington politics, who actually thought he could invigorate the agency while acceding to budget cuts. After less than two years, he fled Washington for a rewarding law practice in Pittsburgh. Armstrong spoke of the vitality of modern Republicanism, and by force of personality was able to stir things up, initiating investigations and talking to the agency's young men of their bright futures at the S.E.C. Some of this was self-delusion, and when Armstrong recognized it, he moved on to become assistant secretary of the navy.

Armstrong was succeeded by Edward Gatsby, an administrator experienced in the ways of Washington and realistic about his possibilities with the Commission. Gatsby managed to get higher appropriations but hardly enough for the demands of the job. "Personnel has been an acute problem for years," he noted with sadness. "It's never been big enough."

In this period N.Y.S.E. President Keith Funston became a major spokesman for People's Capitalism, which he thought was the best answer Wall Street could give to international communism. In the Age of Dwight Eisenhower—and that of Senator Joseph McCarthy—the Commission could scarcely have investigated and chided such a bastion of free enterprise. The Commission had only 770 employees by 1954, and all but a handful of them were clerks, typists, political appointees, rejects from other agencies, time servers, and ambitious young men who hoped to use their employment as a means whereby they could land more worthwhile positions in the financial district.

This was why some Amex administrators and specialists were able to manipulate securities, violate regulations, and in general act in a lawless fashion. The rules of the game as set down during the New Deal were weak enough, and even Douglas conceded that self-regulation could prove a sham once trading volume expanded and a new group of scoundrels appeared in the district. But he had thought there was a safety web at the S.E.C., for in his day the Commission was known as one of the best places for aggressive, intelligent lawyers in the capital. This was no longer so in the 1950s. It appeared to have followed the normal life cycle of regulatory agencies, as analyzed by Marver Bernstein. The S.E.C. had traveled the road from gestation and youth through devitalization to debility and decline. Was regeneration possible? Bernstein thought not, "until some scandal or emergency calls attention dramatically to the failure of regulation and the need to redefine objectives and public policies."*

More than that was required. The S.E.C. also needed an administration in Washington aware of the problems and willing to act so as to rectify past abuses and deal with present difficulties. The election of Joe Kennedy's son as President in 1960—an election which coincided with the culmination of the Amex scandal—provided Wall Street and the S.E.C. with such an awareness and willingness to act.

John Kennedy asked former S.E.C. Chairman Landis to prepare and submit a report on the regulatory agencies, which was on his desk in December, 1960—as the S.E.C. and Amex reformers were pressing McCormick and his crew to resign. Based to a degree upon the Bernstein thesis, the Landis report noted that "many of the commissions have neglected their planning or creative functions." Landis was particularly critical of S.E.C. operations, perhaps because he knew these better than any other, or due to the front-page news of the Amex scandal—or because Kennedy might be interested in an antibusiness crusade.

Whatever the reason, Kennedy asked for, and Congress acceded to, what came to be known as the Special Study of the Securities Market, which was completed in 1963, and the final reports of which were in the hands of the public two years later. This was the first comprehensive study of the securities market since the New Deal. From it came the Securities Act Amendments of 1964, which not only indicated a renewed interest in the district by Washington, but signaled the end of the experiment in self-regulation. The amendments provided for additional disclosures by firms whose securities were traded over-the-counter, asked for more stringent standards for broker-dealers, and gave the S.E.C. new powers to regulate the markets. Kennedy also acted to beef up the Commission, and his work was

* Marver Bernstein, *Regulating Business by Independent Commission* (Princeton, 1955), p. 99.

carried on by Lyndon Johnson. In 1960, the S.E.C. had fewer than 1,000 employees and operated on a budget of little more than $8 million. By the time the last part of the Special Study was released, the Commission had 1,500 employees and a $15 million budget.

"Over the long run, the quality of S.E.C. performance appears to flow from the top down, rather than from the bottom up. That is, the caliber, reputation, interest, and drive of the Chairman and the other commissioners are reflected in the appointment of able division heads, who in turn attract personnel of high quality to perform the functions of the Commission." This was the conclusion of the Special Report and indicated that Kennedy's first chairman, William Cary, had given the decaying agency new life. A former law professor who had criticized the S.E.C. for many years as an inept and even implausible organization, Cary hoped to revive whatever remained of the Landis-Douglas-Frank tradition and oblige the district to accept what he deemed to be much-needed reforms.

Cary did reinvigorate the Commission. Some of the bright young men who came to Washington during the Kennedy years wound up at the S.E.C., where they worked with the remaining veterans of the New Deal—men who were young in the mid-1930s, and senior staffers in the early 1960s. The newcomers performed the legwork and did the research for the Special Report, and some collaborated with the veterans in writing it. Cary and his senior staffers appeared before congressional committees, asking for new regulatory powers. The chairman felt that a central market was on the way, and that the S.E.C. would have a major role in bringing it about. Cary thought Wall Street was in need of an overhaul, that the bull market had attracted many devious characters. At the same time, he conceded that no laws had been broken. Rather, there had been a significant breakdown in the operations of self-regulation, which demanded a more vigorous role for the S.E.C.

Cary made it clear that he expected to lead a new crusade on the Street. For the first time since the late 1930s, an S.E.C. chairman was front-page news. Cary appeared on interview programs, the covers of magazines, and even when placed beside the luminous New Frontiersmen, managed to set off a glow of his own. Then, in 1962, the combination of an overbought market and the Kennedy attack upon the steel industry created panic conditions, and the market plunged downward on heavy volume in May. The uncertainty was over in a week, but it frightened Kennedy and his staff, and caused Cary to moderate his tone.

Cary submitted the first part of the Special Study in April 1963. His letter of transmission indicated a growing sense of caution. "The report demonstrates that neither the fundamental structure of the securities markets nor of the regulatory pattern of the Securities Acts requires dramatic reconstruction," he wrote. "The report should not impair public confidence in the securities markets, but should strengthen it as suggestions for raising standards are put into practice." Yet the body of the report was most critical of N.Y.S.E. operations, in particular, aspects of the specialist system and the failure to utilize automation techniques. An entire agenda for reform might have been extracted from the report, including the outlines of a centralized marketplace. Cary chose to ignore or play down these critical issues. Instead, he put a bland face on the report. The Kennedy efforts at reform had ended almost as quickly and quietly as they had begun.

The Amex had just come through its scandal and had anticipated a much more severe S.E.C. stance. The N.Y.S.E. had been prepared for a call for sweeping reforms, and Funston was eager to defend the integrity of his institution. Only a few months earlier, the S.E.C. had issued a report on mutual funds, which demonstrated that their performances were lackluster and their charges extortionate, while the selling methods clearly required reforms. The "gunslingers" had invaded the Street by then; dozens of wheeler-dealers were engaged in questionable activities in new issues, special funds, and related devices. Yet Cary did nothing about any of these problems. He talked, granted interviews, but would not act.

Then, on November 19, it was learned that the Allied Crude Oil Refining Corporation had filed for bankruptcy. The head of the firm, Tino De Angelis, had used the N.Y.S.E. brokerage houses of Ira Haupt & Co. and Williston & Beane in his transactions. Within a day, the Street learned that De Angelis had been engaged in massive frauds, that both Haupt and Williston & Beane could face criminal charges, and that these brokerages were close to failure. If they did close down, some thirty thousand clients could lose their securities and cash—for both firms had violated S.E.C. and N.Y.S.E. rules and laws in their operations. What would the government and the N.Y.S.E. do about this? Furthermore, what did all of this infer about self-regulation?

Funston called a series of special meetings, and by the morning of November 22 it appeared that the firms and clients would be salvaged. But all involved knew that Cary could utilize the De Angelis schemes and the brokerage complicity as excuses to mount an attack upon self-regulation, and initiate a major investigation of the district. Perhaps now he could reclaim the offensive, and ask for enactment of ideas suggested in the Special Report. All manner of reforms could have emerged from this—including a national securities market overseen by the government.

President Kennedy was assassinated a few hours later, and such matters were forgotten. President Johnson was more interested in pulling the country together than in an anti–Wall Street crusade. A month after assuming office, Johnson told the regulatory agency chiefs that "We are challenged . . . to concern ourselves with new areas of cooperation before we concern ourselves with new areas of control." The old Wall Street had a reprieve.

Cary resigned as S.E.C. chairman the following August, after a frustrating season in which nothing of substance was accomplished. He was succeeded by Manuel Cohen, an able and at times forceful bureaucrat, but a man more interested in enforcement than innovation. Cohen saw new problems developing—the paperwork mess in the back offices, the failure of the exchanges to automate, and even the violation of regulations by brokers and banks. He issued warnings, threatened actions, and demanded changes. But the White House wasn't interested in an anti–Wall Street crusade. Criticisms against Johnson's Vietnam policies were mounting, and the Street was one of the few places where the President had close to unified support. Also, Johnson wanted to avoid disturbing the bull market, one of the last remaining signs that all was well with America.

Cohen did what he could to keep spirits high and push through exchange reforms. He hoped to end abuses at the brokerages and crack down on violations, especially those involving shortages in net capital reserves. He did not see a panic coming, and did not appreciate the dimensions of the problems. But Cohen—an old New Dealer him-self—nagged, criticized, and bullied. Nothing was done; without White House support and a Wall Street willingness to cooperate, the S.E.C. could do little. The Commission sank back into its old torpor. The New Frontiersmen packed up and left, and they prepared résumés and let friends know they were on the prowl for new positions. Cohen did what he could to retain the best of them, but even he was obliged to concede that there was not much hope for reform under the conditions of the late 1960s.

When the need for change was more pressing than at any time since the Great Depression, and the nation about to undergo its greatest economic decline since that time, the S.E.C. was a weak and almost powerless agency.

Other blows were about to come. Seeking business support, and taking note of S.E.C. rhetoric while ignoring its lack of action, presidential candidate Richard Nixon criticized what he called "heavy handed bureaucratic regulatory schemes." In a letter sent to leading Wall Streeters in September 1968, Nixon pledged that his Administration would be more friendly to the district than were the Democrats. In effect, he promised to end S.E.C. abuses and restore a large measure of freedom to the financiers.

The message puzzled many on the Street. Stock prices were high and volume excellent that season. The S.E.C. had been quiet for several months; none of the suggestions made in the Special Report were being considered by Congress or the White House. True, Johnson had hinted at new antitrust actions, but these were to be directed against conglomerates and perhaps a handful of giant industrial corporations, and not the brokerages and the exchanges. Nixon's words pleased the Old Guard—it was pleasant to be courted—and angered the reformers at the Third Market and others who had criticized the exchanges. But they had no appreciable impact at the time, and did not play a role in his close victory two months later.

Nixon named his own chairman of the S.E.C., Hamer Budge, a former Idaho congressman who had been on the Commission since 1964. He was a pleasant, rather bland individual, clearly in the mold of James Caffrey and Edmund Hanrahan, and in fact devoted part of his time to seeking a better-paid post, while telling reporters of his sorrow at seeing so many lawyers leave the Commission for other Wall Street area jobs. Even had Budge been interested in making an impact upon the securities scene, the superheated volume of new offerings and registrations kept his staff working overtime; and so, little energy and imagination were left for other matters. In any case, it was a honeymoon period for the exchanges and the Commission.

In 1969, the N.Y.S.E. named Bernard "Bunny" Lasker as its new chairman. A leading Nixon fund-raiser and one of the president's closest friends in the district, Lasker assured his colleagues that they had nothing to fear from the S.E.C. In fact, the area buzzed with rumors of a Commission investigation of the Third Market, which could result in the closing down of that rival. There was nothing to this tale, but during the Budge era the S.E.C. did little to distress the men of Wall and Broad. And were it not for the market decline of 1969 and the quasi-panic the following year, such an action might indeed have been considered.

The stock market decline and the S.E.C.'s failure to alert the public to dangers demonstrated the flaws in the regulatory pattern. The S.E.C. had not contributed to the collapse, of course, but the Commission had done nothing significant to prevent it, either through publicity or coercion. When framing the Securities Exchange Act of 1934, anti–Wall Street congressmen felt certain that their new agency would halt the kinds of manipulation and speculation which they felt had contributed to the 1929 collapse. It had not worked. While there was less outright thievery in the late 1960s than there had been forty years earlier, it was on a larger scale and was, in some ways, more sinister.

In June 1970, the Penn Central declared bankruptcy, in what was the largest corporate failure in American history. Subsequent investigation demonstrated manipulations by officers, bailouts by insiders, and the submission of false if not clearly illegal reports to the S.E.C. Yet the story was broken by the *Wall Street Journal,* and only afterwards did the S.E.C. initiate its own investigation.

What had the policeman at the corner been doing all these years? For most of the time he simply hadn't been there. This situation suited Budge, but it rankled those Kennedy and Johnson staffers still on the job. They pressured the Chairman to initiate legal actions against obvious malefactors, while Budge himself willingly cooperated with the N.Y.S.E. to rescue several commission houses in financial trouble. For the first time in years, S.E.C. agents were visible and vocal in the district. Budge was obliged to take a stand on the automation issue— weak at first, and hedged, but on balance in opposition to the exchanges. There had to be a S.E.C. stance for or against the central market, and once more staffers called for and got leadership from Budge, though of a meek variety. Congressional committees entered the arena, too, and the chairman of the S.E.C. performed badly during those times when called upon for testimony.

The logic of technology pushed Budge into taking stands; Wall Street's near-collapse in the late 1960s and early 1970s provided the impetus for a new reform movement. Then there was the prodding from S.E.C. staffers and the challenge of the Third Market. Finally, the Special Report offered an agenda for change. It was expounded by several reform journalists and academic critics, elucidated by Don Weeden and others at the Third Market, and liberally cited in articles and books dealing with the district's ills.

Budge had been selected for the chairmanship after Nixon had consulted with N.Y.S.E. leaders—there was no attempt to mask this. He was supposed to be Bunny Lasker's man, though few would have put it that crudely. Budge could be counted upon to deliver pro–N.Y.S.E. speeches whenever called upon. Yet in so acting, Budge had lost control of his agency. Staffers attacked fixed commissions, mounted campaigns against Rule 394, issued reports calling for a revamped market—not necessarily including an unreformed N.Y.S.E.—and in general won applause from academic critics and Third Marketeers.

It was a most unusual situation. The Commission had been moribund in the 1950s, noisy and vigorous but largely ineffectual during most of the Kennedy-Johnson years, and had suddenly emerged as an activist force under Richard Nixon, an avowed defender of Wall Street's status quo. The president hadn't removed reformers from their posts, and in fact named several new ones in 1969–71.

Was Nixon himself a closet reformer? Hardly, for when he did act so as to affect the financial district, it was to aid the Old Guard. Nixon, who had been a Wall Street lawyer himself in the 1960s and had several of his friends in government—among them bond lawyer, and later attorney general, John Mitchell—simply gave little thought to such matters as administration.

The S.E.C. wasn't the only agency where the staff was opposed to politically appointed leaders. The same development was occurring throughout the Nixon Administration; there was some justification for the president's conviction that Washington was filled with old New Frontiersmen out to foil him. The Department of Health, Education, and Welfare, was the most obvious place for such actions, but the regulatory agencies as a group were able to overcome standpat administrators. The president knew of this, but did nothing to alter the condition. He was more concerned with foreign affairs and the broader dimensions of politics and governance. And he was a notoriously poor administrator himself, a situation evident on Wall Street in 1970–71, which would become more obvious, and in more important ways, during the next two years.

Confused and badly bruised, Budge tried to halt the staff's campaign to force fully negotiated rates on the N.Y.S.E. He managed to slow the movement somewhat but could do no more than that without risking wholesale resignations and investigations. He came under strong congressional criticism too. During the debates regarding the need for additional legislation, several Democrats noted caustically that the S.E.C. under Budge could not be trusted to handle the job without a watchdog—to keep an eye on the watchdog. In 1970, Congress passed the Securities Investor Protection Act of 1970, which created the Securities Investor Protection Corporation. But wasn't that supposed to have been the S.E.C.'s job—to protect the investor? Clearly the passage of this act was an open criticism of Commission performance during the Budge years.

With visible sign of relief, Budge accepted a high post at Investors Diversified Services and in early 1971 resigned from the S.E.C.

Nixon promptly nominated William J. Casey to fill the vacancy. It was one of his oddest selections. Casey was a florid businessman-speculator-lawyer who only a short time before had been obliged to defend himself against charges of having violated the securities laws. At the time of his nomination, Casey was a contestant in a civil action. Didn't Nixon realize that such a selection—especially after the criticisms leveled against Budge—would be badly received and precipitate a congressional challenge? (On the other hand, Nixon had done the same with his nominations to the Supreme Court.)

The Casey nomination was bandied about for more than two months before being accepted. During this period, the S.E.C. staff was without leadership, and so free to do what it wanted. In February, the Commission put the N.Y.S.E. on notice that it would not permit fixed rates on portions of orders over $500,000, and that if the Exchange did not develop its own plans for fully negotiated commissions, one would be drawn up by others—the Commission and Congress.

The staffers had little idea of what to expect from Casey, a man who seemed determined to live up to his flamboyant reputation. To some, he seemed a colorful and perhaps corrupt version of Hamer Budge. Casey quickly disabused them of such notions. In a series of public addresses he called for an end to N.Y.S.E. delaying tactics regarding a centralized market, specifically asked for a quick halt to commission fixing, and pledged greater surveillance of the commission houses. Casey went out of his way to be friendly to those Third Market figures who in the past had been politely snubbed by S.E.C. leaders. He told the staff he approved and applauded efforts at making the Commission an active regulatory body, and was quick to commend those who attempted to make it so during the Budge years. Casey asked the White House for supplemental appropriations for new staff and studies.

Casey appeared to be the kind of reformer who would keep the exchanges in line, punish wrongdoers, and help create a more efficient marketplace. He had the staff's loyalty, and the admiration of even those columnists who had opposed his nomination. But Casey was no wholehearted reformer, perhaps because he did not believe that the market could stand drastic change without collapsing. The early 1970s was a bad time to accuse the exchanges of flagrant profiteering and charging monopoly prices, argued Lasker and his circle. The N.Y.S.E. had a string of deficits, and there were rumors that the Amex was in such bad shape as to force large-scale firings and revisions of procedures. The price of seats declined sharply—the Wall Street joke of 1973 was that an N.Y.S.E. seat was worth one quarter of a McDonald's franchise, but was only a twentieth as useful or desirable. So, on the one hand, Casey demanded fully negotiated commissions, while on the other he acceded to increases in the commission rates.

For close to a decade, the N.Y.S.E. had argued that negotiated rates would destroy the old central market, and this claim had been dismissed as hyperbole. There wasn't much to this argument in the mid-1960s, but by 1971, when negotiated rates appeared possible, the logic of decline seemed inescapable. What might happen if the N.Y.S.E. collapsed before a replacement was at hand? The question would have been considered preposterous during the regime of Manuel Cohen. It was seriously debated in the Casey era.

Casey served as chairman for two years. In this period he did not move the S.E.C. into new paths. Rather, the staff had gotten away from Budge, and Casey—with a sure instinct—reasserted leadership by accepting the direction set down by the senior staffers. Fortunately, he had the Special Study as a guide. His speeches were variations on that theme. To the general public, Casey seemed a vivid activist, somewhat erratic perhaps, but a pleasant change from the duller men brought to Washington during the Nixon years. In fact, he contributed relatively little in the way of ideas to the S.E.C., and by the time of his departure in early 1973, was an object of some ridicule at headquarters and to even his followers, an embarrassment.

Casey left to take a post as undersecretary of state. He was replaced by G. Bradford Cook, who at the age of thirty-six was the youngest chairman in the Commission's history. Cook was a quiet, somewhat bland individual, who had previously served as the Commission's general counsel. That he understood the issues involved was not doubted, and he did express an interest in furthering reforms. But Cook wanted to review all materials before committing the S.E.C. to a new market system. He let it be known that he would move slowly— at his age there was no rush—and that the decisions would be delayed for several years. There was even talk of a new Special Study, not to be completed until the end of the Nixon Administration.

What was Cook attempting to do? Was this a delaying tactic, or part of a deal entered into by Nixon with his Wall Street allies to preserve the N.Y.S.E. for as long as possible? There was always the possibility that Cook was sincere, though in the Watergate atmosphere, many Nixon appointees were suspected of one or another variety of chicanery.

Of course, most of the Nixon men at the regulatory agencies had nothing to fear from such suspicions. Cook wasn't one of them. In late April there were rumors of his involvement with Robert Vesco, a financier who had fled the country to avoid criminal charges. Vesco had made a $200,000 cash contribution to the Nixon reelection campaign—it was never learned what he obtained in exchange for the money—and did so through John Mitchell and Maurice Stans. Cook was not implicated in the donation. But as general counsel, he had deleted mention of the donation from an S.E.C. complaint on the matter.

It was a small matter. Had something like this taken place in earlier times, Cook would have been embarrassed but could have remained at his post. As it was, he underwent a day-long grilling by a Senate subcommittee. In the end, Cook resigned, after less than three months in office. The S.E.C. was in limbo, under the leadership of Acting Chairman Hugh Owens. It awaited the selection of the third permanent chairman in less than half a year—and this, by a president under challenge of impeachment, to be ratified by a Congress already talking about means of replacing him.

In early July, with Watergate bombshells bursting around the White House, President Nixon sent the name of his selection to replace Cook to Capitol Hill. He could not risk a rejection this time; his position was shaky enough without seeking additional troubles. The new chairman was to be Ray Garrett, who had served on the S.E.C. staff in the Eisenhower years and then left for private practice. Garrett had a reputation for independence and within his profession was considered one of the ablest experts on corporate debt financing. Those who remembered him from his S.E.C. stint in the 1950s recalled an intelligent investigator who chafed under the inactivity of the Budge era, who was no revolutionary, but who did realize that the marketplace was ossified and unresponsive to the new technology.

Garrett's nomination had little difficulty in clearing the Senate. At the same time another nominee, A. A. Sommer, Jr., went to the Commission, where he joined Owens, Philip Loomis, Jr. (a former S.E.C.

general counsel), and John Evans (who had earlier served as minority staff director of the Senate Banking Committee). All were experienced in securities affairs; all appreciated the nature of the problems facing the Commission—and all had the confidence of the staff, the men who had been dismayed by Budge, and then had their hopes raised and smashed, first by Casey, and then by Cook. For the first time since the Cary years, the S.E.C. had the kind of leadership capable of—and willing to—take a commanding role in the financial district.

Under Garrett, the Commission was more vigorous and effective than it had been in more than a decade. Still, it no longer could claim to be the policeman of lower Manhattan, or the guarantor of fair play. The S.E.C. had failed badly during the crisis of 1969–70, and had waffled on the issues of commission rates, accounting procedures, and the electronic marketplace. These failures resulted in a vacuum of power that was filled by other agencies and institutions. During the New Deal and through the 1950s and early 1960s, Congress had responded to S.E.C. requests for supplemental legislation, trusting the Commission to initiate actions and satisfied to respond to them. Now Congress took the lead, with the Subcommittee on Securities of the Senate Committee on Banking, Housing, and Urban Affairs in the vanguard. Should Chairman Harrison Williams or some other senator require information, he would look first to the S.E.C. The Subcommittee relied upon the Commission for expertise and advice, and in addition was more willing to develop both on its own than previously had been the case. While the Nixon Administration grappled with Watergate-related matters, control over some areas of the executive branch were loosened. Thus, the S.E.C. moved into a congressional orbit in 1973–74. By the time Garrett had assumed office, his agency had become a retainer of Congress, and not the strong arm of the executive branch on Wall Street.

The new alliance could be seen in the Securities Act Amendments of 1975, passed after long and convoluted hearings, designed primarily to hasten the evolution toward a central marketplace. Under the terms of one part of the new legislation, the S.E.C.'s authority over the stock exchanges was expanded, and the agency was given the responsibility of carrying out the congressional mandate.

Garrett was ordered to report to Congress—not the White House—in early 1976 as to whether he considered Rule 394 anticompetitive, and if so, whether the rule should be abolished or severely modified. Since there could be no doubt as to the anticompetitive nature of the rule, clearly Garrett was expected to lead the way in altering it.

The S.E.C. ruling came down in late December 1975. Under the terms of its order, the exchanges would have to drop all restraints imposed upon members regarding trading in shares of listed stock on the O-T-C markets. The change would take place in stages, to be completed by the first trading day in 1977. With this ruling, Garrett signaled Wall Street that his agency had been reborn—with a new parent.

Another part of the Securities Act Amendments ordered the S.E.C. to develop a plan for a central market. If approved, this entity would be imposed upon the exchange community. Garrett organized the National Market Advisory Board (N.M.A.B.) and immediately named John Scanlon, a former vice-president at American Telephone, as its chairman.

The message was direct, and understood by all on the Street. The S.E.C. would create the central market, with or without N.Y.S.E. agreement, and it would come about in 1977, and not at some undisclosed date after endless delays on the part of Wall Street.

Recognizing that the time for adamant opposition to such a change had come to an end, the exchanges opted for cooperation. Needham's departure and replacement by Batten was the most important signal sent by Wall Street to Washington in this regard. The N.Y.S.E. worked with the N.M.A.B. thereafter, and the Board soon came under the domination of Wall Streeters who were willing to cooperate with Congress. The Williams Subcommittee soon was on harmonious terms with Batten and others at the N.Y.S.E., giving rise to suspicions that the wily chairman was in the process of coopting the reformers.

This was not so. Instead, Batten and the S.E.C. both agreed that it made little sense to continue the fight, that technology and political pressures dictated the rapid evolution toward a central market. To some old-timers the situation was vaguely reminiscent of what had transpired in the early days of the New Deal, when a handful of Wall Street reformers united with Kennedy to create a regulatory atmosphere in the district. Batten was making certain reforms would take place, but that the N.Y.S.E. would have a leadership role in determining tactics if not strategy.

One of the keys to this new dispensation was CLOB—the Composite Limit Order Book—another acronym which quickly entered the Wall Stree lexicon. Armed with the electronic capabilities of CLOB, a commission broker anywhere in the country would be able to indicate his desire to buy or sell a security at a specified price. On seeing this order, specialists and market makers would have the option of accepting or rejecting it. CLOB immediately was described as an "electronic book," referring to the specialist's book, and so it was. But in addition, this book was to be shared by all dealers in the stock, and so was a consolidated book in this sense, and a major step in the creation of the national electronic exchange.

Naturally, the N.Y.S.E. specialists opposed CLOB as still one more attempt to erode their monopoly. In the summer of 1976, however, they knew the game was up. The S.E.C. wanted CLOB. Batten went along with the Commission on this crucial matter. It was difficult to tell whether the N.Y.S.E.'s leadership or the S.E.C. was in the saddle. In any case, the specialists clearly were no longer in command.

The renewal of congressional powers and the rebirth of the S.E.C. were not unusual, given the Watergate atmosphere and the attempted revival of the legislative branch during the Ford presidency. Also, one might have anticipated a burst of investigative fervor, given the popularity for uprooting corruption during what former Vice-President Agnew described as the time of "post-Watergate morality." In this period the S.E.C. initiated a round of probes into many aspects of business life in the United States, and the roles played by American corporations throughout the world. Whether or not this had any direct relationship with the Committee's primary role was both questioned and questionable.

The key figure in all of this was Stanley Sporkin, head of the Division of Enforcement. A young man in 1974—41 years old—but a veteran staffer, Sporkin had worked through the Budge-Casey-Cook regimes with little encouragement or support. Now Garrett urged him on, and Sporkin put on a display of energy unmatched in the agency's history. In the past, his division had concentrated on uncovering and stopping stock frauds and manipulations. On his own, Sporkin broadened the mandate to include other forms of corruption not related to shareholders' interests—or at least, this was both the appearance and the charge. He wanted to know which companies paid kickbacks in order to obtain contracts from both domestic and foreign politicians, and in the process uncovered as much or more graft than any other prosecuting body or agency in the post-Watergate era. The Division was responsible for disclosing the overseas payoffs made by Gulf Oil, Lockheed, United Brands, and Northrup. Sporkin's vigor and growing reputation made him a contentious figure, and one to be feared. The slightest hint that his agents were about to investigate a company would precipitate a special meeting of the board, and should word of it reach the press, a flurry in the price of the stock. Over a hundred companies came forth and made voluntary admissions of wrongdoing, most in the hope of forestalling a full-scale investigation, or in the belief that Sporkin was on their trail and was bound to learn what had been going on.

Due in large part to Sporkin's actions, Garrett was able to ask for and receive larger budgets and additional personnel—in fiscal 1974 the Commission obtained $36 million for operations, against $30 million the previous year, and was authorized to hire some 300 additional personnel, which in 1973 numbered only 1,700. The bulk of the new money and agents went to Sporkin, who by 1976 commanded a staff of 600. As always, the Commission had to ration its funds, and the Division of Enforcement was allotted only $1.5 million. Sporkin made do with what he had. This was possible because by then he had won the admiration of the reform element in the district—Ralph Nader said he was "a public servant who takes his public trust seriously"—and had developed a network of unpaid informers. Lawyers, accountants, executives, and others at large corporations knew that a telephone call to the Division of Enforcement would result in a check of charges of wrongdoing, and perhaps indictments soon after.

The Street complained of smears and arbitrary actions, and some of the veterans at the S.E.C. seemed to agree. "I am aware of the resentment our investigations generate and I am troubled by it," said Loomis, but he added, "I don't think you can prove we violate due process." Yet the fact that the issue was raised at all, and so frequently, troubled many observers both outside and within the financial community. Garrett appeared to be trying to cleanse his agency and revive the reformist spirit, but it may well have been that much of the effort backfired.

Sporkin was a hard worker, a moralist, and a person who was convinced large-scale conspiracies existed and that it was his task to expose them. He was a charismatic figure, clearly ambitious, and at times ruthless. To his friends and admirers, he seemed a tribune of the people. Others thought Sporkin resembled no one more than Senator Joe McCarthy, and that his actions were not unlike the abuses of the F.B.I. and C.I.A. in the 1960s and early 1970s. Whenever the Commission brought an indictment against a supposed violator it called in the press, complete with flashguns and tape recorders. A few months later the charges might be dropped, this time with no publicity. Meanwhile, reputations were damaged and large sums spent on defenses which souldn't have been required, if more careful spadework had been performed initially. Sporkin and his defenders replied that more often than not the charges were only the first step in a prosecution. The early diggings into Lockheed, for example, uncovered only a small portion of the corruption. Without publicity and press demands for more information such inquiries might die. To many Americans, who by 1976 believed in conspiracies and thought corporations responsible for much of the nation's ills, this made sense.

Was Sporkin overreaching his authority? All of his work might be required, but was it the duty of the S.E.C. to engage in such activities? Was this not a congressional responsibility? Or one for the Justice Department? At a time when Wall Street was changing rapidly and required government supervision and intervention, Garrett's agency was involved with investigating corruption in Japan and the Caribbean and ignoring its primary tasks. The American Bar Association thought so, and it protested the investigations. By late 1974, Garrett and Sporkin were the objects of sharp criticisms, not only from Wall Streeters, but from civil libertarians. The district appreciated their abilities and intentions, but it was felt that they had gone too far.

This is not to say that Garrett was a failure or Sporkin a witchhunter. They did not transform the agency into a growler and snapper from its previous stance as a watchdog. Rather, the S.E.C. had to face problems for which it was unprepared by law or tradition, situations the New Dealers could not have imagined when they fashioned the enabling legislation in 1934, or when Joe Kennedy arrived at the N.Y.S.E. for a visit as the first chairman. At that time the Commission had been charged with the job of eliminating the debris of the

1920s and cleansing a dispirited community, as well as urging reforms upon a flawed N.Y.S.E. This task took the better part of half a decade to accomplish, and could not have been done were it not for the evolution of the concept of self-regulation. Forty years later, Garrett had to face a district far more complex than that of the 1930s, and not nearly as supine. The N.Y.S.E. and other exchanges were not in need of reform; it wasn't that simple, for perhaps they would have to be eliminated altogether.

In the mid-1930s, one of the most important matters for Wall Street to decide was the issue of a new constitution for the N.Y.S.E. Should the Exchange have a paid president? Should the organization accept outside directors? These were considered revolutionary ideas. Yet four decades later, the specialist system itself was under attack, as was the rate structure and the mode of access to the ticker tape. The New Dealers hit out at peripheral matters; this can be seen in retrospect. Garrett had to deal with issues central to the concept of markets and exchanges, and enter into discussions the result of which could radically alter the nature of securities-based capitalism. And throughout all of this, he would be moved by events, and not vice versa. For example, Garrett worked for fully negotiated rates, and they came about in 1975. For this he was criticized at Wall and Broad—but not too severely, for by then even the most mossbacked of specialists and commission brokers appreciated that given the new technology, little else was possible. The same was true for Garrett's support of a central market. Budge tried to ignore the issue, and in his time this could be done. Casey came out in favor of an electronic marketplace, but fudged on particulars, trying to please both the N.Y.S.E. and the Third Market. As for Cook, what he might have done is unknown, but certainly any administration would have had to accept the concept in one form or another. The same was true for Garrett. He pressed forward in part out of conviction but also because, by then, he had no other option.

To complicate matters, the S.E.C.'s credentials were bad. Kennedy, Landis, and Douglas had hit out at wrongdoers, observing all the while that the new laws would protect investors in the future, and knowing that the quiet markets of the 1930s could be policed with little effort. It was different in Garrett's day. Each of Sporkin's indictments raised the issue anew: Why hadn't the S.E.C. uncovered the abuses while they were taking place? A district joke of the period was that the Commission indeed had behaved like the policeman on the corner—never there when you required help.

Some went so far as to question the need for any such agency. Professor George Stigler of the University of Chicago thought the value of corporate disclosure was overestimated, while Professor George Benston of the University of Rochester saw no significant differences in the nature of market pricing prior to and following passage of the Securities Exchange Act. Garrett tended to ignore such critics, but in early 1976 he stepped down as chairman and was succeeded by Roderick Hills, a California lawyer whose specialty was labor relations, and whose prime recommendation for the job was his marriage to Housing and Urban Affairs Secretary Carla Anderson Hills. The new chairman, somewhat unsure of himself at first, publicized what he called "the Stigler Challenge," though up to that time few outside of the academic community and congressional committees knew of it. Hills debated the effectiveness of his agency; most of the time while on the defensive. The work of the National Market Advisory Board went on, but by early 1977, it seemed to be taking the lead from the Street's reformers, and not those at headquarters in Washington.

By late 1976, some of the momentum generated during the Garrett era had been dissipated. The S.E.C. was not an issue in the presidential election. Nor was Wall Street. Neither was considered that important by Gerald Ford or Jimmy Carter.

Much of this is understandable, given the record of 1969–73. Forty years before, in the early 1930s, the Wall Street tycoons and plungers had been blamed for the Crash. In the middle years of the 1970s it seemed fair to place the onus for failures upon those in the S.E.C. who hadn't been able to spot chicanery and thievery. That this situation will change is questionable. Wall Street generally favored President Ford in the 1976 election, but the district did not fear Carter, as it had McGovern four years earlier. Those doubts regarding the Democrat were derived from his programs—and the lack of them—in the areas of tax policy, fiscal and monetary matters, and style. No Wall Streeter of any prominence voiced fears of a strong, crusading, S.E.C.

Not even Ralph Nader thought the matter important. The consumer advocate found time to attack banks, industrial corporations, the automobile industry, the media, and almost every other major branch of capitalist America. But he said next to nothing about the securities markets; Nader's Raiders did not swoop down on Wall and Broad. Nor did he appear interested in who the next S.E.C. commissioner would be when he decided to support Carter for the presidency. Why place a bet on a dead horse?

This view is as unfair as the mass indictment of business had been in the 1930s—when the S.E.C. had been created and began operations. From the first the Commission had certain obvious weaknesses. It could oblige corporations to reveal information to investors, for example, but could not force the public to act prudently. A later generation learned that by simply telling smokers of the links between cigarette usage and cancer the government could not cut deeply into tobacco sales. The same principle was true for Wall Street speculation in the 1960s.

The Commission had been created in the flush of the greatest reform wave in this century, and given its limited mandate and budget functioned with no little skill and sophistication in the 1930s. Self-regulation as set forth by William Douglas was no bland statement of trust in the Street, but rather the best that could be expected under the circumstances. World War II all but killed the reform impulse; to criticize Wall Street in the 1950s seemed somehow un-American. The S.E.C. was half-forgotten during these two decades, and seemed more akin to a fossil than anything else. Its budgets were small, though adequate for the needs of an indifferent staff in a moribund age. The agency retained an inner core of dedicated lawyers and accountants, but there was little in the way of talent and commitment beyond them.

Yet the agency did point the way for Wall Street reforms. There was that short spurt of energy and activism in the Kennedy era, which produced the Special Report; in it could be found a program for meeting the needs of a different kind of securities market from the one that had existed at the agency's birth. The S.E.C. could have done no more than that without a new mandate from Congress. There were amendments to the Securities Act in 1964, but these were minor, more in the way of housekeeping changes than anything else. The S.E.C. would have required additional powers from Congress to act effectively, and these were not provided.

The Commission, and not Congress, was made the scapegoat for defects in the regulatory situation during and after the 1969–71 collapse. Then Casey and Garrett, each in his own way, tried to expand their agency's powers beyond the boundaries set down by legislation, usually acting without encouragement from the White House and with the opposition of the exchanges. That Garrett was able to accomplish as much as he did in bringing about the unified tape and abolishing fixed commissions was a tribute to his skills and political abilities. Similarly, his successes in moving the district toward a centralized marketplace was a sign of his sophistication in using whatever tools he had at hand and convincing the opposition he had reserves when in fact he did not. Certainly the new alliance with Congress helped him in his work. But would any of this remain when and if the Watergate syndrome came to an end? The impetus for change is present today. Already it has brought competition in the area of rates, and shortly will do the same for prices at exchanges and markets. But some of the credit will accrue to William Batten—and the N.Y.S.E. will remain a power center on the Street.

It seems to be true, as has been indicated, that regulatory commissions pass through stages of youth, maturity, and old age, and in the last phase are somewhat of an embarrassment to those who recall with pleasure that first burst of vigor and enthusiasm. The S.E.C. is no longer feared in the financial district, though several of its top staffers are among the most respected individuals in the industry. On occasion, it can act effectively, but such moments are rare and do not last for long. Such a moment exists at the present time. Is this a sign of rebirth or the last trauma before death? To return to the simile of the policeman, he is now old, arthritic, forgetful, and in need of eyeglasses but unable to afford them. He still can wing a malefactor with his gun, but someone else must aim it for him.

What could be expected from such a guardian? With such a record?

CHAPTER EIGHT

THE INVESTMENT BANKERS

F EW POLITICAL ANALYSTS thought Franklin Roosevelt a man of substance, principles, or programs in the summer of 1932, as he contested for the Democratic presidential nomination. The trouble with
the New York governor, wrote Walter Lippmann, "is that his mind is
not very clear, his purposes are not simple, and his methods are not
direct." That autumn, during the campaign, Lippmann characterized
Roosevelt as a decent chap who, without much in the way of qualifica-
tions, wanted very much to become president. After the election,
F.D.R. went to visit aged and retired Supreme Court Justice Oliver
Wendell Holmes, who pronounced his judgment: The president-elect
possessed a first-class temperament—but a second-class intellect. Both
men changed their minds after the March 1933 inauguration, of
course. But on the basis of what Roosevelt said and did the previous
year, their estimates of the man were not only justified but obvious.

Roosevelt took few daring stands on the issues during the political
campaign. He did not have to, for in 1932 the Democratic nomination
all but insured election. The Hoover Administration had been discred-
ited by the economic collapse, and F.D.R. offered the only alternative to more of the same. Furthermore, the Democrats had a perfect
scapegoat for all the nation's ills, one created by a half-century of reformist history and annealed in the heat of the greatest depression in
American history. Roosevelt would run against the Republicans, to be
sure, but the chief villains were not the men in Washington, but those
in lower Manhattan. Afterwards, F.D.R. would vow to drive the

money changers from the temple, and all knew whom he meant: he would flog the bankers.

Throughout the 1920s, many Americans received a crash course in investments. At cocktail parties on Park Avenue and in drugstores on Main Streets, dabblers in securities spoke knowingly of margin, syndicates, pools, and the latest rumors regarding the activities of the "big boys." Even those who did not participate in the market could scarcely help being aware of it, since Wall Street was front-page news in the late 1920s. Then there were those Americans, a majority in fact, who looked upon stocks and bonds as alien, somehow disreputable paper, vehicles for gambling, and not investment. To them a dollar earned by the sweat of the brow was honest and real, while one obtained through an "uptick" in RCA was ephemeral, especially when the stock was purchased on margin. Such people put their money in banks and trust companies, knowing it would be there when they wanted it.

Yet those who rejected the markets may have had a stake in its movements. For the banks had become a major source for call money—the funds used for margin buying. Large banks underwrote new issues and engaged in direct speculation, often with depositors' money. Not only was this practice within the bounds of law and practice in the 1920s, it was considered traditional, and even important for the health of the economy. Small depositors would place their funds in time accounts, the banker would gather them together, and then use the money to purchase securities in an economic enterprise, which may have provided jobs for the depositors, and certainly turned out goods for consumers.

This was no secret; anyone with a basic knowledge of banking knew the banks and trust companies had investment affiliates that underwrote new issues. At the time, however, few Americans possessed that information. Thus, the man who thought the stock market crash of 1929 and the decline of 1930 were not important to him, since he had no stocks, may have felt differently in 1931 and 1932—when the banks shut down, leaving depositors with passbooks as valueless as the stock certificates in defunct enterprises.

This was on the minds of the president and Congress as both set to work after the inauguration. Banking reform was part of that hodgepodge of legislation passed during the New Deal's famous first hundred days. Most of the measures were pushed through the mill as rapidly as possible, but this did not mean that they were hastily considered. In fact, the ideas that went into the framing of the Glass-Steagall Banking Act, aimed at correcting perceived abuses within the system, could be traced to protests first heard at the turn of the century. Its principal framer, Senator Carter Glass of Virginia, had arrived in Congress in 1902 and quickly established himself as a leading Democratic theoretician in the banking area. Glass went on to help write the Federal Reserve Act and to serve as Wilson's Secretary of the Treasury. Only a few months before the special session of the Congress met in March 1933, Glass had turned down Roosevelt's offer to resume the Treasury position because of age (he was seventy-four in 1933) and his wish to complete work on a new banking bill, which he considered the capstone of his career.

For the past year and a half, Glass had chaired a subcommittee of the Banking and Currency Committee, which held hearings on the matter. Leading Wall Street bankers had given testimony, most predicting a financial paralysis should investment and deposit banking be separated. Their presentations were weak—paralysis had already set in by late 1932. Some bankers, most notably the Chase's Winthrop Aldrich, disagreed. Aldrich conceded the unification of the two functions may have had a role in the bank failures, and announced that even without legislation, his bank would divest itself of its securities affiliate. And while this was going on, Ferdinand Pecora, the special counsel for the full committee, grilled other Wall Street bankers, and in the process uncovered manipulations and deals which, though legal for the most part, were of dubious ''soundness.''

From the first, there had been little doubt that Glass would be able to effect the separation. Working with Representative Henry Steagall of Alabama, he introduced a measure to accomplish this and, in addition, to provide for deposit insurance. The bill had no difficulty in passing both houses, and was signed into law on June 16.

The Glass-Steagall Act created no great stir outside of Wall Street, though most Americans seemed to approve of any measure aimed at punishing banks. So many other things were happening to divert public attention. On the same day that Roosevelt signed the legislation, he also approved the National Industrial Recovery Act, a centerpiece for the New Deal, as well as the Farm Credit Act and the Railroad Coordination Act. Yet the Glass-Steagall Act did bring to a close a major period in Wall Street and banking history. During the next few months such important firms as Morgan, National City Bank, and Guaranty Trust left investment banking completely, either by spinning off their subsidiaries or liquidating them. New investment firms arose from the rubble—Morgan Stanley, Brown Harriman, and First Boston among others—and the Wall Street investment banking community underwent a major realignment. But the adjustments were those of firm names, and not of individuals. The old men did the same business under new letterheads. Within a year most Americans had forgotten the original impetus for the Glass-Steagall Act, and those who did remember considered deposit insurance, and not separation of investment and deposit banking, its major accomplishment.

The reason for this was obvious. Most Americans didn't know the difference between the two forms of banking. They still do not. The same individuals who appreciate the workings of a brokerage are vague about its investment banking function. It is not a secret, however, or a mystery. In fact, investment banking is at the heart of Wall Street, and indeed is its most important reason for existing.

The securities markets play a secondary role. They provide marketability and liquidity for those securities sold to the public by investment bankers. Without markets and exchanges, individuals and institutions would have difficulties in effecting transactions in ''old'' stocks and bonds, but they still could obtain ''new'' ones from the investment bankers. Under the proper conditions, the bankers could provide exchange services of various kinds. They could survive without the markets as presently constituted. Indeed, American capitalism would not be crippled, given a poorly functioning exchange structure.* It could even go on with no markets at all. But without investment banking, there would be no free enterprise capitalism as we know it.

A crude form of investment banking existed some five thousand

* The market collapse of 1929 did not cause the depression, but rather reflected speculative excesses and an economic downturn which had begun the previous year. Economic paralysis came in 1931–32, when the banks collapsed, and not in 1929–30, when the problems seemed confined to the exchanges. But the N.Y.S.E. is a better and more dramatic symbol than any bank. That is why the Securities Exchange Act attracted more attention than the Glass-Steagall Act, and why even today the Exchange receives more journalistic coverage than do the major banks.

years ago in Mesopotamia, where individuals performed functions that would not be alien to money managers at Lehman Brothers or Morgan Stanley. The institution developed in ancient Greece and flourished in Rome. A version of it, merchant banking, fueled the Renaissance. Jacob Fugger made loans to princes and kings, and through them even controlled the papacy. In the nineteenth century several merchant bankers—the Barings, Hambros, and the famous Rothschilds—not only provided corporations with funds, but assisted in managing their affairs and setting their strategies.

Operations were simple enough. These were private banks, in control of a pool of cash, portions of which would be loaned to clients. For this they received interest, backed by guarantees. In order to keep an eye on these loans, the bankers might place a partner on the client's board of directors, where he would act as an official advisor.

Their counterparts existed in America too, though with some differences in style and substance. Nathaniel Prime, for example, generally is considered the father of American investment banking. He arrived on Wall Street in the 1790s, and soon became a leading stockbroker. By the 1820s, he was one of the sages of the Street, a well-connected individual with several major American clients and a handful of European ones, including the Barings.

This was a period when American business was booming, with banks and canal securities leading the way and railroads just about to make their impact. Europeans wanted to invest in these industries, and men like Prime made a good thing of it. In 1826, Prime left brokerage completely to form an investment bank, Prime, Ward & King, which dealt in foreign exchange, but more importantly, entered the securities business on the wholesale end. Rather than buying and selling old securities, he would approach a firm and offer to take an entire new issue of stock or bonds, and then distribute it to clients, many of whom were overseas. Prime, Ward & King retained membership in the New York Stock and Exchange Board, but no longer would deal with clients who, literally, came in off the street.

The essential difference between Prime's earlier work in brokerage and his later career as an investment banker was in matters of focus and stress. Brokers were, and are, interested in securities as commodities—they stand prepared to buy and sell shares and bonds and conduct auctions in them, and in other ways transact business for interested purchasers and sellers. Investment bankers, in contrast, exist to serve the requirements of the issuing corporation or government, which needs money and does not know how to raise it. Prime's most important assets were his connections with potential buyers and his good name and reputation. Prime could float a $100,000 railroad stock offering because he knew beforehand the people and institutions that might want to purchase shares, and these clients would take them because they trusted Prime as a man of good judgment and honor. Later on, investment bankers were generally called underwriters, and although this does not describe all of their functions, it nonetheless is a useful concept, for these houses did underwrite, in the sense that they endorsed the worth of securities sold.

The matter of reputation is one that is readily comprehensible to non–Wall Streeters, who find it hard to believe it precedes all else. This clash of cultures was most strikingly illustrated during the Money Trust investigation of 1912—in which Carter Glass played a significant role. The chief counsel, Samuel Untermyer, was a reform-minded lawyer convinced that a sinister, plutocratic web of power centered on Wall Street controlled most aspects of big business, with money the prime fuel for it all. J. P. Morgan, then in his last years of life, was the symbol of this money trust, and Untermyer questioned him on its supposed operations.

UNTERMYER: Is not commercial credit based primarily upon money or property?

MORGAN: No, sir; the first thing is character.

UNTERMYER: Before money or property?

MORGAN: Before money or anything else. Money can not buy it.

Morgan was one of the most powerful investment bankers in the world, the man who put together a billion-dollar trust and whose reputation in London was greater than that of any president of his time. Nathaniel Prime had been the adjunct of several London firms, underwriting a relative handful of securities, conducting more business in foreign currency transactions than in stocks and bonds. Yet the two men were in the same field and its fundamentals did not change appreciably from the time John Quincy Adams sat in the White House to the incumbency of William Howard Taft.

The major difference was scope, and several innovations introduced by Jay Cooke, the link between the two men. Cooke, a Philadelphia banker who had gone into the investment field in 1861, undertook to sell larger issues than any previous house, and was able to do so because of his ability at organizing syndicates. In his first year, for example, Cooke took a $3 million Pennsylvania state issue as head of a syndicate which included bankers from other eastern cities as well as his own. Together, they sold most of the bonds to selected clients. But in the narrow markets of that period more in the way of distribution was needed. So Cooke advertised in newspapers and paid premiums to salesmen who marketed the issue to small investors as well as to large ones. The bonds were sold; Cooke had helped create a mid-nineteenth century version of People's Capitalism, and in the process became the leading investment banker of his day.

During the Civil War, Cooke's talent were enlisted in the Union cause. Opening a Washington office and establishing strong contacts at the Treasury, he took entire issues, which were sold throughout the nation. Cooke recruited a force of more than 2,500 salesmen, working for his company and members of the syndicates, that sold more than $360 million in bonds by 1864.

Cooke attempted to apply these techniques to railroads in the postwar period. Becoming banker for the Northern Pacific, he sold its stocks and bonds in America and Europe. Then, in 1873, the railroad declared bankruptcy, leaving Cooke with worthless paper and a damaged reputation. Some of the smaller members of his syndicate were able to recover, often by making restitution to large investors who had purchased Northern Pacific on their recommendations. Others, Cooke included, were unable to come back, and closed their doors for good.

The 1873 panic and depression did not discourage foreign investors for long; within a few years they had returned to the American markets, using the facilities of those investment bankers who survived. In the three decades after/ some $2 billion in foreign money—much of it English—arrived in New York for investment in American securities, providing new opportunities for the major houses. By the post-1873 period these included Lehman Brothers, Clews & Co., and Kuhn, Loeb in New York, Drexel & Co. in Philadelphia, and Kidder, Peabody in Boston. As the names indicate, the business was dominated by native-born Protestants (usually with strong London ties) and German Jews, well known on the continent.

Even then, young Morgan was looked upon as the rising star in the field. His father, Junius Morgan, was a partner in George Peabody & Co. in London, where his son got his start prior to the Civil War. Morgan retured to America in 1857, and three years later formed his own firm, which acted as a correspondent for Peabody on Wall Street. Morgan rose rapidly, his company undergoing several changes through combination, and finally merging with Drexel to form Drexel, Morgan, with Morgan the firm's leader in New York.

As has been mentioned, Morgan undertook to sell 250,000 shares of New York Central in London in 1879. The Vanderbilts, who owned the stock and controlled what then was the premier American railroad, wanted to sell in order to raise money, diversify their holdings, and end criticism of their domination of the line. Morgan agreed to act as agent using his excellent London connections, but on his terms. Vanderbilt had to guarantee the stock would pay a large dividend for at least five years and had to give Morgan representation on the Central's board—where he would look after the interests of those to whom he sold the stock, and provide advice and leadership in financial matters. William H. Vanderbilt concurred and Morgan assumed banking control for the line. Others followed—the Philadelphia & Reading, the Chesapeake & Ohio, the Baltimore & Ohio, and more. Jacob Schiff of Kuhn, Loeb had obtained a similar position at the other eastern giant, the Pennsylvania, and between them these two men dominated most of the major lines in that part of the country. Thus was born the money trust that reformers like Untermyer so feared and wanted to destroy, or at the very least, closely regulate.

In fact, there was no money trust, unless by that term is meant a generalized community of interests among investment bankers, who agreed to cooperate, but also worked under rules by which competition was acceptable. The banks would unite to form syndicates to organize an industry and market securities, but an entirely different syndicate might be created for a second industry and marketing operation. Through his banks, John D. Rockefeller acted independently, often at odds with Morgan. Schiff engaged in a series of fierce duels with Morgan, one resulting in a brief but severe panic in 1901, when each was trying to help a client carve a western railroad empire. The critics saw the cooperation, which unquestionably was present, and tended to ignore the competition.

During the next two decades, these investment bankers refashioned large segments of American industry, taking command of financing and in some cases actual management. Together with Lee, Higginson and several smaller banks, for example, Morgan created General Electric. The investment bankers were midwives for trusts in virtually every important segment of American business in this period, culminating with the massive Morgan-led effort of 1901, the molding of the billion-dollar United States Steel Corporation.

Throughout all of this, integrity and reputation remained the paramount considerations in the business. The large and successful investment banks understood that their names as underwriters were warranties to the purchasers, and they knew that should this trust be betrayed, they would suffer at the hands of the public, and also from their fellows, who might exclude them from syndicates. This is not to say the investment bankers always made money for purchasers or raised sufficient funds for their corporate clients. Morgan took great risks in fashioning U.S. Steel and International Mercantile Marine, the latter an attempt to create a trust in transoceanic shipping. The former paid off, though at times Big Steel appeared on the edge of failure, but I.M.M was not so fortunate. Morgan's syndicate was unable to market its paper in 1902, and in the end the members had to "eat" a good deal of it themselves.

When the syndicates did work, however, they performed spectacularly. In 1894, for example, President Grover Cleveland tried to market federal bonds overseas in order to save the gold standard, and he failed. The European investors trusted Cleveland as a man of honor but did not believe him capable of delivering on pledges. The following year, his secretary of the Treasury, William Curtis, went to see Morgan on Wall Street. The financier agreed to sell a $100 million issue in Europe, and the news sent the market higher. In the end, the flotation was somewhat smaller, and was sold with no difficulty. Other flotations followed, and these too were sold.

The message was clear: Morgan could deliver, while President Cleveland could not. The Wall Street investment banks were more powerful than was the United States Treasury.

As might have been anticipated, this growth of private power created a reaction, in the form of the Progressive movement, whose most colorful leader was Theodore Roosevelt. At first Morgan tended to ignore Roosevelt, and when they did meet, the banker treated the President as an equal—no doubt Morgan thought this a compliment. On occasion, Roosevelt spoke harshly of bankers, but Morgan dismissed this as hyperbole. When T.R. attacked one of his interests, Morgan was surprised. If anything was wrong, he told Roosevelt, it could have been cleared up by underlings. T.R. should have sent one of his men—presumably the Secretary of the Treasury—to see a Morgan partner, and between them all could have been made right. Still, Morgan did support Roosevelt in the 1904 election, after which the President opened a new assault on Wall Street in the form of an antitrust crusade. But America was struck by another financial crisis in 1907, one Roosevelt could not end. Like Cleveland, he called upon Morgan's help, and this time he did send his man—Treasury Secretary Cortelyou—to New York to work under the Great Man. Morgan managed to stanch the crisis, while Roosevelt did nothing about antitrust for the remainder of his administration. The bankers had triumphed once more.

The Money Trust Investigation took note of this banker power. The nation was controlled by a handful of private banks—Morgan; Kuhn, Loeb; Lee, Higginson; and Kidder, Peabody were singled out—and some other public institutions which did a private banking business, including First National of New York, National City, Guaranty Trust, and Bankers Trust. All the rest followed their lead.

What should be done to alter this situation? The reformers talked, questioned, and debated, and in the end came up with no concrete plan. The Federal Reserve System was established in 1913, and went into operation on the eve of World War I. It was designed to remove some of Wall Street's power. The system was centered in Washington, but the leading regional bank was in New York—near Wall Street. And the first president of the New York bank was Benjamin Strong, among whose other titles was that of J. P. Morgan's son-in-law.

The war had profound effects upon international finance, one of which was the decline of London and the rise of New York as the premier money market. In 1913, Wall Streeters began the day by asking, "How's London?" Upon learning that prices declined the previous day, they would prepare for a sympathetic reaction at the N.Y.S.E. This changed by 1918, for by then, London followed New York.

This was to have been expected, given the nature of international balances. In 1914, the United States was the world's leading debtor nation. Four years later, it was the leading creditor. The Allies floated well over $2 billion in bonds on Wall Street during the neutrality period, with $1.2 billion of it going to London. In addition, the Allied governments liquidated much of their American stock holdings, usually selling to Americans. After the United States entered the war, the investment banking community both led and participated in the Liberty and then the Victory bond drives, as well as marketing securities of private corporations that required additional funds to produce war materials. In the process, the banks not only enlarged their power but expanded their scope. Individuals who prior to 1917 had savings accounts, some property, and considered all stocks and bonds esoterica, now had experiences in dealing with investment bankers, and learned that they could increase the yields on their savings through the purchase of bonds—and possibly stocks. The initial encounter was followed by others, and this provided the basis "for the vast and credulous postwar market for credit which culminated in the portentous speculation of 1928 and 1929," as historian Edwin Gay wrote shortly after the 1929 crash. Paul Warburg of Kuhn, Loeb, thought the wartime experience, together with several changes in the tax laws, would combine to create a mass market for securities. "The successful distribution of large volumes of new securities can only be carried on by following wealth into the millions of small rivulets and channels into which it now flows, and where it is less subjected to the exactions of the tax-collector."*

Mass marketing did transpire in the 1920s, though the notion that America went stock-market crazy toward the end of the decade is exaggerated. By the late 1920s, however, millions of Americans looked upon bankers as miracle men engaged in an exciting business—the creation and manipulation of wealth. These men became the symbol of New Era capitalism, and so it should not have been surpris-

* As quoted in Vincent Carosso, *Investment Banking in America* (Cambridge, 1970), pp. 238–39.

ing that they emerged as scapegoats by 1930, and were punished by such legislation as the Glass-Steagall Act once F.D.R. took command in Washington.

The new legislation was the classic example of firing a bullet into a corpse. Investment banking was an ailing business by 1933, and would remain so for the remainder of the decade. The Reconstruction Finance Corporation in Washington, and not the investment banks in New York, was the most powerful single force in providing funds for America's industries during the Great Depression, and its chairman, Jesse Jones, wielded more influence than had any investment banker after the death of J. P. Morgan. Jones not only controlled billions of federal dollars, he had special entrée to the White House, where he was considered the most important non–New Dealer in the Roosevelt Administration.

The crusade against the investment bankers continued nevertheless. Several reform committees demonstrated that the industry still was dominated by a handful of Wall Street firms, that in some cases the same individuals who had led the profession in the 1920s were in command a decade later, and that the syndicate system prevailed. The bankers protested that their influence scarcely could be considered important, given the state-centered approach of the New Deal. Weeks would go by without a single major flotation, and in fact some companies preferred to cut back on operations or utilize R.F.C. facilities than to sell new bonds because stock prices were so depressed that their sales were impossible or unwise. Furthermore, many large corporations, still suffering from the traumas of the early 1930s, wanted to remain liquid, as though anticipating a new depression. Expansion was frowned upon, and inventories kept as low as possible. Firms would borrow short-term funds from commercial banks, but the former investment affiliates were avoided. Not even the outbreak of a new war in 1939, or America's entry as a belligerent two years later, could alter the situation. The nation's banks had played a major role in financing the war effort in 1917–18. They stayed on the sidelines during World War II.

Banking remained somnolent in the immediate postwar period. Not only was there no sign of banker domination of industry, there was some question as to whether America would relapse into depression.

Yet in 1947, the Justice Department filed an antitrust action against seventeen investment banks, charging them with violations of the Sherman Act, in that they had conspired to monopolize their industry and restrain competition. The Justice Department brief contained reams of evidence that major Wall Street houses, along with those in other cities, had entered into combinations to bid on new issues and then worked together so as to market them. In other words, the syndicate system was intact.

Apparently the suit had political motivations. Hoping to revive the New Deal spirit after the war, the Truman Administration had warmed over that issue which had served F.D.R. so well in 1932–34. But the motives were transparent, or at least seemed so to presiding Judge Harold Medina, who in handing down his decision in 1954 breathed cold anger and contempt for the prosecution. "I have come to the settled conviction and accordingly find, that no combination, conspiracy and agreement as is alleged in the complaint, nor any part thereof, was ever made, entered into, conceived, constructed, continued, or participated in by these defendants, or any of them."

Medina threw out the charges with prejudice, an unusual move that was a further slap at the prosecution. In effect, he admonished the Justice Department for having embarked upon a punitive case with little in the way of evidence. Medina described syndicate practices not as collusion, but natural and normal, given the nature of the business and industry. His final critique was contained in supplementary materials prepared by his staff, which comprise the most complete history of investment banking available to that time—something the prosecution should have undertaken but had avoided doing. Medina drew from this evidence most of his conclusions, and in such a way as to bring to an end a half-century of governmental warfare against the money trust. Never again would Washington lead an attack against the district's prominent investment banks.

The settlement of the antitrust action coincided with the development of a new bull market, which by the late 1950s had come to resemble the one that expired in 1929. Medina had concluded that cooperation between leading firms and the development of communities of interests were natural in the industry, and that domination by a relative handful of banks was no sign of illegal collusion. Even then, however, investment banking was taking on new aspects, which within a few years would make his decision appear antique.

Four developments in particular altered the industry. One of these was transitory, the second a variation on old themes, while the other two—which also involved commercial banking—were of profound importance, not only for the district but for the future evolution of American capitalism.

The first of these—and the most dramatic and most publicized—was the new-issue mania of the late 1950s and early 1960s, which was a product of the bull era, and stirred the brokerages into action. By then the Eisenhower market had reached the emotional stage, with volume rising and a new generation of investors coming to Wall Street. Memories of the Great Crash had faded by then, and many speculators appeared convinced the upward move would be permanent.

As had been the case with all such periods, dozens of new companies—many in such glamour industries as electronics, space, and drugs—came to Wall Street to sell stock, in effect providing fodder for speculators. The large, established investment bankers, the firms indicted in the antitrust action, would have nothing to do with most of them, for the companies lacked assets, products, and management depth, and in some instances had not even gone into production. Their paper would be highly speculative, a fact noted in their prospectuses, but one which did not dismay even those who read them.*

New underwriters were organized to serve the needs of both undercapitalized corporate clients and the speculators. Some were as shaky and transitory as the firms they served, but for a while they dazzled the district. Their methods were simple and foolproof. The underwriter would bring out a new issue, say one hundred thousand shares of a stock going for three dollars a share. These would be distributed to his clients, who promised not to sell until given the word to do so. Then, with no supply available, the underwriter would encourage other

* As early as 1937, this flaw in the Securities Exchange Act had become obvious to S.E.C. commissioners, but nothing was done to alter the situation. A joke of the period was that a person could organize a firm to encourage people to jump off the Empire State Building, and if the material in the prospectus was forthright, the stock could be sold. The Act was based upon the assumption that investors and speculators would behave prudently if given complete information. This belief was overly optimistic and unfounded in experience, as would be shown in the 1960s.

clients—not as favored as the first set but hoping to become members of the inner group through cooperation—to bid them up. The stock would rise to 6, and then to 12, by which time unwary outsiders would begin buying. Then the underwriter would dump his client's shares onto the market and turn to his next vehicle.

Small investment bankers, such as Michael Kletz, Donald Marron, Stephen Fuller, and Michael Lomosney became millionaires in a matter of weeks in this fashion. New companies such as BBM Photocopy, Nytronics, Wyle Laboratories, and Polychrome came to market, were pushed up, and then collapsed, some to declare bankruptcy. At the peak of the mania, in 1969, close to 1,300 new issues were underwritten, with a net take of $3.5 billion (in contrast, only 24 new issues were sold in 1975, when only the more substantial fresh firms could find sponsorship, and these fetched $230 million).

There was nothing illegal about any of this. The S.E.C. and Justice Department did nothing to curb the brokers.

The new-issue craze demonstrated that entry into the field of investment banking still was possible, but only on the fringes. Kuhn, Loeb or Morgan Stanley hardly would place their names behind such small operations as Faradyne, Belock Instruments, or Microwave Associates. Had Wall Street truly been controlled by a money trust, such firms and dozens of others like them would have failed to obtain sponsorship. As it was, the large banks did not dominate all aspects of the field or regulate entry, and so the groundwork was set for the major bust that came later in the decade.

Still, none of the go-go underwriters of the early 1960s remained in business for more than a few years. The great postwar bull market had demonstrated that admission to the field was not impossible, and that under some circumstances, a shrewd individual with a small amount of capital could make a quick fortune. That was all. Most of the major underwriters of 1976 had long pedigrees, with almost all dating back to the 1920s. Morgan Stanley; First Boston; Halsey, Stuart; Dillon Read; Kuhn Loeb; Blyth; Lehman and others of their kind still were at the top of the industry in the 1970s.

Yet there was a change, a subtle shift in emphasis made necessary by People's Capitalism but really an expansion of ideas set down during the Civil War period by Jay Cooke and his associates. The older investment banks had specialized in finding major purchasers for new issues, in much the same way Morgan had acted for Vanderbilt in the matter of the sale of New York Central to the English investors close to a century ago. In the investment atmosphere of the 1960s, large client lists—often comprised of small investors—could prove useful. This was particularly so for those firms interested in a widespread ownership, either to forestall outside pressures upon management or to provide it with a political constituency of some size, as might be the case for utilities who prefer many owners in its service area. This situation provided an opening for the commission houses to enter investment banking in a major fashion.

Some commission houses had underwritten issues in the past, either individually or as members of syndicates—the former for small companies, the latter for major efforts. Merrill Lynch; Paine, Webber, Jackson & Curtis; W. E. Hutton; Reynolds & Co. and Bache & Co. among others had shown some interest in the area prior to the 1950s, though with the exception of Merrill Lynch all indicated underwriting would be peripheral to other activities. This changed somewhat in the bull-market period. By 1959, Merrill Lynch had emerged as the sixth largest investment banker—behind White, Weld and Blyth, but behind of Kuhn, Loeb and Halsey, Stuart.

The intrusion by the parvenu might have stimulated talk of Wall Street revolution had it taken place at the turn of the century, and might have dominated the rumor mills in the 1940s. But in the 1960s, when the moorings of the district were being uprooted, it hardly merited more than a passing glance. By the end of the new-issue mania, speculators and investors had become accustomed to looking to brokerages for such exotica—which not only might rise rapidly, but could be purchased without paying the usual commission. The hotshot brokerages may have declined and then disappeared later in the decade, but the major commission houses remained in underwriting, so that by the mid-1970s, it scarcely seemed to matter whether a new issue was presented by a syndicate headed by First Boston or Bache Halsey Stuart—the latter the product of a merger between the second largest commission broker and a major investment bank.

The next development was a side effect resulting from an unexpected twist in the evolution of the corporation—the emergence of the conglomerate.

Although they intrigued Wall Street and the rest of the nation in the 1950s and 1960s, conglomerates were neither unusual or new at the time—multi-industry companies had existed in the early national period, and some businessmen (including George Washington) had many diverse interests, and so might be described as personal conglomerates. Prior to their appearance, however, it had been widely assumed that the large American corporations would go in a different direction. Students of the subject wrote that the important firms would expand either in a horizontal or vertical fashion—some might combine them—and become more closely integrated. Furthermore, these corporate giants would be self-financing, an outgrowth of enlarged cash flows and a natural desire to be free of banker controls. The Age of Morgan was over, they said; it would be replaced by that of General Motors or of some other large enterprise, headed by faceless individuals who shuffled in and out of corporate headquarters, each stamped from the same mold.

In some respects this did occur with older, well-established firms. But capitalism retained some of its original vitality. In part as a reaction to antitrust policies and the desire to spread risks and take advantage of tax laws—but also impelled by sheer opportunism—several quite colorful businessmen took command of small enterprises (or founded them) and within less than a decade became masters of billion-dollar operations. Tex Thornton of Litton Industries, James Ling of Ling-Temco-Vought, and Charles Bluhdorn of Gulf & Western, to name only three, did so by engulfing other firms, some with only a few thousand dollars in sales, and several larger than themselves. In order to do this, these "conglomerateurs" needed money, advice, and support. They had daring, but they lacked respectability and connections. Just as J. P. Morgan's cachet was sought by businessmen coming to market in the 1880s and 1890s, so it was that sponsorship by a major investment bank gave legitimacy to many conglomerates in the 1950s and 1960s.

An example of this would be Lehman's relationship with Litton. In 1953, Thornton and some of his associates approached Lehman for help in raising $1.5 million, which was to be used to purchase Litton, then a small West Coast electronics manufacturer. Thornton had a good reputation, earned through stints at Ford and Hughes Aircraft, and Lehman decided to obtain the money, in return for a commission, seventy-five thousand shares of common at token prices, and the position as Litton's banker. From that time to the present, one or several Lehman partners devoted a good deal of time to Litton business, arranging mergers, the sale of new securities, and offering advice on corporate development. In so acting, Lehman performed the functions of a European merchant bank as well as those of an American investment banker, as did banks which advised other conglomerates.

There was a major difference between the two types of enterprise, however. The merchant banks were private institutions, owned and controlled by insiders, prepared to risk their own capital on ventures, hoping to be rewarded through profits and commissions. The American investment banker of the post–World War II period had to develop marketing techniques, and given the fact that the United States has an S.E.C. while no European nation has seen fit to create one, was obliged to be more open in his dealings. In the 1950s and early 1960s some of them went so far as to relinquish partnership status, and enter into incorporation. Then, in 1969, the small brokerage-underwriting firm of Donaldson, Lufkin & Jenrette filed a prospectus with the S.E.C., announcing its intent to go public in order to raise $24 million.

It seemed a good idea. Wall Street was booming, brokerage profits were high, and the prices of new issues inflated. If it made sense for a small electronics firm to sell its shares into this kind of market, in order to enrich its founders and obtain expansion capital, why not apply the same reasoning to its banker? DJL proposed to sell a small portion of its total capitalization, with a book value of $3 a share, for $30. The partners would retain the bulk of the shares which, at the offering price, would be worth more than $200 million. If this would not establish DLJ in the same category as Lehman or Morgan Stanley, it would place the firm in a strong secondary position. The Street saw the logic and beauty of it all, and Merrill Lynch, Reynolds, Hayden Stone, and Bache followed suit, as did many smaller enterprises.

Now the commission houses had sufficient capital to vie with the old-line investment banks for underwritings. That their stock sales took place on the eve of the greatest crash since the 1930s masked the significance of this alteration in the industry's fabric. Investment banking, aspects of merchant banking, and ordinary brokerage are more closely joined today than ever before. Merrill Lynch, for example, may risk its own capital on a new venture, underwrite the firm's shares and offer them to the public, or position them in several trust accounts prior to the official announcement, and all the while run a large-scale brokerage. The same company may manage money in trust accounts; organize, operate, and sell shares in mutual funds; participate as a partner in new enterprises; and conduct an international business. In effect, this firm, and others in the industry, have become financial supermarkets. By 1977, many formerly staid investment banks had entered some of these fields too, and almost all had made the plunge into every aspect of money management.

Of the several developments in commercial banking that impacted upon investment banking, the most obvious concerned attempts to bypass, and in some respects repeal, sections of the Glass-Steagall Act. This is not to say the commercial bankers wanted to get back into the call money business or use deposits to speculate or invest in the stock market; no sane Wall Streeter wants to return to that aspect of the 1920s. Rather, the commercial bankers viewed the 1933 legislation as being more punitive than reformist, in that it had punished bankers for what they had done rather than reshaping the industry in a rational fashion. One of the major functions of banks, they say, is to channel public funds into worthwhile enterprises. At times this means a loan to a new or established company, while on occasion the sale of the firm's stock might be more sensible. Prior to 1934, the same institution might handle both transactions, and its officers would have the right to decide which was the more prudent action. After Glass-Steagall, however, the corporation was obliged to utilize commercial banks for loans, and then go to investment bankers when interested in selling stock, arranging for mergers and acquisitions—or fighting off the same. Morgan Guaranty, a leading commercial bank, stood ready to advise corporate clients on new ventures. So did Morgan Stanley, the descendant of its former investment affiliate. The separation may have made sense a half-century ago, in a simpler world. Was it equally wise in 1977?

Some leading commercial banks thought not, but until 1958 there was nothing they could do about it. Finding a loophole in the Bank Holding Company Act of 1956, First National City, the premier New

York bank and the nation's second largest, organized a holding company, First National City Corporation, into which was placed the bank, as its sole functioning unit. This legalistic alteration had no impact upon the bank's depositors or clients, but the implications were profound and immediately recognized in Washington and in New York. First National City (the bank) was circumscribed by more than a century of laws, both on the federal and state levels, which dictated where, how, and with whom it could transact business. First National City (the corporation) was another matter. It could become a conglomerate, and enter such fields as mortgage banking, leasing, consumer finance, and factoring. Operating units could organize and manage real estate investment trusts, oil drilling syndicates, and the like. There was no reason why other subsidiaries couldn't franchise restaurants, enter manufacturing, or in fact almost any business. After all, such were the rights of conglomerates.

Could the one-bank holding companies purchase or create an investment banking subsidiary? This move, which would have been a challenge to the Glass-Steagall philosophy, was discussed in the early 1960s, but nothing was done.

Other banks appreciated the freedom afforded them by the transformation into one-bank holding companies. Within a half-year of First National City's move, there were almost 800 of them, with assets well in excess of $100 billion. Soon thereafter Congress passed new legislation to limit their growth, but the banks found ways around it. Today, commercial banks under one-bank holding company umbrellas control three out of every four dollars on deposit.

The underwriters were annoyed and more than a trifle uneasy. Clearly the commercial banks meant to expand their merchant banking activities. This meant that client corporations would have less reason to market stocks and bonds than previously had been the case. Still, this was no direct challenge to the investment bankers. Wall Street wasn't certain how to react to amendments to the Bank Holding Company Act, which were passed in 1970, and which contained serious implications for underwriting practices. Under the terms of the new legislation, the one-bank corporations had to limit their activities to those closely related to financial matters—though the specifics were open to interpretation.

Would this encourage the large commercial banks to seek means of entering investment banking? According to the Glass-Steagall Act they were permitted to service municipalities and states, and this included underwriting their securities. Some Wall Streeters thought the next move would be for the commercial banks to ask for alterations in the legislation to allow them to offer their facilities to industrial corporations. By 1970, Wall Street was in a shambles, while the commercial banks seemed in much better shape. To permit them access to this market would increase competition, provide greater liquidity when access to funds was becoming a problem, and further punish Wall Street at a time when such action would be politically popular.

Some large banks did indicate an interest in underwriting, but the industry as a whole was reluctant to mount a strong campaign for revision of the laws. Multi-national dealings and branch banking were more alluring. The larger banks wanted to explore credit card purchases, and those that hoped to invest in securities believed that they could do so more profitably through real estate investment trusts. Supermarket banking was another possibility. The idea was simple enough: shoppers would deposit paychecks on weekly visits to the store—at a bank next door to the supermarket, or in some cases, an integral part of the complex—and then withdraw just enough money to pay for purchases, leaving the rest to earn interest.

The branch bank would become ubiquitous—technology and the demands of the public would make certain of that, just as the same forces were transforming the securities market. After the advent of negotiated commissions, some banks saw the possibility of uniting the two areas. Congress and the S.E.C. spoke loudly and often of the need for more competition and of the lower commission rates that would result. Now that it was coming about, the major commercial banks decided the moment was right for an end run around Glass-Steagall.

It was not portrayed as such, of course. Instead, some banks advertised that just as depositors in the 1940s had placed money into Christmas Clubs, and those of the early 1970s had accustomed themselves to branch banking and the use of bank credit cards that were tied to accounts, so those of the mid-decade would be able to purchase certain stocks—at low commissions—at their branch bank. In effect, the bankbook would also be a brokerage account. All the plans stressed this, and portrayed the purchase and sale of stocks as being little different from ordinary deposits and withdrawals.

So they were. The Chase's Automatic Stock Investment Plan, for example, was connected with checking accounts. The depositor decided which of a list of blue-chip stocks he or she wanted to purchase on a plan basis, and then notified the bank to make regular withdrawals for that purpose. First National City, which as early as 1968 had a program for dividend re-investment, followed suit, as did most of the New York banks. The idea spread throughout the nation—Crocker National in California and Continental Illinois were pioneers in the Far West and Midwest. Chemical in New York made the next step—purchasing blocks of stock on the Third Market, and then selling them to clients, making money from commissions and spreads.

Was this brokerage? The commission houses said it was and claimed violation of Glass-Steagall. The banks said nothing, at least officially. By the end of the decade, however, banks could be doing a larger business in retailing securities than any but the most important brokerages.

The commercial banks deny having any intention of competing directly with their investment banking cousins. They claim there are few areas of overlap in their businesses, or at least this seems the agreed upon position when the subject is raised. For one thing, commercial banks do not offer investment advice; and for another, they do not deal in options, commodities, or offer margin loans. But this stance is quite disingenuous. All major banks have trust departments, in which assets are managed, and the personnel there are interchangable with those at investment banks. Starting in 1965, First National City offered portfolio management for small trust funds, and the other banks followed during the next decade. A client with more than $10,000 to invest has no trouble finding a bank ready to do the job for about one percent of total assets—Marine Midland will manage $8,000 accounts, and for less than one percent. In most respects such management is superior to that offered by brokerages. For one thing, the manager has no incentive to churn accounts—to buy and sell in order to generate commissions—since the bank's earnings rise with the total funds managed, and not through increases in trading volume. This means that when conditions call for it, the clients' funds may be totally in cash, a position few brokerages ever recommend, since to do so would be to lose commission business. Given the greater power of the bank trust departments, they can obtain commission discounts not available to the small investor who acts on his own, and so the management fee can often be offset by savings on commissions.

Still, the commercial banks insist that their forays into brokerage are intended merely as a convenience to depositors. They are more than that, as everyone on the Street knows. To claim that Citibank, Chase Manhattan, Chemical, and the rest are interested in only a bit of the action in securities is transparently untrue. The banks have it within their power to transform Wall Street into a wholesale market, while they handle most of the retail business. In almost all respects they are as well equipped to handle clients as any but the largest and best of the commission houses. And in fact, they are quite capable of performing wholesale functions as well, if given the opportunity—and the right—to do so. The debate between the N.Y.S.E. and the Third Market—which still is not resolved—is minor league compared to the challenges posed by the banks. The Securities Industries Association (S.I.A.) recognizes the threat, and in testimony before Congress in 1975 warned that ''we are witnessing a trend toward the concentration of financial resources into fewer and fewer hands. Adding additional services to an increasingly monolithic banking structure only exacerbates this trend.'' Edward O'Brien, the S.I.A. president, put it bluntly. ''If it comes to head-on competition with the banks, the securities industry can't survive.''

O'Brien and others like him are not engaging in hyperbole or using scare tactics. Nor were they speaking merely of brokerage. Right now the banks are the masters of Wall Street, not only on a residual basis—through the failure of the Exchange or other forces to maintain control—but as a result of their own enormous power. While Washington debates alterations in law and the shape of the new marketplace, the nation's largest banks have fashioned their own methods of dominating securities-based capitalism. There seems no way of legislating changes in this area, for the banks—as a community—are already more powerful than Congress or the presidency in this sphere of national enterprise.

This is the last development transforming the securities industry.

As indicated, the breakup of the seeming oligopoly in commission brokerage and underwriting and the appearance of go-go brokers were elaborations of old themes or of transitory importance. The entry of commercial banks into brokerage was of greater significance, for the district and the nation. But the last development, the molding of a new banker-industrialist nexus erected upon the base of institutional money, is of monumental significance, beside which the squabbles of the N.Y.S.E. and the Third Market seem unimportant. While Batten and Weeden talk of an electronic marketplace, anonymous trust managers manipulate billions of dollars with the sangfroid of a J. P. Morgan. They are deferred to by Arab oil magnates and Third World politicians, who often barely mask their contempt for Washington-based bureaucrats. The fight regarding Wall Street's future shape continues. Whichever side wins, however, the commercial banks headquartered in lower Manhattan will inherit the world.

CHAPTER NINE

INSTITUTIONS

———

THE AGE OF THE tycoon ended just prior to World War I, with the death of J. P. Morgan in 1913 as good a symbol as any for the demise. Power emanated from personality in this period, with the corporation or bank an extention of the man. Money counted too, though not as much as is commonly thought. No American clan had as much raw wealth as did the Rockefellers, though the Mellons were rising rapidly. Yet Morgan, with a fraction of their assets, was the equal of any business potentate. Only he had the influence and power to fashion the billion dollar U.S. Steel trust; no other man could have commanded the legions of Wall Street as he did. And only Morgan had the reputation and ability to calm foreign bankers needed to stem the 1907 panic. These accomplishments were made possible by trust and the creation of confidence, and not a mere outpouring of funds—the raising of money was the result, not the cause, of Morgan's tremendous influence. This was understood and appreciated at the time. Both Republicans and Democrats, those for and against Wall Street, considered the creation of a central bank in 1908; for they knew Morgan was not immortal, and that an institutional structure would have to be fashioned to take his place, since no other individual would ever have his power and influence. Out of this came the Federal Reserve: the greatest tribute his opponents could pay the banker was the power and scope of his replacement.

The underwriters became dominant in the 1920s. Combining the duties of the investment banker with those of the stockbroker, and adding the gimmickry of the snake oil huckster, they raised money for large and small enterprises, and often manipulated their securities as parts of their jobs. In their primes, syndicate managers might control pools of $100 million or so, while speculators like Jesse Livermore and Arthur Cutten—forgotten today but as famous on Wall Street as Babe Ruth and Ty Cobb were in baseball—were looked upon as miracle workers, creators of instant wealth. This period came to an end with the 1929 crash, and for the next two decades financial power seemed centralized in Washington.

During the 1950s and 1960s, Wall Street housed many glamorous individuals, from go-go fund managers to Ivy League professors and their students, who through the use of computers and esoteric techniques claimed the ability to select the right stock at the right time. There were the founders of new companies guaranteed to be "the IBMs of the 1980s," and out-and-out charlatans of the variety that appear with each bull market. Their exploits were followed in the daily press and popular magazines, and they became heroes to small investors who owned mutual funds, or whose pension money was in retirement trusts.

Through all of this, however, the manager of institutional funds and other assets was gaining power and authority. There were few such individuals in the Morgan era, and not many more when Livermore was engaged in manipulating R.C.A. common. For a while it appeared some of the fund managers might emerge as Wall Street's new powerhouses, or at least their celebrity gave this impression. In the 1960s men such as Jerry Tsai, George Chestnutt, John Hartwell, and the "three Freds"—Carr, Alger, and Mates—were lionized. The mutual funds under their management were growing rapidly, and they could wheel and deal with hundreds of millions of dollars. Then the bull market ended. Most of the go-go fund managers no longer are on the Street, while those who survived have lost reputations, assets, and followings.

Little was heard of Carl Hathaway in that period. He did not seek publicity, or for that matter, go out of his way to obtain new clients. Hathaway handled pension funds for Morgan Guaranty. At a time when Tsai's Manhattan Fund was amazing the district by selling over $270 million in shares in a short period of time, Hathaway was charged with trust portfolios in excess of $10 billion, and toward the end of the 1960s bought and sold more securities in some months than J. P. Morgan underwrote in 1901, when he fashioned U.S. Steel.

Who outside of several large commission houses and banks knows Paul Aron, the young investment manager for College Retirement Equity Fund, an entity familiar to college teachers, but unknown to the general public? CREF is not the largest of such funds, but it does have $4 billion in securities, and Aron gets around $400 million a year in new money to invest. Most of it goes into securities.

Individuals such as Aron and Hathaway are not juggernauts or symbols; both men could be replaced without a ripple on the Street. Their institutions are powerful, however, and will be more so in the foreseeable future. In some respects, they will dominate the district and may set the tone for American capitalism as well. There are no tycoons in view—that age passed in the late 1920s—and no large syndicate can expect to be as powerful as one of the trust departments of a major bank.

Those who study the financial district and the reporters who cover it often categorize managers like Aron and Hathaway as "faceless." The characterization is understandable though overstated. The money managers comprise a mixed group, but taken as a whole they include the most sophisticated and knowledgeable men and women in the district, easily a match for their Swiss, British, and Japanese counterparts. Flamboyance may pay off in brokerage, some forms of underwriting, the management of small funds, and the writing of market advisories. It is an avoided quality in those organizations that manage hundreds of millions of dollars, for it is axiomatic there that the individual exists to serve the institution, which, in turn, is supposed to be subordinated to the needs of clients. This is inevitably so, given the long histories of some institutions, and the magnitude of their managed funds. Between them Morgan, Citibank, Bankers Trust, Chase Manhattan, and Mellon National—the big-five trustees—manage close to $100 billion in securities alone. Even the "small fry" on the list of the fifty largest trust operations are impressive forces. American National Bank, a little-known institution which is itself a subsidiary of Walter E. Heller, has over $2 billion in its trust portfolio, and barely makes the roster. Still, American National manages twice as much money as does Massachusetts Investment Trust (M.I.T.) a premier mutual fund.

The trust department and the mutual fund are both in the business of managing other people's money. What the mutual fund provides for the small investor, who often is a novice as well, the trust department does for large investors, including pension funds. Many mutual funds advertise aggressively; the trust departments are more genteel, and in some cases will insist upon an interview prior to accepting a new client. All mutual funds are commingled, which is to say that the money invested by individuals is pooled, a portfolio is created, and the investor receives shares in that portfolio. The newcomer to M.I.T. purchases new shares in an already existing portfolio, and on occasion his money is used to purchase the shares of an old investor who wants to liquidate his position. In such cases, the stock portfolio remains intact, and each investor can scan the morning newspaper to discover how he did the previous day, for results not only are public, but when much better than average, are advertised.

Some trust portfolios are commingled in this fashion, but the practice is still unusual enough to vex the mutual funds but not frighten them. Rather, the owner of a trust account has a manager whose name is known; who can be contacted for chitchat, congratulations in good times and criticism in bad; and who draws upon a staff of analysts and other experts for assistance in managing the funds. When huge pension funds are involved the bank trust officer may be a vice-president, who will travel to the office of the union or company to explain actions, educate his client, and in effect serve as a quasi-officer in the union or corporation, even to the point of being called in during contract negotiations, or when the organization is framing its long-term plans. Such individuals function in a rarefied atmosphere, and no more would advertise their services than they would wear sports clothes to the office or seek interviews from reporters on garish magazines. Even if they are not ''old money'' themselves, they behave as though they were. The Hamptons for a summer vacation are out for such people; they go to Newport or Palm Beach, not only for rest and recreation, but so their clients can be close to the men who manage their money.

As has been indicated, the major economic function of Wall Street today is the channeling of funds from investors to new and old companies, and it is here that the underwriters become vital. Without this money, American capitalism would wilt and shrivel, and in the end metamorphose into fascism or communism of one kind or another. The trust function runs a close second to underwriting, however. Through it small and large investors place today's surpluses for use tomorrow—when the owner of mutual fund shares wants to purchase a car, or when the worker retires and starts receiving his pension.

The underwriter raises money for the company whose securities he is selling, while the trustee invests money for those who seek income and capital gains. Their focuses are different—one obtains capital for enterprises, the other invests the earnings made possible by corporate operations. At times, and on occasion, the underwriter and trustee come together. For example, a blue-chip company may decide to sell $100 million or so in stock so as to obtain additional capital, or it may go to the capital market with a similar amount in thirty-year bonds. These may appear attractive to a fund manager, who may decide to take a few million dollars worth for his portfolios. But the symbiosis is far from complete. If and when the two gigantic forces do come together—when entire underwritings are taken by trustees—the stock exchanges will have become obsolete. For that matter, the Third Market will have to undergo major alterations, perhaps merge with Instinet or some other Fourth Market operation in order to survive.

It may be taking place today, and not through an unslaked thirst for power, manipulation, or conspiracy. Rather, it seems the result of the continuing process of capitalist development. Just as the investment banker wrested control of large enterprises from industrial capitalists at the turn of the century, so the trustees now may be replacing, or at the very least supplementing, the investment bankers. The first change took place when companies needed more capital than their managers could raise on their own. Thus, an Andrew Carnegie gave way to a J. P. Morgan in the steel industry. This new change (which is not all that new, since it began two generations ago) is occurring as liquid assets have flowed to the middle classes, not individually but collectively, though their institutions, which include pension plans, insurance programs, and the like.

As has been indicated, large blocks account for some 70 percent of N.Y.S.E. volume. Without block trading the Third Market never would have become so great a threat, and the Fourth Market would not have come into being. The blocks revealed the flaws in the specialist system, and their growth—both in terms of total trades and size—are a major factor in the current reshaping of the trading complex.

Almost all the blocks come from, or go to, institutional clients. They may trade $500,000 or so of I.B.M. or General Motors to test the water, attempt to unload 100,000 shares of Ford or International Paper in a few days if the proper investment committee decides autos or paper look bad, or dominate both the buy and sell sides of Sperry Rand for a week if of a mind to do so. Needless to say, institutions never deal in odd lots; nor do they consider any but the best Amex or O-T-C stocks. As for margin purchases, the institutions are more likely to lend money than to borrow.

It was quite different at the turn of the century, despite all the talk of concentrated power at that time. There were trustees for the wealthy, to be sure, but they handled private accounts. This was a time prior to the appearance of mutual and pension funds. Almost all the equity capital in America was in the hands of individuals, and these were the people who dominated trading at the exchanges. The small investor in the days of Teddy Roosevelt might purchase odd lots from a Consolidated Stock Exchange broker, or take a few hundred shares of a Curb or O-T-C issue. N.Y.S.E. stocks often were purchased on margin, even by the wealthy. The gamblers were interested in options, and frequented a bucket shop or two. It was the age of the broker; the trust manager was yet to appear.

The situation had altered considerably by 1963, at which time one-fifth of all equity capital was either owned or managed by an institution, with most under the control of pension and mutual funds. This was the last great era for the small investor, and it was to end in 1969. Since then, one in six has left the Street, most never to return. The gap created by this departure has been filled by the institutions. Even had the private investor remained, however, he would have been shoved aside, so great is the impetus of institutional money today. At the present time, individuals own only 60 percent of all stock; the pension funds by themselves have between 15 and 20 percent in their portfolios, and the share is increasing rapidly.*

* In a contentious work, Peter Drucker claims pension funds own a quarter of all equity today, and he goes on to predict that by the year 2000 they will own two-thirds of all eq-

No Wall Streeter of Cornelius Vanderbilt's day predicted the rise of institutional power. It was not anticipated during the Morgan era, either by socialists or capitalists. The former believed private property would be eliminated by now, while the latter talked of the need for concentration of economic power in an age of mass production, distribution, and consumption. Shortly after the turn of the century, Thorstein Veblen, the brilliant and erratic economist, wrote of the internal problems of modern capitalist enterprise, and hinted at the separation of ownership from control. The theme was taken up and amplified in *The Modern Corporation and Private Property* in 1932, as the New Dealers prepared to assume power in Washington. Its authors, Adolph Berle, Jr. and Gardiner Means, thought that shareholders no longer had a proprietary feeling toward those companies in which they owned shares. Given decent dividends and growth in equity, they would be satisfied to retain whomever sat in the executive suites. Thus, a deal was struck, though no one put it in so many words: managements would retain power and perquisites by means of paying off the legal owners—the shareholders. Should the shareholder dislike or distrust managements, he would not lead a crusade to eject them, but instead sell the stocks and seek elsewhere for dividends and capital gains. The idea was repeated by Thurman Arnold in *The Folklore of Capitalism,* published in 1937, and in other New Deal books and articles. As assistant attorney general charged with a sweeping antitrust campaign, Arnold often noted that he was obliging large-corporation executives to demonstrate a sense of responsibility that faded once ownership and control were divorced. In an earlier age, the stockholders might have accomplished this; by the late 1930s, he wrote, government had to do the job. Such were the adjustments necessary to control those who had power without responsibility.

From that time to the present, there have been many attacks upon the power of large enterprises, as well as waves of antitrust indignation. Increasingly, the stockholders in the companies under fire have lost their proprietary sentiments regarding such firms—the owner of a round lot of Lockheed does not feel he has engaged in illegal acts, and

uity plus a major portion—say 40 percent—of bonds. Both his figures and projections have been contested. See Peter Drucker, *The Unseen Revolution* (New York, 1976), pp. 1-3 ff.

sentiments of betrayed trust are overshadowed by outrage at a ten-point decline in the stock's quotation.

Even this limited kind of reaction might not take place were the shares in Lockheed—or Penn Central, Equity Funding, or some other disaster stock—held in a commingled trust or a pension fund, for participants in these may receive only annual reports on the status of portfolios, and not learn (unless they read the fine print, and few do) of in-and-out transactions during the year. Mutual funds issue quarterly reports, but these too mask many trades, and "dressing up the portfolio" by selling losers and buying winners just prior to the end of the quarter for the sake of appearances is commonplace. Without new legislation to control the large pools of money, and a concern on the part of the participants regarding the way their money is being managed, the situation will not change. There is little evidence that either alteration is in the making.

The concept of the separation of ownership and control of large corporations intrigued and angered the New Dealers, who for the better part of a decade tried to alter the situation and failed to do so appreciably. The idea filtered down to college freshmen by the 1950s, and in the next decade it appeared in high school texts. By then it no longer was novel, or even considered insidious. That such separation would continue was deemed natural and, to some, vaguely desirable—some hybrid form of People's Capitalism. When Ralph Nader tried to stir public interest in the matter in the late 1960s, and when anti–Vietnam War demonstrators took up the beat, they quickly learned the issue lacked bite, and so dropped it and turned elsewhere.

Meanwhile some management philosophers approached the issue from the other end, that of changes in the nature of the corporation and the workers' relationship to their work. In early 1950 Peter Drucker began talking and writing of the impact pensions would have on the corporation and labor unions—ignoring stockholders and Wall Street in his discussions. Drucker took some of the ideas of Veblen, Berle and Means, and Arnold, provided several new twists, and presented what he called "pension fund socialism." It was as though the Chinese or Japanese, without knowing of Columbus and those Europeans who followed, came upon the California shores in 1600 and claimed to have found a new continent. This is not to say that Drucker was ignorant of the writings of these critics of American corporate and finance capitalism, but that he presented their ideas from a radically different perspective.

Drucker traced the origins of pension fund socialism to ideas set down by General Motors President Charles Wilson in 1950, but added that the thoughts had been percolating at G.M. headquarters since 1944.* During contract negotiations with the United Automobile Workers that year, Wilson proposed the establishment of a workers' pension fund, to be managed by company-designated trustees, or "asset managers." According to Drucker, the union's leaders were wary at first, fearing it was a management ploy to undermine the loyalty workers had for the union. Additionally, the labor leaders weren't particularly pleased with Wilson's plan to have the bulk of the fund's assets invested in common stock.

Yet neither idea was wholly novel, and certainly not revolutionary, the harbinger of socialism. There had been employee pension funds in the 1870s, and at the time of the General Motors negotiations, some two thousand were in operation. Most of these were invested in government bonds, as they had been from the start. This resulted from tradition and an unwillingness to subject retirement accounts to the vagaries of Wall Street—especially in the light of the 1929 stock market crash and the kind of markets that existed in the 1930s and early 1940s.

Toward the end of the war, however, some funds started to invest in corporate bonds and preferred stocks. Those of utilities in particular interested the fund managers, and by the late 1940s they were turning to industrials as well. By 1950, close to half the capital of private uninsured pension funds—which at the time had slightly below $8 billion in assets—was in corporate bonds, and another 18 percent in corporate stocks, mostly preferred. Only a quarter of the assets were invested in federal securities of one kind or another. And the drift was in favor of private paper, especially stocks.

In the end the United Automobile Workers (U.A.W.) accepted Wilson's ideas, and the General Motors pension plan was set up along

* Drucker started on his seminal study of General Motors, *Concept of the Corporation*, in 1945, and it was released the following year. His article, "The Mirage of Pensions," appeared in *Harpers* in February, 1950, and was an outgrowth of his G.M. experiences.

the lines he proposed. The concept was appealing, and since it came out of G.M., had the cachet of respectability. Then too, the market was rising in the early 1950s, and so the fund was able to report good results from its inception. Others imitated the General Motors idea; within a year, according to Drucker, some eight thousand new common stock–based pension plans were in existence.

The number and scope of these plans expanded in the Eisenhower, Kennedy, and Johnson years. Part of the reason for this was the persistence of the bull market, the longest-lived in American history. Then too, as old union members who remembered the Great Crash were retired, and their places filled by relative youngsters to whom the 1930s were textbook tragedies, the demand for growth increased while the need for complete security seemed less important. Fears of inflation replaced the threat of depression; fixed annuities such as several provided by federal paper–based funds were less appealing than those dependent upon the upward swing of stock prices for benefits. This was the situation with the Teachers Insurance and Annuity Association, which had been organized in 1918 by the Carnegie Corporation and the Carnegie Foundation for the Advancement of Teaching. As was the case with almost all retirement funds, TIAA was based upon investments in government bonds and mortgages, and so was dependent upon money rates, and not securities prices. Interest rates were relatively low in the late 1940s and early 1950s, when stock prices began their rise. TIAA responded by creating CREF—the fund managed by Paul Aron—in 1952, with the understanding that no one would be permitted to place more than a quarter of his retirement bundle in the equity-based plan. The CREF unit price was $10.43 at its inception. By 1965, the price was over $39.00, while the original unit, with reinvestment of dividend income added, stood at $56.32. Participants demanded the right to place more of their money into CREF and less of a percentage into TIAA, and with some reluctance the trustees agreed to permit the professors to make their own allocations—to do less would appear strange, for virtually every academic economist was a member of TIAA–CREF. As anticipated, there was a large-scale swing over to CREF. This took place on the eve of the market decline of the late 1960s and early 1970s, an unfortunate and somewhat embarrassing situation for participants. Yet with all of this, by the end of 1976 the value of that original CREF unit of 1952 was above \$80.00, assuming reinvestment of dividends.

The other plans went over to equities more rapidly than did TIAA. By 1955, one-third of all private pension fund assets—which had grown to \$18 billion by then—was in corporate stock, and most of it in common shares. Ten years later, half the \$73 billion in assets was in common stock, and less than 5 percent in government securities. This was at the peak of the go-go years, when insurance companies were straining to obtain permission to sell variable annuities based upon common stock. Despite the collapse that followed and the bitter residue left during the subsequent recovery, approximately 60 percent of private pension fund assets are in common shares today, with only 3 percent in government paper. This, out of the well over \$110 billion in such funds and plans.

It goes without saying that no two funds operate in identical ways. Each had its own investment advisor; some utilize more than one, each in open competition with the others, the winner receiving a larger share of the total portfolio to manage as a reward. But some stocks appear in almost all portfolios—I.B.M., Xerox, Exxon, General Motors, Merck, and American Home Products are among the leaders in this area. There are several important reasons for this situation. Many asset managers were raised under, or still are controlled by, the "prudent man rule," which was promulgated in Massachusetts in 1833, and stated that trustees had to manage other people's money in the way a prudent man would take care of his own assets. In the twentieth century, many states and municipalities drew up lists of such prudent man investments, which consisted of government bonds and the like initially, expanded over time to include industrial bonds, and then utility bonds, preferred stocks, and finally, common shares, not only of utilities and leading railroads, but "sound" industrials—such as I.B.M. and the rest. Another factor is lack of imagination and fear of solitary risk. Should a good many of the pension funds own General Motors, for example, a portfolio manager could accumulate a million or so shares in the knowledge that he has powerful company—other managers who have concluded that G.M. was a good buy or hold at current quotations. If the automobile industry entered a slump, and the stock fell more than a few points, the manager could defend his purchase by noting that almost everyone had been taken in on that one. Furthermore, he might elect to hold onto the stock, or even purchase a few hundred thousand additional shares at lower prices, for the historical record shows that General Motors and stocks in its exclusive category tend to "come back," even if the coming takes a decade. Meanwhile, the dividends are usually both safe and high; cuts do take place, but these are rare, and are reinstated as soon as possible, both as a matter of honor, and to enable the G.M.'s of the investment world to maintain their positions.

There are other reasons, however, not as obvious to outsiders, but which carry weight with fund portfolio managers.

The managers like to purchase shares in companies that have large equity bases—a hundred million shares or more—in which management is secure in its place, and impervious to raids and outside pressures—especially from fund managers. The first attribute insures a degree of liquidity. A manager who decides to sell 100,000 shares of Merck or Xerox knows other managers carry the shares in their portfolios, and might be interested in buying the block, or taking a portion of it. Such a manager might use one of the Fourth Market firms to contact the would-be buyers, using a block positioner at one of the several brokerages that specialize in such work. Or he might contact other funds directly, or seek out an insurance portfolio manager, the director of a mutual fund, or someone else in that privileged category.

After a while this shuffling of shares takes on the aspects of a game, with a fixed number of pieces, which include those stocks already named plus a handful of others, such as Coca-Cola, Procter & Gamble, Kresge, and Minnesota Mining. On occasion new pieces are permitted into the game, but no more than a small number in any given year. Burroughs made the grade in the early 1970s, along with Avon. Once in this club, it is difficult to drop out. Polaroid came in during the early 1960s, along with Control Data. It took a series of very bad years to convince the managers that the latter issue should be expelled. As for Polaroid, it remains a "portfolio stock," despite some rocky times and flat earnings, due in part to the hopes and dreams of a handful of portfolio managers. To be sure, the stock took a sharp dip during the recession, but many managers held on, and helped nurse it back to relative good health.

The phenomenon of portfolio stocks made the so-called two-tier market of 1973 possible. Most of the N.Y.S.E. stocks declined badly that year, but the favored issues not only held their prices, but in some cases actually rose. The press publicized the two-tier market, with some writers creating the impression the institutions possessed the power to maintain prices, no matter what the rest of the list did. This was not the case, of course, and in the end of the first-tier stocks followed the second into collapse.

Paradoxically, the portfolio managers might be dissuaded from purchasing shares in a stock that might be controlled in this fashion. Wall Street lacks a taste for paradox, however, and so the idea eluded most writers.

Control of a stock is quite different from control of a company. To have the latter requires only possession of key offices. The officers of most multi-million share companies own only a small portion of outstanding shares. But they do have the stockholder lists, and given a halfway decent performance, can use them to maintain their positions. The large funds, which taken as a whole could exercise control of many huge companies, prefer to go along with management—after all, leadership was one of the reasons they purchased their shares. They can unite to oblige management to refrain from mergers or to accept them, or to fight or bow to government edicts, but this is rare, and usually such coercion takes place when the institutions find it difficult, perhaps impossible, to liquidate their positions. With great reluctance, and only when locked into a stock, will the funds go to management and make their feelings known. But if a company has a record of such interventions, it wins the reputation of being insecure and erratic, and so portfolio managers are dissuaded from taking positions. Thus, susceptibility to such control might lead to gradual eliminations of the stock from institutional portfolios. Should that happen, the stock would lose a good deal of its glamour and decline, perhaps never again to rise.

There is no rule of thumb for such things, but a lemming effect does exist on the Street, in that institutions tend to follow the leader when committing funds or withdrawing them. But there, unlike the situation with lemmings, the leadership is on a rotating basis. News that several large pension funds have accumulated blocks in XYZ Inc.—

have anointed it, as it were—would lead other institutions to make their purchases. In this fashion, a stock selling at a price to earnings ratio of ten to fifteen may be elevated to twenty or thirty. XYZ, which had anticipated earnings of $2.00 per share and is selling at 25, for example, could be lifted to 50, with no discernible alteration in the company's future. In the early 1970s, it might have been done in a matter of weeks—a few days set off sparks in the mid-1960s. At present, elevation to the first tier may take months. This is so because like many small investors, the large funds bear the scars of the 1969–73 decline and debacle, and tend to hesitate prior to taking the plunge.

Still, such large aggregations of money are managed by individuals who, one might think, would be immune to such traumas. A pension fund with about a billion dollars in equities could see the net value increase or decline by more than $50 million during the course of a trading day. And new money is always coming in, providing the fund not only with additional chips for the game, but a replenishment of portfolio liquidity. Veteran Wall Streeters know that the speculator who risks hundreds of thousands of dollars on his knowledge and instincts usually is far less nervous about conditions than the novice investor who purchases an odd lot of General Electric, and whose pulse quickens when the stock rises or falls by a major fraction in midsession. In addition, the fund managers have access to the best information available, along with the advice of Wall Street stars—whoever they happen to be at any given moment.

Had the novice purchased his shares through a conventional commission house, he would have spoken with a registered representative, whose recommendation of General Electric would have been derived from a report put out by his research arm, or more likely, from his knowledge of the client's needs (psychological as well as financial), the market, and the company. Novices don't ordinarily have accounts at discount brokerages, of course, but if this one did, he would have received no advice at all, and would have had to come to the broker with his ideas already established.

It was quite a different situation for institutional clients, especially prior to the advent of negotiated commission rates. As indicated, the institutional client who purchased ten thousand shares of G.E. had to pay the same commission per share as the small investor out to add a few hundred shares to his portfolio, and the work involved in the large transaction wasn't much greater than that for the small. Brokerages competed with one another for institutional business, which in practice meant seeking ways around the rules. Most would promise to keep large balances in checking accounts at the major banks and trust companies handling the portfolios, accounts which did not bear interest, and which could be used by the financial institutions for profit-making purposes. Some would find roundabout methods of offering the trustees reciprocal business. Of course, the institutional clients would be entertained lavishly; for example they might be guests at an investment seminar—held in Bermuda, with all costs borne by the commission house.

More than a few institutional clients felt somewhat uneasy regarding this kind of deal, even though it was not dishonest or unethical in and of itself. No one could criticize special handling of institutional clients in the area of research, however, and this was the most important form of reciprocity. Was the client interested in the potential of General Electric? The commission house would have its top electronics and consumer goods analysts draw up a report on the stock, and then go to the client's offices to make a personal presentation. Was the customer concerned with the implications of foreign currency transactions on the prospects of a security in his portfolio? The commission house might ask a former Treasury Department bureau chief to analyze the situation and make his report to the client. In other words, institutional investors had the advantage of special handling, special analysis, and in some cases, inside information.

All of this still goes on today, but with the added kicker of negotiated rates. The client in search of a large block of General Electric might compare net prices at several commission houses prior to making his choice, and in addition receive much in the way of special treatment. Taken together, this makes large block transactions far less profitable on a unit basis than previously had been the case. But the business is growing, and so profits are rising in the aggregate.

One might imagine that this situation would enable the funds to outperform the novice investor. There is no evidence that this is so. In fact, there are signs that the small investor has become more sophisticated—or perhaps has hit a streak of dumb luck—in recent years. He

had sold prior to large declines (such as in 1972) and reentered the
market just before rises (in 1974 and 1975). Meanwhile, the large
trusts remained in the market throughout, their portfolios undergoing
remarkably few changes.

In part this was due to their sizes. The manager of a large union
trust fund, worth about a billion dollars, might decide that the fund
was overinvested in glamour issues, and want to unload such stocks as
I.B.M., Burroughs, Coca-Cola, and Xerox, to the tune of $200 mil-
lion worth of paper. If this were all there was to it, the manager might
accomplish the task in two or three weeks, without upsetting the markets in these stocks. The lemming effect would be at work, however—
other fund managers would have had the same idea, and would be in
the market on the sell side on these securities. Thus, the propitious
time to have sold Coca-Cola may have been in February, but the fund
might not have been able to liquidate its position until July—when the
price could be much lower.

Some institutional managers have tried to eliminate this problem
by turning over portions of their funds to different individuals. A $1
billion pension fund might then be managed by ten people, each
charged with $100 million. Initially this may seem a good idea, but
what it really means is that ten people might be selling Coca-Cola (and
in competition with one another) but in smaller blocks, or it could be
that half the managers take an opposite view, and could be buying
from those who are dumping, thus generating commissions but with
no net change for the whole. It is as though a person decided he could
not eat an entire pie, and so sliced it into ten portions and then tried to
consume it. In the end, it's the same pie.

The difficulties faced by managers and trustees of large pension
funds and trust accounts are enormous, their power potentially great,
and their impacts upon the securities complex shattering. Almost all
readers of financial pages are aware of the role played by institutional
investors, yet most do not make the connection between them and the
retirement plan where they work. Probably this is so because the plan
was obtained for the worker by his union, and news of its operation
cannot be found in the papers. It might be different if the individual
worker had the right to select from among several managers of pension
plans, or if he could opt for one of many ongoing plans. Performance

records would have to be made available, and the workers could trace them and read of investment philosophies and objectives. Probably only a small minority of workers would take the trouble to do all the work necessary to make an informed judgment, but the requirement and option would suffice to keep the managers skittish, and provide them with a stronger sense of public awareness than they demonstrate at present.

Right now, managers are hired by trustees, and they keep their jobs as long as their records are respectable and their personal contacts are intact. Trustees also seek out well-established trust departments of major banks—after all, no matter what the performance, a trustee could not be faulted for placing funds with Morgan or Citibank. Until some drastic alteration is made, the clubby atmosphere surrounding the management of pension and trust funds of various kinds will remain intact. Additional money will flow into accounts each month, will be invested, and the performances will not be monitored as carefully as they should be.* In other words, in order for pension funds and their managers to be more responsible they would have to come to resemble mutual funds.

There is an old cliche to the effect that mutual funds are sold, and not bought, and a generation ago their performance wasn't as important as the size of their sales force. Along the Street and throughout the nation, mutuals were known as the vehicles by which many little guys made their first contact with the market. Hundreds of thousands of salesmen, most working on a part-time basis, or viewing the funds as a sideline, entered the field, and they urged novices to buy their share of the nation's future through front-end load funds. These salesmen had the persistence of life insurance agents, but for the most part lacked their training, knowledge, and experience. In the 1950s they sold fund shares to individuals who had never been in the market

* Market analyst and *Forbes* columnist Heinz Biel long has criticized the work of trustees. He has noted that a major West Virginia bank with a $200 million trust portfolio once advertised for a person to manage 350 accounts worth $70 million or so. In addition, the manager "may also manage common trust funds." The requirements? "2–3 years of trust experience," for which he would have a job "with minimum supervision and decision-making freedom." As Biel put it, "When a bank promises minimum supervision to a man with minimum experience, it is best to go elsewhere." *Forbes*, August 15, 1976, p. 93.

before—an entire generation of investors was lost in the 1930s and 1940s—promising them outstanding performance and safety. The market was rising in the Eisenhower years, and in some cases those who purchased shares did quite well. However, many never made up the load factor on their funds, which usually was over 8 percent, and they dropped out, embittered by the experience, or intent upon purchasing shares directly, and not through the funds.

Meanwhile, the salesmen did their jobs well. In 1950 there were fewer than one hundred mutual funds, less than a million accounts, with assets of $2.5 billion. The industry peaked in the early 1970s, when there were more than 400 funds, 11 million accounts, and $60 billion in assets. Then the funds were hit by redemptions, while the industry struggled to keep pace by offering new forms of funds with differing objectives. At the end of 1976 there were over 500 of them, but their net assets were down to $50 billion.

Prior to the 1969 decline, it had appeared that mutual funds would become the major source of institutional power on the Street. The industry had been on a hot streak—the number of accounts had doubled in the 1960s, while assets had tripled. Fred Carr of the Enterprise Fund was deemed the wonder man of the district. That year his mutual racked up close to $600 million in sales, and Enterprise had become a billion dollar giant. It is different today. Carr no longer is at Enterprise, and the fund's assets are down by 80 percent.

Depending upon how the term is defined, mutual funds originated in Greece during the pre-Christian era, in Belgium in the early nineteenth century, in Scotland in the mid-century, in Britain soon after, or in the United States at almost any time in the nineteenth or early twentieth centuries. Greek merchants in the time of Pericles pooled their assets in risk-taking ventures which had a limited life, and some informal organizations continued on for several years. In 1822, William I of the Netherlands established the Société Générale des Pays-Bas "pur favoriser l'industrie nationale." This was a fund to which private investors subscribed, which was supposed to develop the Belgian economy. Scots investment trusts took shares not only in British companies, but overseas ones as well. The American cattle industry was bankrolled to a large extent by Scottish-American Investment Company, Scottish-American Mortgage, Matador Land and Cattle, Prairie Cattle, and similar trusts. Soon after a group of London bankers organized Foreign and Colonial Government Trust, while others incorporated Government Stock Investment Company, American Investment Trust, Municipal Trust, and many more. As their names indicate, most were invested in government paper, some stocks and bonds, and American shares, with the railroads taking most of the play.

Some historians believe the first American investment trust to have been organized by the Massachusetts Hospital Life Insurance Company in the early nineteenth century. Little is known of this small fund, but given the nature of investment practices at the time and the securities available, it must have concentrated upon government paper, with perhaps minor forays into canal and railroad securities.

Other, similar trusts followed, with few leaving more than a faint trace upon the record. The vast majority of Americans had little interest in such paper. The European middle classes may have placed some of their surplus funds into railroad and industrial securities; the Americans preferred to buy land directly or with a mortgage, or to control their own businesses. When they did turn to paper in the early 1860s, the investments were due to a combination of patriotism, the promise of good returns, and safety.

The rise of a national market for railroad securities, together with several speculative manias that intrigued middle-class individuals, resulted in the creation of mutual investment funds in the post–Civil War period. The New York Trust, formed in 1889, was patterned after the Scots operations, and may have been started by émigrés from Dundee and Aberdeen. The Boston Personal Property Trust, organized in 1893 when that city had the nation's largest market for industrial securities, began with an initial capital of $100,000, and was designed for those Brahmins who wanted to take a plunge into that area of investment. Others followed, with almost all of the trusts small, managed by bankers, and located in Boston, New York, or Philadelphia.

Those who purchased shares in these trusts did so in hope of capital gains distributions. None of the pre–World War I funds was listed on any stock exchange, none offered shares on a continual basis, and as far as can be determined, they were not bought or sold actively on the Over-the-Counter market. Families and friends owned shares in the same trust; these were not for most investors.

This situation changed drastically in the 1920s, when the boom attracted hundreds of thousands of newcomers to Wall Street. It was the decade of the hot tip, the insider, and the manipulator. Most novices realized that they lacked access to all three. What was needed was an manager with a good reputation, who would sell shares in an investment trust, use the funds to make wise speculations, and then shower the capital gains upon the shareholders after deducting his fee. Several funds of this type were organized—United States & Foreign Securities, Goldman Sachs Trading Corporation, Tri-Continental, United Founders, and Lehman Corporation were among the most prominent. All were highly leveraged and offered to the public with great fanfare. Their prices quickly rose to a premium—which means they sold for above the net asset value of their underlying securities. In early 1929, these trusts had assets of over $1.5 billion, and market values far in excess of that figure. Then came the crash, and all fell in value, with some declaring bankruptcy. By 1931, those that remained sold at discounts. Such is the situation today with those trusts, which are known as closed-end funds.

The closed-ends are not currently much of a factor in the market. Tri-Continental, which is the largest of them, had less than $600 million in assets at the end of 1976, while Lehman Corporation, in second place, was slightly above the half billion mark. Like the others, they can be purchased for a substantial discount from their net asset values, usually over 25 percent. Some investors consider the closed-ends a bargain for this reason; the owner of Madison Fund, for example, can have five dollars in assets working for him for every four dollars he pays for shares. If the gap is closed—should Madison, Lehman and the others rise to their underlying prices—the owners would do quite well. But the gap rarely has been closed for any of them. Yet it could be, and with relative ease. All the closed-ends would have to do in order to accomplish this would be to amend their charters and transform themselves into open-ends—mutual funds.

The Massachusetts Investment Trust, the first of the modern mutual funds, was founded in 1924. M.I.T. differed from closed-end trusts in that it was not leveraged, and owners of shares could redeem them at net asset value. One purchased M.I.T. through its salesmen, and not at a commission house, so from the first a commitment to mutuals appeared to have more in common with life insurance than with speculation in securities. Management records could be discovered on a daily basis through reference to net asset values, and not the quotations afforded the securities by the give and take on the N.Y.S.E. floor. Initially these factors worked against the mutuals—very conservative investors still preferred insurance, while those seeking professional management with a speculative kicker purchased closed-end trusts. With only a relative handful of funds and shareholders, then, the mutuals did not suffer a stigma when the market collapsed in 1929–33. As was the case with the rest of the securities industry, the mutuals stagnated in the 1930s, when safety was prized above all else, and Wall Street was synonymous with chicanery.

This attitude was altered somewhat by passage of the Investment Company Act of 1940, which placed the industry under federal regulation. At the time there were only sixty-eight funds, with three hundred thousand accounts and assets of below a half billion dollars. But the industry was well-positioned for the boom that arrived a few years later, when for a while mutual funds were the national rage.

Until then, the commission houses and trustees gave little thought to mutuals. In the 1950s, however, they came to realize that the funds could become a serious challenge, and even divert hundreds of thousands of potential clients from direct investments in securities.

The commission houses watched the growth of fund sales forces with no little trepidation. In 1950, for example, Hamilton Management had seventy-six salesmen, and its fund reported assets of $7 million. Five years later, Hamilton's fund had $31 million in assets, and shares were being sold by over 600 representatives. In 1961, the sales force was up to 7,800, most of them part-time, and the fund had $271 million under management.

These salesmen and those who worked for other funds received most of their income from commissions, which came out of the load charged the clients. In this respect their remuneration was earned in much the same way as was that of insurance salesmen or Fuller Brush men. Like them, the mutual fund salesman would visit the client in his

home or office, use the hard sell, and in that period, showed little inclination to stick to the facts when pushing shares on the unwary.
Even then there were some funds which operated on a no-load basis,
with no salesmen. In order to purchase these the client had to contact
the company directly. The no-loads did advertise, but received little of
the play.

The rising trend of fund sales precipitated several responses from
the investment community. Some commission houses entered into arrangements with established funds whereby the registered representatives would offer shares and receive commissions on sales. A few
organized their own mutual funds—even Sears Roebuck and American
Express entered the industry later on—and tried to motivate their
brokers to push them on clients. None of this worked; the load mutuals
continued to grow, with the commission houses remaining on the periphery of the industry. Nor was the N.Y.S.E.'s response much more
successful. In 1954, with great fanfare, President Keith Funston announced the beginning of the Monthly Investment Plan, through which
small investors could purchase listed shares on what amounted to a
plan basis, and do so through their brokers. The M.I.P. fizzled and
sputtered, and recently, quietly, was terminated.

Yet the industry did change, due more to internal pressures and the
growing sophistication of its clients than to any effort on the part of
the brokerages or exchanges. Few of the funds were able to put
together a long string of advances well ahead of the rise of the Dow-
Jones Industrials. A *Forbes* study conducted in 1953 indicated that the
funds, in aggregate, did not do as well as the popular averages, and
two years later *Business Week* ran an article which showed that the
forty-one largest funds had performed only half as well as the Standard
& Poor Index. A wide-ranging study by the Wharton School, commissioned by the House Committee on Interstate and Foreign Commerce,
arrived at the same conclusion. "With respect to the performance of
mutual funds, it was found that on the average it did not differ appreciably from what would have been achieved by an unmanaged portfolio consisting of the same proportions of common stocks, corporate
bonds, government securities, and other assets as the composite portfolios of the funds." The report also criticized sales methods, commissions, and in particular, front-end load plans, under which the client

paid most of the commission on a long-term plan from his early purchases, and so suffered losses should the plan be terminated prior to completion.

These reports and the publicity given to them, combined with the growing sophistication of the new generation of investors, made it more difficult to sell shares in the 1960s than it had been in the 1950s. This is not to say that investors rejected the idea. Rather, they went into no-loads, and toward the end of the decade, speculated with the go-go funds. It took the traumas of 1969–73 to put a lid on growth. Waves of redemptions swept the industry in this period and afterwards, leading to fears that several large and many small organizations would be faced with a liquidity problem: they would not have sufficient cash to redeem shares.

This did not take place. Instead, troubled organizations sought mergers, either with others in their circumstances, or with stronger partners. The industry remained important. Doubtless the number of accounts will grow again, once yet another new generation of investors comes to the Street seeking entry into the investment arena. For the time being, however, this is not a propitious period in which to be a mutual fund salesman.

Some twenty years ago, it appeared that the funds might not only become the major vehicle for individual investment, but in time come to dominate large industrial corporations. An aggressive manager, with several billions of dollars in his fund, might become an important figure on the corporate scene. None of the leading companies in the field—including Wellington Management, T. Rowe Price, and Investors Diversified Services—have aspired to that status and position, and the go-go managers did not have the time or inclination to make the attempt. More important, most owners of mutual fund shares are conservative individuals, and except for the mania months toward the end of the 1960s, did not want glamour or excitement from their investments. Every survey on the subject indicates that preservation of purchasing power and dividends, combined with moderate capital gains, is what they desire. "Capital formation is shifting from the entrepreneur who invests in the future to the pension trustee who invests in the past," wrote Peter Drucker, and so it is with mutual funds. This is what the shareowners want, and for better or worse, what they usually get—

unimaginative, solid portfolios, which tend to move with the popular averages.

What kind of people are we talking about? The typical mutual fund shareowner earns more than $20,000 and less than $50,000 a year, is between the ages of thirty and fifty, and holds at least one college degree. Most are white-collar workers, who own their homes, are married, and have children. Their fund shares will be used to help finance college educations, supplement retirement benefits, and provide additional insurance. In other words, these are long-term investments, made by individuals who lack the interest, the knowledge, or the zeal to follow the financial pages with any degree of regularity. Were it not for the existence of mutual funds, these people would have placed their money into banks and savings and loans, or government bonds. At one time, mutual funds were looked upon as a means whereby novices could make their initial foray into investments in securities. Today they are havens for individuals who do not care that much about finance, and who are, in effect, hiring managers to oversee their investments in stocks and bonds.

In the latter part of the nineteenth century, manipulators and gamblers were the lions of Wall Street. Shortly before the turn of the century investment bankers took over. Syndicate managers were powerful in the 1920s, their exploits covered in tabloids and their power exaggerated by commentators.

Then the institutions took command, but unlike the others, they were less concerned with power than with profit. Contrary to expectations, they did not attempt to direct the affairs of firms in which they held shares. Ownership and direction of these large enterprises remained separate, as a generation of liberal critics had observed. For the most part, the banks, trustees, and funds remained content to clip coupons, collect dividends and seek capital gains. As Drucker and others have remarked, the age of the tycoon and entrepreneur appears to have ended, and that of the bureaucrat to be in full bloom.

These individuals do not seek to control Wall Street, and their unwillingness to assume power has left a gap that no one else could fill. This lack of firm leadership is a major reason why the district's future cannot be predicted, and why it depends more upon the developments of technology than the dealings of power brokers. Still, the institutions do need the market for two reasons. First, trustees and fund managers have to have a place to buy and sell their blocks of shares. Such a market could be strung together from wires and transistors; it need not have a floor, or even a specific geographic location. But it must be a market that can provide liquidity and marketability.

The second reason leads one to believe that that market will have at least one feature common to both the N.Y.S.E. and NASDAQ. It will have posted prices, and at the end of each trading session, provide closing quotes to newspapers.

This may seem a relatively minor point, but it is of vital concern to most institutions. Mutual funds calculate their net asset values each day, and base their bid and ask prices upon it. A sudden flurry of buying in a stock like I.B.M. at a time when few shares are being offered can cause its price to rise three or four points. A majority of the mutual funds and pension accounts have I.B.M. in their portfolios. Each time the stock rises a point, the value of I.B.M.'s paper increases by $150 million. That minor rise could cause the value of a small fund to go from $10.00 a share to $10.05 or so, and could mean a few more cents or dollars per month in pensions. The stock list is a scoreboard, then, upon which money managers can tell who is ahead and who is lagging.*

This hardly conforms to the vision presented by some reformers of a Wall Street controlled by the institutions, banks in particular. That the banks will grow in influence and scope cannot be doubted seriously. They will own property, direct the developments of regions and even countries, and negotiate with potentates as though they themselves were governments. But they are not seeking domination of Wall Street. This is not because they fear conflict with the ancient powers of the district, or even with the government. Rather, the institutions will not take command, because it would not be worth their while to do so.

---

* There always is the danger that the players will attempt to rig the scoreboard. For example, a fund which has a large position in XYZ Corporation might go into the market and buy stock aggressively in order to raise the quote. There is nothing illegal about this, though it is a form of manipulation by some definitions of the term.

CHAPTER TEN

IMAGES

H ALF A CENTURY AGO, at the height of the great bull market, newspapermen would mingle with speculators and brokers in downtown saloons, and reporters would flit in and out of the financial district as a matter of course. For in those days the markets not only were front-page news, but the two communities lived side by side. Park Row, known to locals as Newspaper Row, was a few blocks to the north of Wall Street, across the way from City Hall. Almost all of the major dailies had main offices there. The *Herald Tribune*, the *Evening World*, the *Sun*, the *Times*, the *Evening Telegram*, the *Journal*, and other sheets were within steps of one another, while old-timers recalled the period when several defunct papers—the *Mail & Express*, the *Press*, the *Star*, and the *Recorder*—had offices on the Row. Nearby were other important papers, including the *News*, the *Graphic*, and the *Post*. All had at least one reporter covering Wall Street. It was not looked upon as a prime assignment.

New York had emerged as the preeminent world metropolis at the close of World War I, but most people still thought London retained the central role. New York editors were more interested in local news than national, while international events (excluding wars and the doings of royalty) took third place. Most recalled the time when the city had a small-town flavor, and the newspapers had located themselves close by City Hall to be near their main source of news. That building, and not the N.Y.S.E., was the locus of interest, even while the Exchange was the world's leading securities market. Mayor Jimmy

Walker received more press coverage than did any bull or bear leader.

Further downtown, closer to the financial district, was Dow Jones & Co., publisher of the *Wall Street Journal,* which in that period was a small newspaper whose interests were confined to area events and financial tables. Today the *Journal* is the second largest newspaper in terms of circulation in the United States, and the only one that can truly claim to be national in reach. In the late 1920s, however, it seemed more akin to one of the several neighborhood papers that barely squeaked through in Manhattan.

The 1920s are often considered the silver age of American journalism, when radio had not yet made its major inroads in the news field, television did not exist, and a literate population looked to the papers for information. Millions of Americans read Walter Lippmann, Arthur Krock, and Mark Sullivan, some of the premier political columnists of the day. Franklin P. Adams had a grip on political humor no successor ever equaled. It was the period when Grantland Rice and Ring Lardner were almost as well known as the football and baseball players they covered. H. L. Mencken was a national figure, more important than many politicians. From a small newspaper in the Midwest, William Allen White wrote editorials that had impact in New York and Washington.

This was supposed to be the greatest era in Wall Street history, when it seemed half the nation was in the market with the other half watching the moves as though at a sporting event. Naturally, the district attracted newspaper coverage, and one might have assumed the Wall Street beat to be a prize. After all, the other journalists could tell you what transpired in government or the sports arena; a good financial writer might offer clues to help readers earn money. There was room for a dozen such journalists in the 1920s, and yet there was none—no Lippmann, no Mencken, no Rice. One of the odd aspects of Wall Street and journalism is that they never have combined to produce a national columnist of note.

This is not to say that some of the men who covered the Street in the 1920s were not able, and even outstanding. Rather, they tended to be anonymous. One of the most respected financial journalists of the decade was Alexander Dana Noyes, who in 1920 went to the *Times* from the *Evening Post.* Prior to Noyes, financial columns either were agency handouts or tout pieces. Noyes was the first journalist on a nonbusiness newspaper able to combine economic analysis and a knowledge of the market in such a way as to interest the general reader, and he did it with professional integrity. His column, "The Market Place," contained some of the most perceptive writing on Wall Street ever to appear in the general press. Noyes saw the bull market coming in 1923, and in late 1928 he began warning readers that a decline—perhaps a collapse—was on the way. His track record was better than that of any other writer in the national press—on almost any subject—and the tone he established for his column remains the standard today. Had Noyes been able and willing to utilize his talents on the sports page or in a political column, he would now be considered a giant of journalism, and his reports would be studied in the journalism schools. However, the wrote for the financial page, and so is unknown except to a handful of old-timers and historians.

Journalism was a haphazard profession—or trade—in the 1890s, when Noyes was a general reporter on the *Post*. Few of his contemporaries had much in the way of academic training. Reporters got their starts in the print shops or worked for a while as newsboys before going upstairs to the editorial offices. A large number of them were failed teachers, actors, or ministers, and their capacity for alcohol appears to have been prodigious. Most stories involved straight reporting—the accumulation of material on who, what, when, where, and how the event happened—and/or gossip. The political reporter did not have to have a deep knowledge of the political system in order to ferret out corruption in City Hall, or to write glowingly of a mayor who slipped him a few dollars or cases of booze. The Wall Street articles of the time reflected the reporters' preparation and interests. One could learn of prices and movements by scanning financial pages, and perhaps read of the gossip along the Street. But economic analysis was a rare commodity. When this was desired the reporter would peruse some columns by Walter Bagehot in the London *Economist* and try to paraphrase them for an American audience. When Wall Street followed the lead of Lombard Street and few Americans knew of Bagehot, this was not only proper, but expected.

In 1896, Noyes wrote a short pamphlet opposing William Jennings Bryan's money policies. Horace White, editor of the *Post*, had known of Noyes' interest in finance, but did not know that the young reporter was capable of such a closely reasoned essay. Noyes was called in, given a raise, and assigned to Wall Street. Every Sunday he would write a long analytical piece, while during the week Noyes contributed the usual why-where-when-how articles. This gave him plenty of time to send articles to magazines—including Harvard's *Journal of Economics*—and write several well-reviewed financial histories, which resulted in his transfer to the *Times*, which Adolph Ochs had succeeded in transforming into a sober, responsible, but somewhat dull newspaper. Noyes began "The Market Place" at the *Times*, and in addition was named to the editorial staff.

Noyes quickly became the American counterpart of Walter Bagehot, which is to say that he was read by serious students of the market and had a trans-Atlantic audience. This was an amateur's market, however, a game more akin to football or baseball than investment or even speculation in the old sense of the terms. Newspaper readers in the 1920s wanted tips from touts, and not economic analysis and lessons in finance. The newspapers were willing to provide rumor columns, assigning some of their most exciting writers to the district. All knew where Wall Street was located, but few understood what went on there. But they did understand sports, realized most new speculators wanted to place wagers, and wrote accordingly.

There was a difference in predicting a Yankee victory over the Giants in a World Series and an upward move in RCA. The reporter was in no position to influence the outcome of the baseball game, but if speculators acted upon his advice and predictions, they could influence the way RCA and other securities moved. (Jay Gould and his fellow Wall Street speculators had purchased New York newspapers in the late nineteenth century for just that purpose.) Syndicate managers appreciated the situation too, and several of them worked out deals with leading financial journalists. In return for payments—usually a few hundred dollars—the newspapermen would print favorable or unfavorable stories regarding specific stocks. No one need find out, said the managers. After all, if the columnist touted XYZ and the stock doubled, those readers who bought the security would be overjoyed, the editor would beam at his resident genius, and the syndicate manager would have cleaned up. It wasn't as though there would be losers;

in such an arrangement, all would win, or so it appeared prior to 1929.

Some of the most important and best known journalists, at virtually all the New York papers, were on the take. Raleigh T. Curtis of the *News* received $500 to tout a stock, and several thousands for a full-scale campaign. Stanley Prenosil, the well-known financial editor of the Associated Press, worked for and with several major syndicate managers, his items praising their stocks appearing in newspapers throughout the country. Others who accepted payoffs were William White (the *Evening Post*), W. J. Gomber and Richard Edmondson (both of the *Wall Street Journal*), Charles Storm (the *American*) and F. J. Lowther of the *Herald Tribune*. Several *Times* reporters took money for stories, including Colonel W. F. Wamsley, the financial news editor.

All of these men and others who accepted bribes left their newspapers in the early 1930s, but some reappeared on different sheets, while many received posts at brokerages they had worked for (without advertising the fact) in the previous decade.

Financial journalism in the 1930s was what it had been prior to the great bull market—the refuge for unwanted and uninterested—and usually inept—men and a few women. With the exception of Noyes, who was close to retirement, and Leslie Gould of the *Journal-American,* who was an informed and intelligent—though at times erratic as well—muckraker, almost all were bland, mediocre, and unsophisticated in the ways of finance. Given time and application, some of them did a creditable job, but the field was filled with journeymen, and no masters.

The corruptionists were gone; the scandals and the poverty of the Street took care of that. Reformers saw no need to flay such a dead horse, and so turned elsewhere for interest. Some newspapers had difficulty in finding even barely qualified reporters and columnists, and so turned to academics and retired brokers, who became transformed into journalists. The former had no taste, training, or time for legwork, while the latter concentrated upon digesting and spewing out brokerage house releases issued by old cronies. If Wall Street had appeared glamorous in the 1920s and corrupt in the early 1930s, the place seemed faded and outmoded by mid-decade. Certainly it was no place for a young reporter out to make a mark.

By then, too, Park Row was being transformed into a neighborhood of small shops and marginal factories. Most of the newspapers either merged with one another and moved uptown or simply went out of business. The speakeasies and restaurants where newsmen mingled with speculators closed down, since both clientele and prohibition were gone. Some converted into dry goods stores, pet shops, or hobby centers—Nassau Street became the center for the city's tropical fish fanciers and stamp collectors. The *World* was the last to go, folding in 1931, with what was left merging into the *Evening Telegram*. The new *World Telegram* moved uptown, to join the *Sun, Times, Herald Tribune,* and soon-to-be created *Journal American*. All that remained was the old building, which soon thereafter was sold to Pace College, then a business school catering to accountants and others who might be interested in Wall Street careers. The brokers and bankers on Wall Street did not mind the change, perhaps because they found they had more in common with the eager neophyte businessmen than with the reporters, most of whom barely masked their dislike for what went on at the commission houses, banks, and exchanges.

Journalism as a profession and most newspapermen individually cannot be said to be well-disposed toward banking and securities-based capitalism. This is to put it carefully and cautiously, for such generalizations cannot be proven in any scientific fashion, but must be based upon reactions over a long period of time to the way financial news is handled. Reporters and columnists are supposed to allow the evidence to dictate the conclusions, but in practice they bring to their work a sincerely felt disposition for or against big business, and more often than not it was the latter.

All professions have some of the attributes of ethnic groups, including a special language, traditions, values, ethics, and historic dislikes and fears. One of the hallmarks of journalism today is skepticism, especially toward those in positions of great power. Newsmen either have this attitude when they get their first jobs, or adopt it by following the models all around them. Reputations in the field come from attacking the mighty and defending the weak, no matter what the virtues of the former and the defects of the latter. Often such a stance serves the interests of the public as well as that of the newspaper, but only so long as coverage is not marred by prejudices and irrational hates, often born of ignorance.

The earliest American newspapers were decidedly pro-business. In fact, they arose from the need of business to have commercial information, and actually performed as adjuncts of enterprises. Did the importer need facts regarding shipping and prices? He would find it in newspapers. Did he want to inform potential clients of his wares? He would advertise in the same journal.

The situation changed in the 1830s and 1840s, with the development of Jacksonian Democracy—a reform movement which on its face at least opposed "special interests"—and the appearance of the penny press, independent newspapers which relied upon large circulations rather than business favors for their existence. Reform was in the air, and reform journalism became the vogue, even among conservative publishers and editors.

James Gordon Bennett, the owner, publisher, and editor of the *New York Herald,* was one of these. A staunch Democrat who admired the cotton South and despised the commercial Whig aristocracy of the North, he considered the "paper-changers" of Wall Street little better than criminals. While others sweated to produce goods that could be seen and used, the speculators and brokers sat in offices, manipulated securities, and made fortunes from their meager efforts. In 1837, Bennett announced his newspaper would institute a financial column. He assigned young Jay Cooke to the Wall Street beat, where he not only unmasked manipulations, but learned the craft of investment banking from experts. "Until this epoch of the world the daily newspaper press has been a mere organ of dry detail—uninteresting facts—political nonsense—personal squabbles—obsolete rows—tedious ship news—or dry quotations of the market. I have changed all of this," wrote Bennett, and he promised readers that he would demonstrate how Wall Street ran the country, and was trying to manipulate the North into a war against the South.

The other New York newspapers followed Bennett's lead in assigning at least one reporter to cover Wall Street, though few were able or willing to match his verve and interest in the subject. Bennett would go to the Street himself, when his reporters proved unable to uncover chicanery, and try to ferret out news. Bankers claimed he manufactured scandal when none was to be found, and on several occasions he was waylayed by brokers, and fistfights occurred, which Bennett related with gusto on the editorial page the following day.

The tradition of sensationalist muckraking established by Bennett and imitated by others in the 1840s and 1850s continued in the post–Civil War period. America seemed on its way to becoming a business civilization, with Wall Street as its heart. This also was the beginning of the most corrupt period in national, state, and municipal history. It was a great time to be a journalist, especially in New York. The city's papers were read from coast to coast, this made possible by cheap postal rates. *The Herald,* the *Times,* the *Tribune,* and lesser sheets were located across the way from Boss Tweed's City Hall and a Wall Street controlled by such pirates as Commodore Vanderbilt, Jay Gould, Jim Fisk, and Daniel Drew. The front pages of newspapers in Chicago and Cincinnati contained stories of what was happening within a few steps of Park Row. Reporters and editors saw the scandals close up, and brushed past the leading protagonists while walking to work or having lunch.

There was a financial panic in 1873, made possible by manipulations on the Street and compounded by political corruption. Then followed close to a quarter of a century of depression-recession, broken by only a few years of recovery. Farmers were in despair, and workers received inadequate wages, while it appeared that business leaders were rising to new heights in Washington and New York. A group of publisher—editors, led by William Randolph Hearst and Joseph Pulitzer, unmasked the Wall Street–Washington nexus, and showed how it reached into City Hall and Albany as well. A generation of writers and intellectuals, disgusted by venality and corruption, abandoned politics for a while, and when they returned asked little more than honesty and decency from leaders rather than programs and policies. To them, too, Wall Street was the origin of much of the country's ailments. Under Pulitzer and other journalists, they became newspapermen, and they continued their anti–Wall Street crusades from the editorial pages of leading journals.

The cynical attitude so many reporters had toward the Street in the late nineteenth century was created and reinforced by this combination of factors. Even after the return of prosperity in the late 1890s and close to two decades of liberal reformism and crusade, the financial district appeared the prime instigator of national malaise. By the end of World War I, however, J. P. Morgan and his crew were gone, to be replaced by lesser men and worse symbols. The overwhelming majority of Americans rejected liberalism and crusades, while Wall Street seemed to have been transformed from the arena for giants to the playground for small investors. The same reporters who had castigated the manipulators of 1910 made heroes of the syndicate managers of the 1920s. Morgan had seemed rapacious, willing to destroy his rivals in a quest for power. Jesse Livermore, on the other hand, only wanted money, and the cynical reporters could understand this. In a battle with fellow manipulator Arthur Cutten, some investor-speculators would bet on him, while others pinned their hopes on Cutten. Then the contest—say, to manipulate the price of RCA—began, with the winner taking the chips. What was so sinister about that? In some respects it was no different from the World Series or the Rose Bowl, and reporters treated the contest accordingly. It was as though they had suspended political and economic judgment—and professional ethics— and turned finance into a game rather than a serious matter for national concern. It may have been this combination of cynicism tempered with self-deception that encouraged some journalists to enter the game themselves, by cooperating with the manipulators in order to lay down a bet of their own. Sports writers did the same, in accepting gifts and entertainment from club owners, for which they had been expected to write favorably of the team. If the sports writer could be a quasi– public relations man for the New York Yankees, why could not a finance reporter do the same for Cutten or Livermore?

Just as Spiro Agnew and others argued that they were the victims of a "new morality" after Watergate, so some of the finance writers who were ejected from their jobs in 1932–34 felt little guilt or remorse. Finance in general and Wall Street in particular still made the front pages, but the stories were now written by political reporters, as New Dealers investigated the Street and succeeded in making it the scapegoat for the depression. Once again liberalism was in vogue, and it was fashionable to be antibusiness. The muckrakers returned in the early 1930s, and found more than enough to keep themselves occupied for the rest of the decade.

There was no revival of interest in finance during or after World War II. Most newspapers did not have financial reporters on their staffs, and relied upon the wire services for whatever news came out of lower Manhattan. The financial page of the larger big-city newspapers became known as a dead end, and was avoided by ambitious young journalists, who yearned for foreign assignments and political reportage. One might have thought this would change with the arrival of the bull market of the early 1950s, but such was not the case. Instead, the level of financial journalism in general-interest newspapers remained low throughout the decade and afterwards. Many newspapers with over five hundred thousand circulation had no financial page at all, much less a financial section. Instead, they would print wire service releases and let it go at that.

The situation is not much different today. There are several reasons for this lack of coverage and the poor quality of much that does get into print. Absence of reader interest is not one of them. Given the number of shareholders, the opposite should be the case. Publishers and editors apparently assume these people will subscribe to the *Wall Street Journal,* to get needed information, and they may be right. In fact, the lack of financial news in most newspapers is a significant reason for the nationwide popularity the *Journal* enjoys.

One reason for this gap is a matter of space and cost. For a morning tabloid to run complete N.Y.S.E. and Amex tables, and no more than that, would require at least five pages. Add three or four pages of columns and news stories and the paper would have a respectable financial section—in which finance space would be equal to that of local and national news coverage, with a horoscope thrown in for good measure. Editors could not countenance such a use of space, especially when they considered how the tables would be used. No single reader would want to go through all the statistics. The owner of a round lot of General Motors and a dozen shares of I.B.M. might need only a few numbers on the five pages and not even glance at the rest. So the tabloids couldn't afford to run tables. Without them, they lost many readers interested in finance, and the next step was simple enough: if you don't have financially oriented readers, you don't need finance columnists. So morning tabloids—which increased in number after World War II—couldn't be counted upon to cover the Street in an adequate fashion.*

* Some morning and evening tabloids recognized the problem, and tried to serve readers by offering closing quotes over the telephone. Readers were invited to call the newspa-

The general level and direction of economic education and sophistication in the United States is a second factor. At one time, prior to the war, economics tended to be historical in nature, which is to say that college classes were concerned with the origins, rise, development, and present structure and workings of such entities as organized labor, the corporations, specific industries, the financial apparatus, and the like. Students learned of the interplay between societal forces, individuals, and these institutions. One could emerge from a course of study with a general idea of the nature of the electrical industry, for example, its problems and potential, along with an appreciation of how funds are raised. In a way, the student learned some of the material of fundamental analysis.

In time, such a person might be attracted to the market to buy one hundred shares of General Electric or Westinghouse. Certainly he was well-equipped to read financial commentaries in newspapers, and in fact might have been encouraged to enter financial journalism itself.

After World War II many economists tried to transform their discipline into a science, doing so by introducing quantification wherever possible. The development of the computer aided in their efforts. Instead of investigating the electrical industry, the student would be introduced to national income analysis through the study of several mathematical models. In fact model making in its many forms tended to replace the study of institutions. After a while, students became aware that in order to rise above the basic level in the discipline they would have to acquire mathematical skills, up to and including calculus.

The number of students enrolled in economics courses increased substantially, as the nation's businesses and governments demanded more economists to fill important and well-paying jobs. But these new professionals were technicians and theoreticians, to whom the information and approach of the economic historians were not only alien, but irrelevant. They had learned theories of capital formation, but were unsure as to the actual workings of the Federal Reserve, commercial and investment banks, and other parts of the financial district. This is not

per to obtain the prices of their stocks, which were given to them by clerks from the Dow Jones ticker. But most of these services were short-lived. They provided no income, and apparently the goodwill was not worth the cost.

to say that the economists themselves could not read a well-written financial column. Rather, there was little in their approach to prepare their students for an appreciation of such matters, or to stimulate interest.* Thus, the nation was in the paradoxical position of having more trained economists than ever before, with more students in courses than at previous times, but students whose knowledge of finance—and interest in seeing financial reportage in newspapers—was on the decline.

The third factor is the increasing complexity of the district, and the rapid alterations in its structure over the past decade. This is quite a change from the days of James Gordon Bennett, who in following the manipulations of a handful of tycoons was able to report upon the district as a whole—since Wall Street was a small community at the time, with only limited power and that more regional than national. In the era of Morgan and Schiff, journalists could concentrate upon colorful giants, through whose activities one could understand happenings at the markets as well as the banks and trust companies. One of the major failures of finance journalism in the 1920s—in addition to the venality and ignorance of reporters—was the attempt to portray syndicate managers as the new Morgans and Schiffs. Had the journalists tried to understand the workings of the Federal Reserve and the role of the commercial bankers, they might have anticipated the 1929 collapse and its aftermath. As it was, the vast majority of reporters and columnists had no clear idea of the meaning of the panic and its economic causes.

A similar situation existed in the 1960s, when it appeared the market had torn loose from its traditional moorings and was headed into the stratosphere. Beginning in 1964 and 1965, several financial publications—the *Wall Street Journal* and *Barron's* in particular—began running stories of tricky bookkeeping, manipulations, and

* One need only compare the treatment of banks in any basic college text to that in a trade book like *The Bankers*, by Martin Mayer. College text writers know of banks through theoretical tomes. Mayer, who is not a banker or even an economist, approached his subject with few preconceptions, and insisted upon learning it from the ground up—and writing his book in the same way. The result was a work in institutional economics (though to have called it that would have killed sales) which instructed many thousands of students (and their professors) on how banks actually worked, in contrast to the theories offered in texts.

unrealistic valuations for common stocks. Neither publication was overly impressed by the "gunslingers," those bright young men who dominated the public's imagination in this period. *Barron's* unmasked chicanery at the Penn Central, National Student Marketing, and other hot situations; Abraham Briloff and Alan Abelson did outstanding work in this area. On occasion one might find well-thought-out pieces in the *Institutional Investor,* a journal which was read by the Street, but could not be obtained by the general public. Myron Kandell, at the time editor-publisher of the *Wall Street Newsletter,* issued several alarms regarding back office problems and capital deficiencies at the commission houses. There even were articles on the subject in *Forbes,* which usually aimed for a more general readership. Little appeared in the *New York Times,* however, though in Robert Metz and Michael Jensen it had two reporters of exceptional ability. There were a handful of old-timers on the regional papers whose analyses of events were clear and forthright, but they were too far from the scene to undertake major investigations. Beyond them was a wasteland. Reporters working for the wire services relied more upon handouts and press releases than on investigative reporting.

All the while, however, coverage of economic matters increased in importance. Eileen Shanahan and Leonard Silk of the *Times* provided daily journalism of a higher level than had ever been seen in American newspapers, and others at the major regional journals also were well-trained and perceptive. They did not cover finance, however, but instead concentrated upon economics, and there is an important difference between the two. Reporters, columnists, and editors who covered economic issues tended to view the "big picture"—and increasingly it came from Washington, not New York. A rise in the unemployment rate, a trade conference, devaluation of the dollar—such items would result in a Shanahan article or a Silk analysis. When placed beside these stories, the growth of options trading, the emergence of a new central market, or even a scandal, seemed weak tea. Today the action is with economics in Washington, and not with finance on Wall Street. Reporters look at it that way and, more to the point, so do editors.

So Wall Street became a relatively easy beat to cover. The reporters there require only a fundamental grounding in economics and finance and contacts at commission houses and exchanges. One can flesh out stories on day-to-day events with a few afternoon telephone calls and an occasional visit to banks and trust companies. Editors aren't too demanding when it comes to financial news, perhaps because they lack an understanding of the subject and interest in the area.* Covering Wall Street happenings is as close to having a part-time job for a full-time salary as exists in modern American journalism.

This helps explain why newspapers missed the big stories of 1969 (always excluding the *Wall Street Journal* and, on occasion, the *Times* from the indictment). Even now, financial reporters have difficulty conveying complexities regarding currency rates, the options markets, and commodities to their readers. Outside of New York, few journalists have considered the relationship of Wall Street to City Hall in New York's financial crisis. Not until Felix Rohatyn appeared as the emissary of Wall Street to the Mayor's office did the journalists perk up. They had difficulties understanding the whys if not the wherefores of municipal tax-free bonds, or the importance of the financial center to the city's health, and other related factors. Give them a glamorous mystery man, however, and the reporters could function. So they did, distorting the story by transforming it into a chronicle of the machinations of Rohatyn and his fellows. Similarly, the conflict between the N.Y.S.E. and the Third Market was presented as a clash between the

---

* Chris Welles, formerly of *Institutional Investor* and now the leading free-lancer in the field, has written of what he calls "The Bleak Wasteland of Financial Journalism" in the July/August, 1973 issue of the *Columbia Journalism Review.* Welles illustrates his point by quoting Richard Harwood, assistant managing editor of the *Washington Post,* certainly one of the nation's leading newspapers and one proud of its record in investigative reporting. Harwood was asked why his paper gave more coverage to sports than to finance. "I guess it is because we think sports is more interesting to readers than business and economics. I know it is to me." The *Post,* and other Washington newspapers, afford little coverage to economic and financial news, even when it breaks in the Capitol or the White House. On such occasions, the story is assigned to a top-notch reporter, whose background more often than not is in politics rather than economics, while analysis is limited to columnists and short editorials. One hardly would assign Woodward and Bernstein to cover the economic intricacies of the Penn Central collapse or the Equity Funding scandal. As intelligent and persistent as these reporters are, they would need a year or so in business school before understanding the lay of the land. And even had they managed to find a Deep Throat within the Penn Central, would the story truly interest the readership?

Old Guard—the Club—and brash young upstarts who wanted to bring Wall Street up to date, and sweep away past privilege and abuse. Here too the personal symbolism worked. The N.Y.S.E.'s James Needham—stocky, a trifle ponderous, dark of visage, with a poor sense of humor—was pitted against Don Weeden—athletic, bearded, witty, and mercurial. Reporters were able to write stories about personalities, but the complexities of the issues usually eluded them.

Finally, there remains a culture gap between reporters and financiers that is difficult to bridge. Ever since the 1929 crash, leading Wall Streeters have mistrusted the press, feeling that a large majority of reporters are antibusiness by instinct, breeding, and training. For their part, reporters tend to view the district as being stocked with mediocre people getting far more money than they deserve, shallow individuals who have no interests outside of money grubbing, and manipulators out to grab the main chance. Most reporters are middle class in terms of the way they live and view the world. Their wives more often than not hold jobs and belong to the P.T.A. They own station wagons and live in three-bedroom houses in the suburbs. A seasoned reporter may make $25,000 a year, a good salary but hardly extravagant by Wall Street standards.

Reporters know the earnings capacities of the people they cover. A young bond trader, barely out of graduate school, receives as much money as a veteran reporter. Some analysts, whom the reporters consider dull-witted, though capable of providing quotes on the market's actions, may be in the $70,000 class, while hotshot brokers possessing the glibness of sideshow barkers take home $100,000 and more. In one deal, Felix Rohatyn can earn more than a reporter does in a few years.

Are the journalists resentful? Some are, of course, while a handful are impressed and the rest wonder about the nature of reward in a capitalist system. It shows in their writing.

Thus, a reporter may first learn of trouble at the Penn Central by reading about it in the *Wall Street Journal*. Yet he knows almost nothing of railroading, cannot read the annual report with any great degree of sophistication, and is at a loss as to what to write. So he ignores the subject initially, or offers rehashes of the *Journal* article, or tries to find some friend in academia who can help out with a crash course in the subject. After a while, when the story breaks, he covers it as though it was a political news event. The reporter describes and does not analyze, and so his readers are at a loss when it comes to understanding what has transpired. If the newspaper is large enough, it may commission an article for the Sunday supplement. Or if it is in the giant class—the *Times*, for example—there could be a series of articles by special reporters later on as well.

Where is the interested reader to find information on the present workings of the Street, and how can he learn why the marketeers behave the way they do? Daily journalism is not the answer, and most readers lack access to insider publications. *Business Week* provides material for students of the market, but only after the facts had been sketched by the daily press; like *Newsweek* and *Time*, it does not engage in investigative reporting.

Perhaps it is this combination of complexity and attitude which has led the newspapers to play down financial news. Whatever the reason, aggressive and intelligent business journalists who cannot find an opening at the Dow Jones organization or the *New York Times*, and who are not interested in magazine work as a full-time career, often leave journalism completely; it is far better for them to do so than to write two-hundred-word market summaries for a local newspaper, a job that both stultifies the imagination and damages one's self-esteem. Several excellent journalists are in the field today, but as free-lancers, and not assigned to any single newspaper or other news organization.

John Brooks is the best known of these free-lancers, and is, perhaps, the only writer of business books and articles with a large and assured readership of nonprofessionals. At one time, Brooks had aspirations as a novelist, but his early efforts were not well received, and so he turned to magazine journalism. Some of his short pieces were accepted by the *New Yorker*. Longer ones followed, and he soon had a fairly secure market for his work.

It was the early 1950s, when Wall Street was heating up and the new bull market was underway. The *New Yorker* had a traditional interest in the district, dating back to the 1930s, when Matthew Josephson contributed essays on speculators and the nature of the collapsed market. Now Brooks went to the district seeking the same kinds of stories. Unlike Josephson, he had little in the way of a business background, and as a novelist he was more interested in people than in their institutions. Some of these articles were collected into a book in 1958, entitled *The Seven Fat Years*. It deals with such individuals as David Jackson, an Amex specialist, Robert Young (who was in the midst of a proxy fight for the New York Central), and Hugh Bullock, one of the leaders of the mutual fund industry. The book was a success—as were the articles from which it was drawn—and Brooks was established as the leading translator of Wall Street to the educated but nonprofessional public. He was perhaps, the most popular regular contributor to the *New Yorker* in the 1960s and after, and his work appeared in other quality magazines as well. Additional books followed, most consisting of collections of articles or rewrites of them in book form. *Once in Golconda,* published in 1969, was concerned with the district in the 1920s and 1930s, with the most effective chapters devoted to Allan Ryan and the Stutz corner, and the rise and fall of Richard Whitney. As before, Brooks was fascinated more with people in business, than with the business itself. *The Go-Go Years,* released in 1973, continued the tradition with chapters on several manipulators of the 1960s, more business adventures, and sketches of prominent Wall Streeters of the time. Brooks went deeper into business organization in this book than he had in the others, however. Toward the end of the work it became clear he looked upon the 1969–70 collapse as an analogue to the 1929 crash. Thus, he repeated a theme first presented in *Once in Golconda,* that the years of excesses had to be paid for in the end. Both books contained elements of Greek drama; the hero's hubris precedes his defeat. Underneath it all, Brooks is a moralist, a man who wants to see good rewarded and evil punished. It shows in his novels, just as it does in his Wall Street essays.

This is both the strength and the flaw in much of his work. No other writer on Wall Street has ever captured character as well as he. If his understanding of institutional structure is not as profound as is that of many academics, he is capable of explaining the functionings of markets and banks more clearly than anyone else. Together with this, there is a tendency to overdramatize events. It might be just and right if the 1960s ended with a crash similar to that of the 1920s and 1929. If this had occurred, the morality play concept would have been intact. But there was no great crash in 1969, and the recession that came a few years later wasn't caused by Wall Street chicanery, but by a collection of factors including the Vietnam War, Federal Reserve policies, shifts in trade patterns, the Eurodollar mess, the price of money, and even an alteration in the spawning habits of certain North Sea fish.

Drama is neater than life, because the writer can manipulate his fictional characters to conform to his view of reality and morality. He cannot do the same for flesh and blood individuals. His experience with fiction has provided Brooks with a dimension lacking in most other important writers on Wall Street topics. It also has gained for him an audience that otherwise would not be interested in reading about the subject. But it also leads at times to simplifications and moralizations. *The Go-Go Years* will be read a half-century from now as the classic account of the market in the 1960s, much as Frederick Lewis Allen's *Only Yesterday* is considered the major work on the 1920s. But readers in the twenty-first century may be drawn to Brooks more for his style and the quality of his mind than for his handling of Wall Street topics.

Chris Welles lacks Brooks' ability to turn a phrase, his psychological insights, his subtlety and flare. Welles cannot evoke the atmosphere and smell of the Street as vividly as does Brooks, or weave as colorful a tapestry. But he does have a deeper knowledge of the complexities of money and banking, a finer appreciation of institutional problems, and a clearer grasp of the minutiae of American finance. Most important, he knows the district better than any other finance writer. Brooks is read on the Street by those who want to discover how the country perceives specific actions. The same people read Welles to find out what is happening, and why. Brooks is viewed as an outsider peering in; Welles is a working journalist. He is a reporter, not a philosopher. And unlike Brooks, Welles can be harsh and deeply critical of what he studies, and is a far more controversial person.*

After graduating from Princeton and working for a while as reporter and business editor at both *Life* and the *Saturday Evening Post,*

* In a television encounter with Richard Ney, the actor-turned broker-turned Wall Street muckraker, who claims to have used new techniques to make profits, Welles asked how well the Ney portfolios performed. Ney replied he had never been asked that question before. Welles was bemused, and he reflected that the lack of such questioning indicated the state of finance journalism today.

Welles became a columnist and editor for *Institutional Investor* and *New York*. In the late 1960s and early 1970s, he became recognized as one of the best of the "new breed" of journalists coming out of *Institutional Investor,* a group that was led by George Goodman—better known to the general public as "Adam Smith," the author of the 1968 best seller, *The Money Game.* Welles was looked upon as a precise writer who, although lacking Goodman's verve and humor, was more adept at illuminating complex problems and setting forth solutions. In this respect, he had become the most respected financial journalist working the area today.

A few years ago, Welles left his regular columns and assignments for free-lancing, and one product of his work was a book, *The Last Days of the Club,* which was released in 1975. As the title indicates, Welles believes the district—and the N.Y.S.E. is particular—is dominated by a Club. At no point does Welles precisely identify the components of this Club.* But he clearly means a community of interests erected upon traditions, supported by veterans who seek to maintain their institutions in the face of what others believe to be an evident need to adapt to new circumstances. In this sense, the N.Y.S.E. does contain a Club, which extends to the investment banking community, to the commercial banks, and in fact to most of the district's financial institutions. For that matter, the club idea can be found in corporations, universities, military establishments, and newspapers and magazines. Every profession and organization has rules, the most important of which are unspoken. All possess leadership cadres that attempt to maintain these rules. And in each there are individuals who want to preserve the *status quo,* some who want to alter it, and even a few who hope to destroy it completely.

Welles' point is that the old order is passing—but so are all organizations, in the sense that they are continually evolving in order to meet new challenges. For example, in the 1920s the N.Y.S.E. had a cartel, created by forcing competitors either to go out of business or submit to

* On the dust jacket of *The Last Days of the Club* is written: "The 'Club' is the membership of the New York Stock Exchange—for 180 years an unbreachable, government-sanctioned monopoly that rolled up enormous profits by insulating itself from competition and charging investors exorbitant fees for executing stock transactions." In the book itself, however, Welles extends Club membership to banks and other financial institutions.

its leadership. Included in the nexus were investment and commercial banks, trust companies, and other financial institutions. The Exchange wasn't central to the system, but it had become an important symbol.

Such was the situation in 1929, when the crash began. Four years later the S.E.C. was on the Street, the Exchange under pressure to write a new constitution, and through various New Deal laws the freedom of the marketplace was circumscribed. Was this the end of the Club? In a way, yes, for the men and institutions had to adapt to the new situation. This they did, and the resulting establishment was an altered Club, the one that Welles believes is collapsing today.

The Street is undergoing another metamorphosis in the 1970s. This time the challenges come from a band of outside brokers united in a Third Market and utilizing a new technology, plus an invigorated S.E.C. They are correct in arguing that should one have to create a market mechanism de novo, it would be erected along the lines of NASDAQ, and not the specialist system. Clearly parts of the N.Y.S.E. way of doing things are obsolete, as are other methods of conducting securities business—including the securities themselves. But one does not build upon level ground when creating a social order or a market. There are old institutions that keep getting in the way. These are not controlled by fools and mossbacks, but rather by intelligent and astute individuals who are at least as able to adapt to change as were their grandfathers when confronted by the New Deal. And they have, coming to terms with negotiated commissions, regional markets, electronic devices, altered membership rules, and all other challenges that came along. The N.Y.S.E. attempted to destroy the competition under James Needham, and when that failed, he was dumped and replaced by William Batten, who is trying to negotiate a settlement and reform the Exchange from within. It may work, but if not, Batten will be ejected and a new man will take his place, perhaps with a mandate to sign a peace treaty with the Third Market, effect a merger, or try some other policy that will enable the men of Welles' Club to continue working on Wall Street. That they will survive seems beyond doubt, even though their methods of conducting business will change. After all, there never has been a revolution on the Street, if by the term one means a radical overthrow of institutions and men and their replacement by new forces. Continuity is a more important element in American finance than is change, more so perhaps than in any other part of big business in this country.

Does this infer that Welles is incorrect in his diagnosis? Not necessarily, for underneath what is a thin veneer of hyperbole is the most complete and intelligent analysis of how the Street functions in the literature. This kind of work has been attempted by others—most recently by Martin Mayer, whose *Wall Street: Men and Money* offers a clear picture of how the district functioned in the mid-1950s. None of his predecessors had Welles' experience and knowledge, and of course none could have written about a more interesting and eventful period.

Welles seems to believe that the old Street is doomed by forces the individuals who work there cannot control. In contrast, Brooks portrays the operations of individuals and shows how they can manipulate the destinies of large enterprises. In Welles, the arrival of computer technology dooms the specialist system; Brooks demonstrates how a series of accidents and happenstances in 1969–70 prevented a crash on the order of 1929. In some respects, it is the old conflict between those who believe in predestination and the others who opt for free will. Welles is engaged in a serious flirtation with the former group, while Brooks, as befits his training in fiction, appears to believe the individual makes history and can alter its direction. Neither writer suffers from monochromic vision; Brooks and Welles do not subscribe to devil theories. It appears evident they have contempt for some Wall Streeters and admiration for others. They view a good many bankers and brokers with amusement, and each appreciates the gamelike quality of much that transpires on lower Broadway. Both are far superior to all but a few journalists working for the daily papers on the Wall Street beat. If there are no Alexander Dana Noyes in financial (again, as opposed to economic) journalism, it is because his type is no longer in demand by newspaper editors and he writes magazine articles and books instead.

Rarely has the district produced a great interpreter of its workings and rationale for the general public—or even for its own members. No major memoir or autobiography has come out of the exchanges, commission houses, or banks. American novelists have produced many books dealing with business and businessmen, and some with bankers. But there is no great Wall Street novel. One might have expected such a book in the 1920s, the great decade of Wall Street. But none appeared. Instead, Sinclair Lewis made his Babbitt a small town real estate salesman, while F. Scott Fitzgerald's Jay Gatsby was a bootlegger. Yet the district was filled with Babbitts and Gatsbys in the 1920s. But not for these and other major American novelists.

Why this occurred is difficult to comprehend, unless one takes the view that many Americans do not understand the paper economy that is centered in lower Manhattan, or if they do, are somehow embarrassed by it all. We can admire a person who creates a large economic empire founded on products—a Ford, an Edison, a Thomas Watson—and eulogize image makers in television and motion pictures. Wall Street, on the other hand, is concerned with the creation, care, and reaping of paper wealth, the direction of paper assets into enterprises—what economists call the allocation of resources. It is an exciting and in some ways romantic enterprise, and certainly is necessary. Welles writes of the death of the Club, but not of its functions, for without them there could be no American capitalism. But this is not how many investors look upon the district. They are interested in the preservation of their funds and their possible appreciation. To the vast majority of Americans, $100 earned by and through the creation of a product or service is honest and admirable, while the same amount of money, received when General Motors common rises a point, is comparable to picking the winner in a horse race. One enjoys the race, and is happy to win, but it really isn't productive, and doesn't add to the general store of goods and services. In this respect, the Street is a place of mystery to those who own shares, while the individuals who work there are too busy and preoccupied with their tasks to attempt to interpret their actions to the public.

Many journalists treat the markets as gigantic versions of the numbers game. Economics writers rarely show the relationships between products and services and the money that makes them possible. Money itself is not clearly understood, even by people who own a good deal of securities.* The public receives images of the Street and

* John K. Galbraith, one of the few economists able to reach a general audience—largely due to his clear writing and sense of humor—has not been conspicuously successful in this regard. One of his most famous books, *The Great Crash, 1929* (1955), does contain a fine description of how the markets and the economy were interrelated a

the reason for its existence but knows little of reality.* This situation is not likely to be altered, no matter what direction the district goes in the coming years.

---

half-century ago, even though some might question his conclusions. But his more recent book, *Money, Whence It Came, Where It Went* (1975), is almost completely silent on the matter, and in this respect at least is a disappointment.

* In early 1977 some of the nation's leading businessmen, academics, and government figures were asked to name the top five financial journalists. The results were published in the April, 1977, issue of *More,* in an article by Steve Robinson entitled "The Best in Business." The top five were: Alan Abelson of *Barron's,* Joseph Livingston of the *Philadelphia Inquirer,* Carol Loomis of *Fortune,* Hobart Rowen of the *Washington Post,* and Leonard Silk of the *New York Times.* That all are distinguished journalists is beyond doubt, but with the exception of Abelson, they do not cover the Wall Street beat today. Loomis has moved on to bigger things at *Fortune;* that magazine's stories dealing with the district are covered by other writers. Silk and Rowen are more interested in national economic problems than with the narrower confines of investment finance capitalism. Livingston writes from Philadelphia, and so is not on the scene most of the time.

Omitted are reporters from the *Wall Street Journal.* Charles Elia and Victor Hillery, to name just two, are financial writers and reporters who might be on such a list if it were confined to that segment of the field. Also, the same issue of *More* carried an article by Chris Welles on the "Problems at *Forbes,*" which demonstrated effectively why he too belongs on the roster.

CODA

_____

WALL STREET used to celebrate the coming of Christmas with a roar. At the turn of the century, specialists would run into the street, make snowballs, and rush back to stuff them down the backs of their fellows. Such horseplay might draw a fine—50¢ levied by an indulgent vice-president. Children from nearby schools and orphan asylums would come to the Exchange to sing Christmas carols and receive presents. The grog shops would offer free hot toddies to brokers preparing for the return trip home. The celebration might last for a week—in a good year. And after trading stopped in the final session prior to New Year's Eve, brokers and specialists would go to the windows and throw dollar bills and coins to onlookers.

In 1976, Wall Street celebrated the Christmas season with a round of office parties. Departments at most brokerages had their usual uninspired catered affairs, mostly cold cuts and booze. Partners filtered in and out of the rooms to congratulate big producers and nod at the lesser fry. It had been a good year for the Street, with the Dow Industrials up close to 18 percent, but the partners complained that negotiated commissions had cut deeply into profits. There were not a great number of bonuses in 1976—at least, not as many as in the glory years of the mid-1960s. Some of the big bond houses were able to shower their people with money, but the commission firms held back to husband resources. A few weren't certain they would be there through all of the next year. Only a week prior to Christmas it was learned that Unterberg, Tobin, a well thought of and aggressive underwriter, would be merged into L. F. Rothschild, which was attempting to round out its capabilities in that arena. The merger movement for most American industries peaked in the 1960s; it was just getting rolling on the Street in 1976, with some industry experts predicting that close to a quarter of the member firms would merge or go out of business within the next three to four years.

As usual, the press party at the N.Y.S.E. was a district highlight. There was Chairman William Batten, mingling with reporters and columnists, seeking them out with a joke, or at the very least a friendly smile. He seemed loose, fit, and actually enjoying himself. In terms of personality, Batten was closer to Keith Funston than to James Needham (his immediate predecessors). Needham endured these gatherings, and left as soon as possible, while like Funston, Batten actually relished contact with the press.

Unlike the situation at the brokerages, there was no question that the Exchange would be there for another party at Christmas 1977. But one of these years, before most of the new people have left the scene, there will be a gathering at one form or another of a United States Stock Exchange, though it may go under a different name.

Batten's joviality did not imply that he was in complete control of the organization which he had inherited a half-year earlier. On one side were Batten and his allies—including many members of the S.E.C. and the National Market Advisory Board—wanting to broaden the trading arena through CLOB and other innovations, while opposing them were many of the prominent specialists, who feared that to open the N.Y.S.E. too far would be to dilute the value of memberships. Furthermore, once the barbarians were within the gates they might act in an irresponsible fashion, altering the structure in such a way as to harm both specialists and established commission brokers.

Batten had suggested that nonmembers be permitted to use the N.Y.S.E.'s facilities for an annual fee. Under one version of his plan, those new participants who actually appeared on the floor would be charged $25,000, while traders represented by electronic consoles would pay $13,500 per annum.

The N.Y.S.E. could use the money fetched by such fees. The Exchange's expenses are bound to rise over the next few years if only to pay for the new electronic gear. Under the circumstances, Batten isn't likely to recommend an increase in either listing fees or other charges.

While recognizing the merits of such a proposal, Batten's opponents argued that the presence of these new people would dilute the value of their membership, if not of their equity in the N.Y.S.E. Batten responded that increased participation would make the seats more valuable, and so their prices would advance. Perhaps several Third Market firms would rise to the bait and eventually soften their criticisms of the Club. The best way to silence potential revolutionaries is to give them a position in your organization. Machiavelli said as much almost five hundred years ago; William Batten seems to know his Machiavelli.

As recently as November 1976, an N.Y.S.E. membership changed hands at $40,000, less than a seat at the C.B.O.E. The price was back to $80,000 by Christmas, and one was transferred at $85,000 in early January 1977. But this advance had more to do with speculation as to the nation's future under Jimmy Carter than confidence in the N.Y.S.E. under Batten. Some of the gloomier members thought the quote for a once-prized seat could go as low as $25,000. One old-timer at the Christmas party noted that at the height of the 1929 bull market, when it appeared finance capitalism's New Era would continue forever, a seat changed hands at $625,000. Thirteen years later an N.Y.S.E. membership was offered at $17,000 with no takers. It could happen again, he thought, remarking that his seat had cost him in excess of $150,000, and he never expected to see the money again. To this, another broker added that $17,000 in 1942 was worth more than $40,000 today. By this logic, the seat price of November 1976 had been the lowest in the twentieth century.

Clearly the matters raised by Batten, pushed by the S.E.C. and the N.M.A.B., and opposed by some specialists, would not be easily resolved without a residue of rancor. Three weeks after the Exchange's party, however, the N.M.A.B. released reports recommending the introduction of CLOB and the rapid transformation of existing exchanges into parts of a unified system. Some legislators thought the time right for the creation of a National Market Regulatory Board, to act as the rubric for the new system, but the N.M.A.B. held back, in part due to a growing confidence that Batten could be counted upon to reform the specialists. With this, one reporter noted that Batten might well have wished that he was back in his office in the executive suite of J. C. Penney, where all he had to worry about was competition from Sears Roebuck and the like.

Paul Kolton has no such problems at the Amex, where tradition is as strong as anyplace else in the district, but the instinct for survival is more sharply honed. For the past few months rumors regarding a merger with the N.Y.S.E. had been making the rounds, and apparently there was some foundation for them. Kolton wasn't sure he liked the idea. He has better control over his members than does Batten on the other side of the churchyard, as well as more options, both figuratively and literally. Should a merger take place, all stock trading could be done at the N.Y.S.E., while the Amex would become an options market. Of course, there would be a single class of members. The Amex people would receive the cachet of respectability old-timers there used to yearn for.

But the N.Y.S.E. would get far more—an experienced organization plus the new trading vehicle: the option. This kind of a merger would not dilute the value of a seat; it might cause the price to rise.

Was Kolton receptive to such a merger? In late 1976, he was in an enviable position. He could join with the N.Y.S.E. or remain independent; in either case, the Amex would do well. So would he, personally, for according to rumors, Batten would be chairman of the new exchange, and Kolton its president and chief operating officer. Given the comparative ages of the two men, clearly Kolton would be the most important figure in the exchange community within a few years at the very most. And in order to put additional pressure upon the Amex, the N.Y.S.E. authorized the admission of options trading to its own floor.

Kolton didn't appear impressed, though he did call for an S.E.C. investigation. His mind was on other things. Early in 1977, he initiated talks with political leaders in New Jersey and Connecticut regarding a physical move from the district to avoid New York's taxes. Thus, the Amex may join Weeden & Co. in New Jersey before it unites with Batten at Wall and Broad. Or Kolton could take his exchange to Stamford, Connecticut, which has offered many lures to the Amex. This would place the exchange within hailing distance of the NASDAQ facility north of Bridgeport.

Mayor Abe Beame appreciated the dimensions of this problem. He proposed ten sites on Manhattan, including three in the new Battery Park complex—assuming it is completed. Kolton remains mute on this subject. He is in a position where he can afford to wait for the best offer.

The financial community hadn't been giving Mayor Beame much joy or good news. It did help save the city from bankruptcy through the creation of the Municipal Assistance Corporation, and several Wall Street houses have marketed M.A.C. bonds, while the banks have taken large bundles of them for their portfolios. Was this a rescue operation, based upon confidence in the city's future and a true desire to help? Or were the bankers engaged in a holding mission, during which time they would slowly withdraw from the entire area of municipal finances, leaving others—especially the civil service unions— holding the bag? Some banks acted in this fashion during the last year of the Penn Central; before that corporation collapsed, the banks issued optimistic reports, while positioning themselves for the bankruptcy.

During Christmas 1976, there were rumors that Stanley Sporkin of the S.E.C. might launch an investigation of the M.A.C. This kind of news would shake the corporation badly and might help precipitate a crisis, which is why Sporkin may hold back. In any case, he hardly can act until the Carter Administration assumes office, with a new S.E.C. chairman taking command. Already Roderick Hills has announced his intention to return to private law practice on January 20. On the other hand, several Washingtonians at the N.Y.S.E. party said Carter wants to end this kind of rotation at federal agencies, and may ask Hills to stay on for a while.* Furthermore, the president-elect has just told Beame he will not permit New York to sink into bankruptcy.

What does all of this mean? Historically, Wall Street has come to expect S.E.C. activism during Democratic administrations, though there have been exceptions. As the Street celebrated the end of a good

* In March, Carter announced the selection of Dean Harold Williams of the UCLA Graduate School of Management as Hills' successor, and he took office on April 18.

year for trading and prices and awaited the coming of Carter, this was one of the more interesting questions to be resolved.

Technology does not wait upon presidential inaugurations and S.E.C. actions, however. Shortly after New Year's Day 1977, the Securities Industry Association released a report written by Professor Michael Keenan of New York University, which noted that the important technological changes in bookkeeping and the decentralization of trading meant New York would lose additional exchange and banking jobs in the future. "Perhaps 50,000 jobs in close proximity to the financial community will be replaced by 5,000 jobs associated with a national clearing and depository service." This does not imply that Wall Street will become a desert, said Keenan. "People talk of the industry getting up like the Giants and moving out. I don't see that happening." Instead, the exodus will be slow, "until you have an office with 50 executives left. That's the real danger."

Keenan wasn't telling the industry anything it didn't already know. Increasingly pressure for trading at the regionals and NASDAQ was making itself felt, and so the commission houses had begun to switch assets and personnel. At Paine, Webber, Jackson, and Curtis, for example, the diffusion of energies was well under way. The large firm's New York operations employed 1,784 workers that Christmas, against 1,638 in 1970—for a gain of 146 over that recession year. But Paine, Webber's total employment had risen from 3,900 to 4,791 in this period, and so the proportion of New York workers had declined. The commission house had fifty-nine branches outside of New York in 1970 and three within the city. The same three were open in 1976, but the non–New York offices had expanded to 130.

James Devant, president of Paine, Webber, gave the reason: costs, especially taxes. "There are tremendous disadvantages for security firms to remain in New York," he complained. Besides, there was no real reason to stay. Gesturing toward a Telequote machine, he said, "You can have it as well in Fort Lauderdale as here," while another executive added it would be easy "to pick up the plant and move it out of the area. We could service Wall Street from a remote site."

That remote site looked less remote than ever in early 1977. The brokers and specialists came back to their desks and posts after New

Year's Day to the news that private corporate placements were growing; industrial firms were bypassing the underwriters to offer securities
directly to the public. Several large banks were readying new plans by
which depositors could invest money without ever talking to a
broker—or paying him a commission, or providing income for specialists and exchanges. Pressures for a unified market structure were
growing; on December 4, a story had appeared on the wire that unless
the Street came up with a plan in the next year, one would be imposed
upon it by Washington.

January 5, 1977. Cornelius Vanderbilt died a century ago today.
The anniversary went unnoticed on the Street; the community was
tired of celebrations, having just come through the Bicentennial, during which time the district was flooded by tourists looking for the
place George Washington was sworn into office as the first president.
Besides, brokers were more interested in the health of the market than
in the death of the tycoon. On December 31, the Dow Industrials had
crossed the 1000 mark again, for the fifteenth time in 1976. This time
the sentiment was quite bullish. President-elect Carter seemed more
moderate with each statement, and lowered prime rates helped fuel the
upward sweep. But prices declined on January 3 and 4, falling to the
low 980s at one point.

The decline continued until January 5, closing the day at Dow
978.06. For the first time in two weeks strong bearish rumblings
were heard, with several analysts hedging their bets for 1977. Nowhere on earth can the mood turn a full 180 degrees as rapidly as in a
financial district.

Insofar as the future of the district was concerned, the volume figures were most interesting. Slightly more than 25 million shares were
traded at the N.Y.S.E. Between them, the Pacific Coast, Midwest,
and N.A.S.D. accounted for trades in 3.6 million N.Y.S.E.–listed
shares, and even the Amex took 11,800 shares, an insignificant figure
to be sure, but one that seemed certain to grow. The total O-T-C trading that day was 8.4 million shares. The C.B.O.E. reported its volume
at 107,000 options, which represented one hundred times that number
of shares—10.7 million—almost all of which were listed on the
N.Y.S.E. Figured this way, the C.B.O.E. had trades on 40 percent of

the Exchange's turnover. And the Amex options also traded at a respectable pace—55,000 that day, representing 5.5 million shares of common stock.

It is difficult to find an N.Y.S.E. member who believes that there is a new golden age in the offing, that one day his seat will be worth $200,000, not to say a half-million dollars. Instead, the Exchange's share of trading in its listed stocks is bound to decline, while the commission and underwriting businesses undergo important transformations. All of this probably will transpire on Wall Street. But it could happen someplace else.

There are no giant figures like Cornelius Vanderbilt in the district today. This is not because present Wall Streeters lack talent, ambition, or brains. Rather, the stage for their activities bears little resemblance to that of 1877. A century ago, the technology was somewhat crude, and in any case could be controlled by man. Today, technology calls the tune. And the message is, "Adapt or disappear." The Street has no intention of disappearing, and so it will adapt.

Within a decade, at the outside, the district will be altered more than at any other time in its history. The eventual form to be taken by the new securities nexus is not clear as yet, but that it will be startlingly different from what now exists is beyond doubt.

Still, the N.Y.S.E. building will be there, as will the House of Morgan across Broad Street, and the Subtreasury. The ghosts of Alexander Hamilton and Albert Gallatin will continue to haunt Trinity Churchyard. And the streets will be the same.

FOR FURTHER READING

THERE ARE SEVERAL fine bookstores in the financial district, and some do a lively business. Most display best sellers in their windows, but they always have a row of recent works on the securities markets. Every month or so the displays change, in order to lure customers into the shops and also to reflect the continuing interest in the subject. As might be expected, most deal with ways to make money—in stocks, options, commodities, warrants, and so on. Few have more than transitory appeal, leading one to wonder why publishers invest in the manuscripts. There must be a market for them, though almost all are rewrites of previously unsuccessful books. Several are worth more than a passing glance, and these may be found in the following list, together with the essential works dealing with American finance in the district. For those who want a more complete and comprehensive bibliography, there is *A Bibliography of Finance and Investment* (Cambridge, 1973), compiled by R. A. Brealey and C. Pyle, and James Woy's *Investment Methods: A Bibliographic Guide* (New York, 1973). Sheldon Zerden's *Best Books on the Stock Market: An Analytical Bibliography* (New York, 1972) contains short reviews of works on the history and sociology of the Street as well as investment methods.

Several outstanding books have been published since these three guides appeared, and some have been referred to in the text. Chris Welles, *The Last Days of the Club* (New York, 1975), James Stone, *One Way for Wall Street* (Boston, 1975), Martin Mayer, *The Bankers* (New York, 1974), and John Brooks, *The Go-Go Years* (New York, 1973), should be required reading for all those who hope to understand how and why the district functions. For an appreciation of some of the origins of the present discontent, see Hurd Baruch, *Wall Street: Security Risk* (Washington, 1971).

With all of this, there are gaps in the literature. Vincent Carosso's *Investment Banking in America* (Cambridge, 1970), is a superlative study of the pre-1933 period and contains a section on the New Deal reforms, but is weak on events of the past quarter of a century. Michael Jensen, the perceptive Wall Street reporter for the *New York Times,* has written *The Financiers: The World of the Great Wall Street Investment Banking Houses* (New York, 1976), but by design it is episodic and not analytical. Wolfgang Quante's *The Exodus of Corporate Headquarters from New York City* (New York, 1976), is a useful study, with only peripheral reference to the Wall Street area, however. We still lack a major book on the Securities and Exchange Commission in the post–New Deal period. There is no history of the Over-the-Counter Markets, and none in the works. No major investment bank or commission house has had its hitory written, though Vincent Carosso presently is working on a volume about Morgan Stanley. Wall Street rarely deals with self-analysis, at least in the community sense. It will do so under congressional or S.E.C. pressures, and of course some of the best works on Wall Street have come out of the national legislative branch and are covered in the bibliographic volumes previously mentioned.

BIBLIOGRAPHY

Armour, Lawrence, and the staff of *Barron's*. *How to Survive a Bear Market*. Princeton, 1970.

Barron, Clarence. *They Told Barron*. New York, 1930.

Baum, Daniel Jay, and Stiles, Ned. *The Silent Partners*. Syracuse, 1965.

Berle, Adolf. *Power Without Property*. New York, 1969.

———— and Means, Gardiner. *The Modern Corporation and Private Property*. New York, 1968 ed.

Bishop, George. *Charles H. Dow and the Dow Theory*. New York, 1960.

Black, Hillel. *The Watchdogs of Wall Street*. New York, 1962.

Bloom, Murray Teigh. *Rogues to Riches*. New York, 1971.

Boyle, James. *Speculation and the Chicago Board of Trade*. New York, 1929.

Bracker, Lewis, and Wagner, Walter. *The Trouble With Wall Street*. Englewood Cliffs, 1972.

Brooks, John. *Once in Golconda*. New York, 1969.

————. *The Seven Fat Years*. New York, 1958.

Bruce, Robert. *Bell: Alexander Graham Bell and the Conquest of Solitude*. Boston, 1973.

————. *1877: Year of Violence*. Boston, 1970.

"Brutus." *Confessions of a Stockbroker*. Boston, 1971.

Bullock, Hugh. *The Story of Investment Companies*. New York, 1959.

Cawelti, John. *Apostles of the Self-Made Man*. Chicago, 1965.

Chandler, Alfred. *Henry Varnum Poor: Business Editor, Analyst, and Reformer*. Cambridge, 1956.

Churchill, Allen. *Park Row*. New York, 1958.

Clews, Henry. *Twenty Eight Years in Wall Street*. New York, 1888.

Cootner, Paul, ed. *The Random Character of Stock Market Prices*. Cambridge, 1964.

Cormier, Frank. *Wall Street's Shady Side*. Washington, 1962.

Crane, Burton. *The Sophisticated Investor*. New York, 1964.

Crosse, Howard. *Management Policies for Commercial Banks*. Englewood Cliffs, 1962.

Crum, Lawrence, and Richardson, Dennis. *Competition for the Commercial Banking Industry in the Establishment and Operation of an Electronic Payments System*. Washington, 1971.

DeBedts, Ralph. *The New Deal's SEC*. New York, 1964.

Drucker, Peter. *The Unseen Revolution*. New York, 1976.

Dyer, Frank, and Martin, Thomas. *Edison, His Life and Inventions*. New York, 1929.

Eames, Francis. *The New York Stock Exchange*. New York, 1894.

Edwards, Robert, and Magee, John. *The Technical Analysis of Stock Trends*. Springfield, Mass., 1967.

Elfenbein, Julien. *Business Journalism*. New York, 1947.

Elias, Christopher. *Fleecing the Lambs*. Chicago, 1971.

Ellis, Charles. *Institutional Investing*. Homewood, Ill., 1971.

———. *The Second Crash*. New York, 1973.

Elton, Edwin, and Gruber, Martin. *Security Evaluation and Portfolio Analysis*. Englewood Cliffs, 1972.

Filer, Herbert. *Understanding Put and Call Options*. New York, 1971.

Forbes, Malcolm. *Fact and Comment*. New York, 1974.

Fowler, William W. *Inside Life in Wall Street*. New York, 1874.

Frank, Robert. *Successful Investing Through Mutual Funds*. New York, 1969.

Friend, Irwin, Marshall Blume, and Jean Crockett. *Mutual Funds and Other Institutional Investors*. New York, 1970.

Fritz, Sparta, and Shumate, A. M. *Making the Dow Theory Work*. New York, 1960 ed.

Fuller, John. *Fleecing the Lambs*. Chicago, 1971.

———. *The Money Changers*. New York, 1962.

Funston, Ketih. *Wanted: More Owners of American Business*. Boston, 1954.

Galbraith, John K. *The Great Crash, 1929*. Boston, 1955.

Goldsmith, Raymond, ed. *Institutional Investors and Corporate Stock*. New York, 1973.

Gould, Leslie. *The Manipulators*. New York. 1966.

Graham, Benjamin. *The Intelligent Investor*. New York, 1973 ed.

——— and Dodd, David. *Security Analysis*. New York, 1934.

Hagin, Robert, and Mader, Chris. *The New Science of Investing*. Homewood, Ill., 1973.

Hamilton, William. *The Stock Market Barometer*. New York, 1960 ed.

Hammond, Bray. *Sovereignty and the Empty Purse*. Princeton, 1970.

Harbrecht, Paul. *Pension Funds and Economic Power*. New York, 1959.

Hazard, C. C. *Confessions of a Wall Street Insider*. New York, 1972.

Hazard, John, and Christie, Milton. *The Investment Business*. New York, 1964.

Heilbroner, John, et. al. *In the Name of Profit*. New York, 1972.

Huber, Richard. *The American Idea of Success*. New York, 1971.

Investment Company Institute. *The Money Managers*. New York, 1967.

Kaplan, Gilbert, and Welles, Chris. *The Money Managers*. New York, 1969.

Kennedy, E. D. *Dividends to Pay*. New York, 1939.

Kirkland, Edward. *Dream and Thought in the Business Community, 1860–1900;* Chicago, 1956.

Klein, Frederick, and Prestbo, John. *News and the Market*. Chicago, 1974.

Knowlton, Winthrop, and Furth, John. *Shaking the Money Tree*. New York, 1965.

Kretetz, Gerald, and Marissi, Ruth. *Money Makes Money, and the Money Money Makes Makes More Money*. New York, 1970.

Krooss, Herman. *Executive Opinion: What Business Leaders Said and Thought on Economic Issues, 1920s–1960s*. New York, 1970.

——— and Blyn, Martin. *A Hitory of Financial Intermediaries*. New York, 1971.

Lefevre, Edwin. *Wall Street Stories*. New York, 1901.

Leffler, George, and Farwell, Loring. *The Stock Market*. New York, 1963 rev. ed.

Leinsdorf, David, and Eltra, Donald. *Citibank*. New York, 1973.

Livingston, Joseph. *The American Stockholder*. Philadelphia, 1958.

Loeb, Gerald. *The Battle for Investment Survival*. New York, 1965 ed.

Loeser, John. *The Over-The-Counter Securities Market*. New York, 1940.

Loll, Leo, and Buckley, Julian. *The Over-The-Counter Securities Market*. Englewood Cliffs, 1973.

Magee, John, and Edwards, Robert. *Technical Analysis of Stock Trends*. Putnam, Vt., 1954.

Malkiel, Burton. *A Random Walk Down Wall Street*. New York, 1973.

Martin, Ralph. *The Wizard of Wall Street*. New York, 1965.

Mayer, Martin. *The New Breed on Wall Street*. New York, 1969.

Medbery, James. *Men and Mysteries of Wall Street*. New York, 1870.

Mittra, Sid. *Inside Wall Street*. Homewood, Ill., 1971.

Moody, John. *The Art of Wall Street Investing*. New York, 1906.

———. *Profitable Investing*. New York, 1925.

Morgenstern, Oskar, and Granger, Clive. *Predictability of Stock Market Prices*. Lexington, Mass., 1970.

Nadler, Marcus, Heller, Sipa, and Shipmen, Samuel. *The Money Market and its Institutions*. New York, 1955.

Neill, Humphrey. *The Art of Contrary Thinking*. Caldwell, Idaho, 1954.

Neilson, Winthrop and Frances. *What's News—Dow Jones*. Radnor, Pa., 1973.

Nelson, S. A. *The ABC of Stock Speculation*. New York, 1903.

Ney, Richard. *The Wall Street Jungle*. New York, 1970.

Noyes, Alexander. *The Market Place*. Boston, 1938.

Parrish, Michael. *Securities Regulation and the New Deal*. New Haven, 1970.

Pecora, Ferdinand. *Wall Street Under Oath*. New York, 1939.

Plummer, A. Newton. *The Great American Swindle, Incorporated*. New York, 1932.

Prochnow, Herbert, and Prochnow, Herbert, Jr. *The Changing World of Banking*. New York, 1974.

Regan, Donald. *A View From the Street*. New York, 1972.

Rhea, Robert. *The Dow Theory*. Colorado Springs, Colorado, 1932.

Robbins, Sidney, and Terleckyj, Nestor. *Money Metropolis*. Cambridge, 1960.

Robinson, Roland, and Wrightsman, Dwayne. *Financial Markets*. New York, 1974.

Rolo, Charles, and Nelson, George, eds. *The Anatomy of Wall Street*. Philadelphia, 1968.

Russell, Richard. *The Dow Theory Today*. New York, 1960.

Salmon, David. *Confessions of a Former Customers' Man*. New York, 1932.

Sarnoff, Paul. *Puts and Calls*. New York, 1968.

Schwartz, Robert. *You and Your Stockbroker*. New York, 1967.

Selden, George. *The Psychology of the Stock Market*. New York, 1912.

Smigal, Erwin. *The Wall Street Lawyer*. New York, 1964.

Smilen, Kenneth, and Safian, Kenneth. *Investment Profits Through Market Timing*. New York, 1961.

Smith, Adam (George Goodman). *The Money Game*. New York, 1967.

Smith, Matthew. *Bulls and Bears of New York*. New York, 1872.

Smith, Ralph. *The Grim Truth About Mutual Funds*. New York, 1963.

Sobel, Robert. *Amex*. New York, 1972.

———. *The Curbstone Brokers*. New York, 1970.

———. *N.Y.S.E.* New York, 1975.

Soldofsky, Robert. *Institutional Holdings of Common Stock, 1900–2000*. Ann Arbor, 1971.

Sparling, Earl. *Mystery Men of Wall Street*. New York, 1930.

Stedman, Edmund. *The New York Stock Exchange*. New York, 1905.

Sturgis, Henry. *Investment: A New Profession*. New York, 1924.

Sutton, Francis, et. al. *The American Business Creed*. Cambridge, 1956.

Tilove, Robert. *Pension Funds and Economic Freedom*. New York, 1959.

Tyler, Poyntz, ed. *Securities, Exchanges, and the SEC*. New York, 1965.

Van Antwerp, W. C. *The Stock Exchange From Within*. Garden City, 1913 ed.

Washburn, Watson, and DeLong, Edmund. *High and Low Financiers*. New York, 1932.

Weissman, Rudolph. *The New Wall Street*. New York, 1939.

West, Richard, and Tinic, Seha. *The Economics of the Stock Market*. New York, 1971.

Weston, J. Fred, ed. *Financial Management in the 1960s*. New York, 1966.

Williams, John. *The Theory of Investment Value.* Cambridge, 1938.

Wise, Tom. *The Insiders.* New York, 1962.

Zahorchak, Michael. *Favorable Executions: The Wall Street Specialist and the Auction Market.* New York, 1974.

Zarb, Frank, and Kerekes, Gabriel, eds. *The Stock Market Handbook.* New York, 1970.

INDEX